25 Portland

WESTMORELAND AND PORTLAND PLACES

The History and Architecture of America's Premier Private Streets, 1888–1988

By Julius K. Hunter

Foreword by James Neal Primm

Essay on the Architecture by Esley Hamilton

Color Photography by Robert Pettus and Leonard Lujan

University of Missouri Press

Columbia, 1988

Copyright © 1988 by
The Curators of the University of Missouri
University of Missouri Press, Columbia, Missouri 65211
Printed and bound in Japan by Dai Nippon Printing Co., Ltd.

Second printing, 1989

∞™ This paper meets the minimum requirements of
the American National Standard for Permanence of Paper
for Printed Library Materials, Z39.48, 1984.

Library of Congress Cataloging-in-Publication Data

Hunter, Julius K.

   Westmoreland and Portland places: the history and
architecture of america's premier private streets, 1888–1988

   1. Westmoreland Place (Saint Louis, Mo.)—Social life and
customs. 2. Portland Place (Saint Louis, Mo.)— Social life and
customs. 3. Saint Louis (Mo.)—Social life and customs. I. Title.
F474.S26W474   1988   977.8'65   87–38079
ISBN 0–8262–0677–8 (alk. paper)   Includes index.

This book is published in memory of Edward Mallinckrodt, Jr., by virtue
of a grant made by his granddaughter Rosalie Randolph Mallinckrodt.
Edward Mallinckrodt, Jr., lived for more than fifty years in the
award-winning house that he had built at 16 Westmoreland Place.

To Barbara, Jennifer, and Julia

FOREWORD

by James Neal Primm

The long stretches of Westmoreland and Portland places, with their grand houses one after the other, on and on, offer a scene of cumulative magnificence seldom if ever matched. Visitors to St. Louis in the World's Fair era thought their effect "marvelous," "inconceivable," better than could be found in any combination of other cities. Now, in the 1980s, when public attention has been fixed on downtown refurbishing and rebuilding, highlighted by the restoration of the distinguished Union Station, the current owners of the West End private places have been polishing and grooming their slightly faded monuments. Their love of beauty, if not their political and economic roles, rivals that of their predecessors.

Restoration of formerly wealthy and middle-class streets has been underway in the city for decades, but many of the nineteenth-century private places are long gone. Westmoreland and Portland, perhaps because they were the finest and best protected, survived two world wars and many other threats in ghostly grandeur, and now they seem to be quietly pulsing with new life, prestigious addresses once again. Few who have seen them would deny that they, along with Forest Park, the Missouri Botanical Garden, and Union Station, give credibility to St. Louis's claim to be a beautiful city.

Beauty speaks for itself, as the illustrations in the present volume demonstrate, and it was beauty that attracted Julius Hunter's attention to the private places. But contemplation of handsome structures leads finally to questions. Who built them and why, what sort of persons were they, what kinds of lives did they lead, how were they perceived by others, how did they relate to the larger community? Julius Hunter has asked these questions, and he addresses them in this volume. Since his account deals primarily with the hundred-year span since

Westmoreland and Portland came into existence, a glimpse of those who held power and prestige in St. Louis before that time will set the stage for the story Julius tells.

Even as a remote outpost of the Spanish Empire two centuries ago, St. Louis had its elite. In reporting to their superiors in New Orleans, the lieutenant-governors in charge here made rank distinctions among the king's local subjects, giving honorific titles to the leading merchant-traders, especially those born in France rather than in Illinois or Canada. Slave-owning, military rank, and literacy were other marks of distinction.

Because of their connections with Pierre Laclede, their profitable monopoly of the trade with the Osage Indians, and their undoubted talents, the half-brothers Auguste and Pierre Chouteau were the leaders of Upper Louisiana when it was relinquished to the United States in 1804. Their English-educated brother-in-law, Charles Gratiot, and a handful of French and Creole in-laws shared the pinnacle with them. For another generation these and other Creole traders shared power with territorial officials William Clark, J. B. C. Lucas, and Frederick Bates. An aggressive Spanish Creole named Manuel Lisa and American lawyers, merchants, and land speculators such as Edward Hempstead, David Barton, Rufus Easton, and William C. Carr played prominent roles during the territorial period. Several talented Irishmen, including Joseph Charless, Edward Walsh, John Mullanphy, and Thomas Brady, added to the mix, intermingling and intermarrying with the Creole families.

That Creole political power was on the wane was evident in 1823 when St. Louis elected a flat-broke Pennsylvania doctor as its first mayor. But Creole connections, especially if accom-

panied by the ability to make a lot of money, such as that demonstrated by Pierre Chouteau, Jr., and Louis Benoist, insured social prestige. The French writer August Laugel, visiting St. Louis during the Civil War, lamented that the "rich, esteemed French population" were ruled politically by people they barely knew.

From the 1820s to the 1850s, when eastern and foreign arrivals swelled St. Louis's population from under 4,000 to 161,000, the city's energy level was lifted mightily by an infusion of entrepreneurs from the Northeast, the border slave states, and abroad. Yankees Thomas Allen, Hudson Bridge, Daniel Page, O. D. and Giles Filley, Carlos Greeley, William Greenleaf Eliot, and Erastus Wells; border Southerners Henry Taylor Blow, George R. Taylor, Samuel C. Davis, James Harrison, James Yeatman, Wayman Crow, Frank P. Blair, Jr., and Derrick January; and Gerard Allen, Robert Campbell, Henry Shaw, and the Finney brothers from the British Isles were busy in every corner of the vast St. Louis hinterland, or in conducting the mercantile, banking, manufacturing, cultural, and legal business of the city. By the eve of the Civil War, Thomas Allen (who had married the wealthy Anne Russell), Bridge, O. D. Filley, Harrison, and probably several others were multimillionaires, as were the scions of older families, such as Charles P. Chouteau, James Lucas, and Louis Benoist.

By midcentury, the wealthy were enjoying an elaborate lifestyle. Hudson Bridge, for example, whose son was a charter homebuilder in Westmoreland/Portland, kept a summer residence in exclusive Newport, in addition to his large estate (Glendale) southwest of St. Louis on the main line of the Pacific Railroad. His wife and daughters wore Paris gowns, and the family traveled extensively and often in Europe and

Great Britain. Jefferson Clark's Minoma (built by his father William) was a summer and weekend playground for Clarks, Kennerlys, Glasgows, and other relatives and friends. Jefferson's older brother, Meriwether Lewis Clark, had developed an interest in horse racing at a nearby track that culminated in his founding the Kentucky Derby at his father-in-law's Churchill Downs in Louisville. Just to the west of Minoma, in Normandy, clustered the Hunts, Lucases, and Turners—closely knit descendants of J. B. C. Lucas. In addition to their banking, real estate, and transit interests, these wealthy folk—some of them—involved themselves in horse racing, baseball, and various philanthropies.

In 1876 Erastus Wells, the street railway and gaslight magnate, built the West End Narrow Gauge Railroad, from the Grand and Delmar vicinity to Florissant. This was a great amenity for those commuting between their town houses and their summer and weekend homes. Between Normandy and Wells's estate, Wellston, near the post-1876 city limits, the powerful "Big Cinch" leader David R. Francis—grain broker, bridge builder (the Merchant's Bridge), mayor, governor, secretary of the interior, the last U.S. ambassador to pre-Bolshevik Russia—had his country home. Francis later built mansions in Vandeventer Place and on Maryland Avenue, the latter occupying an entire city block, while his son J. D. Perry Francis built an impressive house on Portland Place. Beyond Normandy toward Florissant, Derrick January and numerous Mullanphy descendants, Harneys, Frosts, Grahams, and Chamberses—had large estates. South of St. Louis, in magnificent isolation, Louis Benoist's Oakland, designed by George I. Barnett, was the scene of many ante- and postbellum galas, the setting for some of the action in Kate Chopin's daring novels.

These country estates were a response to the same imperatives that inspired the series of elegant enclaves that culminated in the ultimate jewels—Westmoreland and Portland places. Carr Square, Washington Avenue, Chouteau Avenue, Lucas Place, Lafayette Square, Benton Place, Compton Heights, and Vandeventer Place were increasingly ambitious efforts of the wealthy, the socially secure, and the socially

aspiring to wall out the world, to exclude from their line of sight and smell all that was unpleasant in city living. The noise and smoke of industry; the swarming masses of the poor; the stifling heat of the treeless downtown streets; the risk of epidemic disease—all these could be avoided, or at least minimized, by distance and by enforced isolation. Even better, as Thorstein Veblen suggested, living in baronial castles validated their occupants' claims to aristocratic status, to others and to themselves.

Large country estates limited socialization; in the city the private place was the answer. James Lucas acted on the idea first, in 1851. Having inherited his father's huge downtown holdings north of Market Street, he created Missouri Park at the site of the home of his youth and gave it to the city, blocking vehicular traffic from the east, and then between the park and Eighteenth Street he set aside land for a development he called Lucas Place. With George I. Barnett he planned an exclusive private street and invited those who could afford it to build there. Eventually he built a mansion there himself, combining profit with like seeking like. The newer Yankee and border-South businessmen responded, mingling with a few of the older families. Except for the First Presbyterian Church and Mary Institute, only residences were permitted. Lucas Place was the right address for several decades, but it was too close in and not isolated enough to withstand the rapid post–Civil War industrial expansion. (Fortunately one of the beautiful homes has been preserved, the residence of the noted fur trader Robert Campbell.) As Lucas Place faded, Julius Pitzman was busy planning Vandeventer Place, the first of his private streets in the area added to the city when it tripled in size in 1876.

St. Louis's population doubled in the last quarter of the nineteenth century, to nearly 600,000, and the city confirmed its early position as a major distributor of groceries, dry goods, and hardware. Fortunes were made in distilling (despite a major national scandal), flour milling, and tobacco manufacturing, before they began to decline in the 1890s. Brewing was gaining, but the rising stars were chemicals, iron and steel, textiles, utilities, electrical machinery, and shoe manufacturing, especially the last. Dozens of other important industries dotted the city, remarkable for its economic mix. Many of the barons of business and industry whose fortunes

were either made or maintained by these enterprises built impressive mansions in Westmoreland and Portland.

St. Louis had no Rockefellers, Carnegies, Morgans, or Vanderbilts, but it had more than one hundred millionaires at the turn of the century. Ironically, its most baronial figures, Adolphus Busch and James Campbell, were not strictly a part of "society." Busch, a merchandising genius whose support of Bismarck's Kulturkampf made him a familiar figure at the German chancellery and Court, lived in a mansion near his brewery, a power in the city's business, but not a member of its exclusive clubs. He apparently was not devastated by this. Campbell, who came to St. Louis as a messenger boy on General Frémont's staff in 1861, had clawed his way to the top by 1900, the head of a utilities empire that covered several midwestern cities including St. Louis. He bought a mansion on Westmoreland, but he had little use for society, and he helped finance Reedy's Mirror, which heckled, taunted, and outraged the city's first families for twenty years.

In their business and social outlook, the wealthy and powerful of St. Louis during the several decades after the Civil War were typical of an era that seems ruthless and callous in retrospect. They disliked muckrakers and reformers, "knockers," as they called them; they were not moved by compassion in their labor policies; and some of them were dishonest in their business practices. Several of the most prominent were directly involved in bribing the Missouri legislature (not hard to do at that time) in the Pacific Railroad Scandal in 1868. On the other hand, the bribe-givers' most relentless adversary was their fellow director Hudson Bridge, who took the railroad away from them in 1870. Bridge was against bribery, especially with company funds. In 1873, the Whiskey Ring investigation revealed that several St. Louis distillers, including the bearer of one of the city's proudest names, had been defrauding the government for years. And in 1902, as Julius Hunter notes, city attorney Joseph W. Folk exposed the "boodlers," high-placed businessmen and bankers who bribed members of the city council and house of delegates for franchises and other favors.

Giles Filley set a local standard for labor relations in 1877, when the first general strike in American history paralyzed St. Louis business. He fired fifty suspected union men and planted a cannon at the entrance of his Excelsior Stove Works to

keep the marching strikers away, which it did. In 1900, St. Louis Transit Company workers went on strike after the monopoly's president, Edwards Whitaker, reneged on a promise to grant them a ten-hour day and rehire workers fired for union activity. In an episode Julius discusses, Whitaker, with the help of federal Judge Elmer Adams, brought in strikebreakers from Cleveland, which outraged the public, except in the West End. After weeks of violence on both sides, Whitaker agreed again to some of the union demands, and again he broke his word. The strike resumed for several more weeks, but their families' desperate condition finally forced the workers to surrender. Whitaker, Judge Elmer Adams, and their allies had won the battle, but the ethnic middle and laboring classes were confirmed in their belief that they were victims of a heartless elite conspiracy, the "Big Cinch." Public projects and programs for the next two decades, if they were perceived to have downtown–West End backing, had plenty of trouble at the polls.

The energetic entrepreneurs who lived in the West End mansions contributed heavily to the city's dynamic economic growth. St. Louis's broad hinterland, stretching from central Illinois to the Gulf, to the Mexican border and the Sierras, was created in large part by its marketing and manufacturing leadership. Thomas Allen, O. D. and Giles Filley, Hudson Bridge, Walter McKittrick, E. C. Simmons, Samuel C. Davis, A. F. Shapleigh, Wayman Crow, Samuel Cupples, Robert Brookings, Alanson and George Brown, John C. Roberts, Murray Carleton, James Campbell, Samuel Kennard, Charles Clark, W. K. Bixby, Henry Clay Pierce, Erastus and Rolla Wells, Julius Walsh, James and Edward Harrison, the Benoists, the Maffitts, and their competitors and successors created tens of thousands of jobs and promoted the city's interests wherever and whenever possible. The Louisiana Purchase Exposition, remembered as one of the great World's Fairs in history, would not have happened without the leadership of David R. Francis, Rolla Wells, William H. Thompson, John Scullin, Breckinridge Jones, James T. Blair, and dozens of other West End movers and shakers.

Only a minority of the elite were involved in the corporate and municipal scandals; no doubt many of them frowned on such activities. Hudson Bridge despised the railroad ring and made a public scandal of its corruption, and shoe industry chiefs such as John C. Roberts and George Brown and drygoods wholesaler Murray Carleton backed the Folk prosecutions and contributed generously to Folk's successful campaign for governor. But a majority of the wealthy seemed to feel that it was not quite right to arrest businessmen who were simply trying to deal with the world as it was. All the same, it was hard to refute critics who pointed out that the maze of interlocking relationships between the transit lines and the downtown banks made every bank stockholder a partner in the enterprise. Julius Hunter demonstrates that connection.

The moral contradictions in what Thomas Cochran called the Age of Enterprise have been pointed out repeatedly by historians and social critics. Mark Twain and Charles Dudley Warner called the postbellum period the Gilded Age, gleaming on the surface with base metal inside. The enormous philanthropies of Rockefeller, Morgan, Harriman, Stanford, and Huntington do not obscure the wreckage their ruthless careers left behind them. Theodore Dreiser's "Financier" had his counterparts in every major city in the nation. In St. Louis, even before the Folk disclosures, *The Iconoclast* charged the "local nobility," which controlled the banks, the transit companies, and the utilities, with buying aldermen "like cattle." Yet, according to the writer, they were all "religious and moral men, their crookedness purely commercial and political."

The conspicuous display of wealth, no matter how acquired, attracts the attention of those who do not have it. Yet the public hostility to the West End power elite was impersonal. There were no invasions of Westmoreland and Portland planned or carried out, and those who lived there were not in danger of deliberate violence. But the antipathy was real; it ran deepest among the southside German and Kerry Patch Irish ethnics, and it spread throughout the state. When Joseph Folk ran for governor in 1904, Mayor Rolla Wells, Harry Hawes, and the rest of the city's Democratic establishment, backed by the wealth and power of the city with the exceptions noted above, did everything possible to deny him the nomination. But the Democratic farmers of the state, delighted by Folk's assaults on the "gold-bug" aristocracy, swept the crusading reformer to a one-sided victory. In the general election, Folk carried the state by 30,000 votes, while the Republicans took all the other state offices.

The first residents of Westmoreland and Portland were set apart from the day-to-day lives of the majority of St. Louisans by their wealth and power, as well as by the privacy they gained from living in their enclave. The stories of their lives are intriguing, partly because of the imperfections of some of those who lived in these private places. Both as monuments to the power and prestige they wielded and even more importantly as structures of surpassing beauty, the houses they left behind them remain for us to appreciate today.

Interior of 38 Portland.

PREFACE

Working on this manuscript for the past three years has been a true challenge, a rewarding learning experience, and an intense labor of love. The Westmoreland/Portland story is an intriguing episode in the history of St. Louis, the midwest, and the nation. The sheer survival of America's two premier private residential places attests to the ingenuity involved in their conception, the craftsmanship used in their construction, and the unflagging care with which they have been maintained through the prominence and wealth of those who have been their guardians for one hundred years.

When I was seven years old I lived with my family on Windsor Place—the narrow street built for the servants who worked just one block south in uniquely grand and opulent Vandeventer Place. Even at that age, and with no polished appreciation for history or architecture, I was astonished and saddened by the cruel devastation of the headache ball as it leveled this magnificent private residential gem to make way for a monstrous hospital of government architectural design.

Westmoreland and Portland places are in no jeopardy of extinction, but I am thrilled that their story is now set in print forever. No such work was written to keep alive detailed memories of Vandeventer Place.

This is a book about people, life-styles, and architecture. It is the chronicle of how the two best examples of the private places in the United States came to be created in St. Louis.

There are many, many devotees of Westmoreland/Portland who helped me assemble this fascinating story, and an expression of my gratitude is due all of them. First, I would like to thank the trustees of Westmoreland and Portland for the commission to write this book.

The three-year research efforts of Mary Cunningham and Alice White were absolutely invaluable. They were able to supply me with detailed information when given some of the most impossible requests. The more remote and obscure the data, the more Mary and Alice seemed to enjoy the assignment. Charles Brown of the Mercantile Library was also extremely cooperative in researching points I needed to correct, clarify, or confirm. Betty Burnett is to be commended for executing her commission to edit the text from 97,000 words to 60,000. She is responsible, therefore, for your being able to lift this book.

Historian James Neal Primm's prepublication review helped me write a more historically accurate account, and for his scholarly insights I am grateful. I also thank Professor Primm for his Foreword.

Architectural historian Esley Hamilton's scholarly research is a valuable addition to this book. I greatly appreciate Esley's contribution, as you will, particularly as you take your strolling tour of Westmoreland/Portland.

Two extremely talented photographers added masterful touches to the book. The photographic artistry of Robert Pettus is greatly evident. Bob, a descendant of one of the charter residents of Westmoreland Place, exhibits keen sensitivity in his exterior photos to the unique architectural qualities of each house. Leonard Lujan's interior photography, as well as his few exterior shots, is also brilliant, warm, and sensitive to the subject matter. His is a valuable contribution to all who have yearned to get a glimpse inside Westmoreland/Portland's imposing mansions.

William Julius Polk, who grew up at 28 Westmoreland, should be recognized and thanked for his personal reflections and sharp memories about some of the early residents of Westmoreland/Portland.

Long-time Westmoreland resident Norris Allen has been an invaluable human resource and living reference from the very beginning of this project. All who know him can attest to how readily Norris will take one on a trip down Memory Lane . . . or Westmoreland Place . . . or Portland Place. This work would not have reached this point were it not for Norris's inspiration and support.

This book project was infinitely blessed by the supererogatory efforts of a former trustee of Portland Place, John Byrne. Jack has served ably as executive producer, coordinator, researcher, editor, executor, and "trail boss" for this publication effort. We can all be grateful to Jack for being there to see this project through five years of its development.

I would be remiss if I didn't express my appreciation here to my wife, Barbara, and to my two daughters, Jennifer and Julia, for granting me yet another sabbatical leave to spend the time necessary to complete this book.

And finally, a word of thanks to all the residents of Westmoreland/Portland present and past who opened up their homes, photo albums, and memories to ensure that the story of America's two premier private places can be told again and again.

J.K.H.
December 1987

View of Portland Place

CONTENTS

The Westmoreland/Portland Neighborhood in the 1980s
(the only entrance is by Lake Avenue)

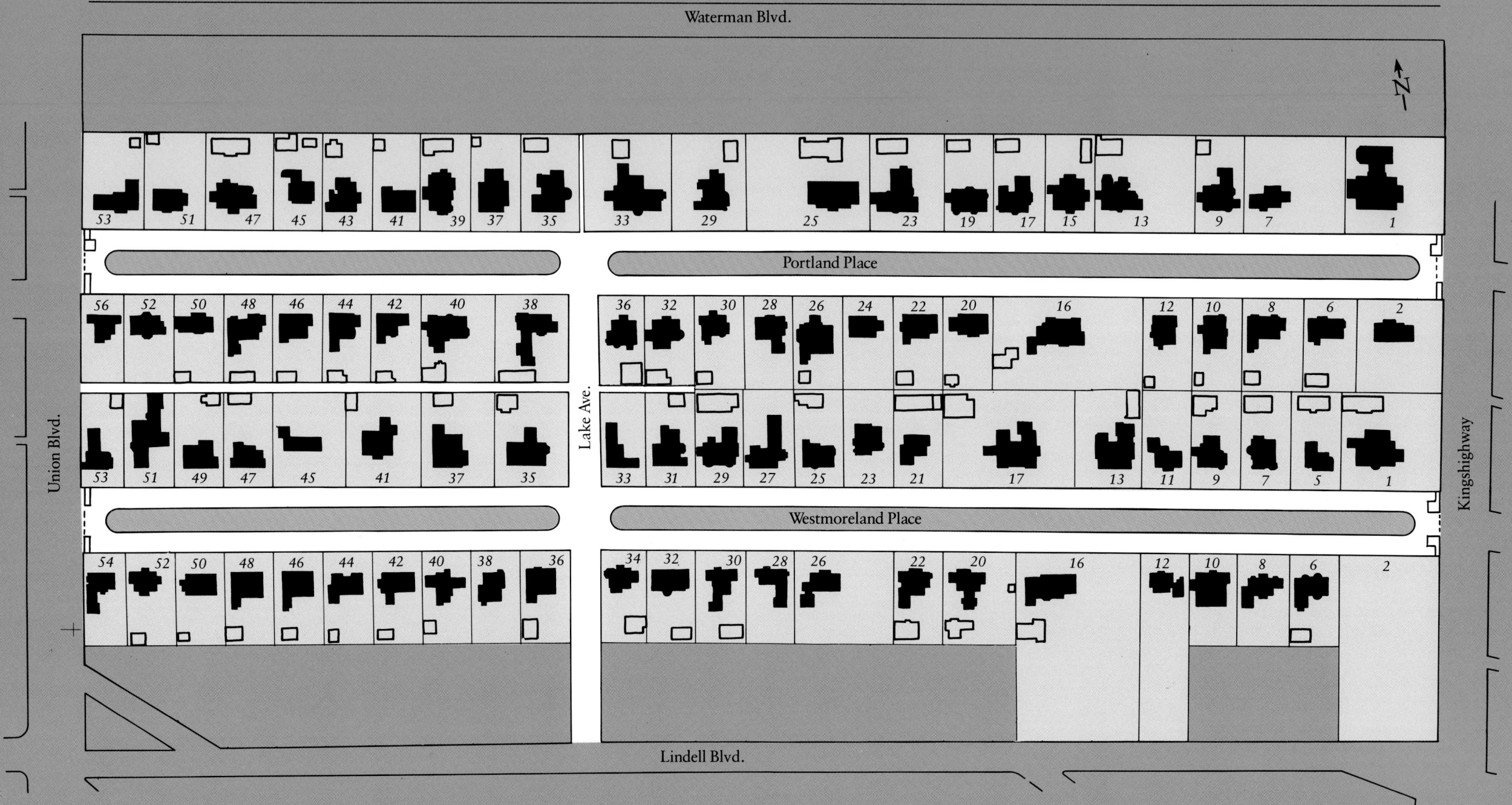

Waterman Blvd.

Portland Place

Westmoreland Place

Union Blvd.

Lake Ave.

Kingshighway

Lindell Blvd.

Forest Park

0   100 150 200 ft.

1. WESTMORELAND AND PORTLAND: THE GENESIS

1887 was ushered in with the shrieking of steamboat whistles, the clanging of bells, the sounding of horns, with noise of every kind and description.

—*The Missouri Republican*, January 2, 1887

It was an appropriate celebration for the birth of a year that would see so many new beginnings, so many changes, controversies, and hardships, so much excitement and so much sheer fun.

This was the year of Queen Victoria's Golden Jubilee, the worldwide commemoration of her fiftieth year of reign over the British Empire. Elsewhere in Europe the new year began with the rattling of sabers. In a January address to the Reichstag, Chancellor Otto von Bismarck accused French War Minister Georges Boulanger of being the greatest obstacle to peaceful coexistence between France and Germany. The specter of war in Europe loomed as an even greater possibility when Russia refused to renew a treaty with Germany and Austria.

The events in Europe were watched with interest in St. Louis. Ties to the Old World were strong, and virtually every nationality was represented in the city's ethnic neighborhoods. By 1887 there were distinctive Italian, Irish, Afro-American, German, French, Polish, and Bohemian neighborhoods.

In 1887, with help from all the ethnic groups, St. Louis was in the midst of a great industrial boom. Mayor David R. Francis proclaimed in his annual message to the municipal assembly, "The growth of the city during the past year has been great. Real estate has advanced, building has been extensive, manufacturing has taken new life, the unemployed are comparatively few, and the city's commerce has increased. A sanguine feeling as to our future prosperity seems to pervade the entire community."

The United States was fast becoming the world leader in the production of steel, heavy machinery, and durable goods. A new class emerged—the industrial entrepreneurs who risked capital and reputation to build factories and develop new products. Typically aggressive and self-confident, some of these industrial barons elbowed their way into the St. Louis power structure in the late nineteenth century, joining powerful survivors of the older mercantile, banking, industrial, real estate, and professional families in a somewhat more broadly based local elite. Following an already established St. Louis pattern, they built palatial homes in exclusive subdivisions, supported cultural institutions, and used their leverage in politics to their advantage.

Mercantile progress and cultural sophistication were concomitant elements in the late nineteenth century. It was during that era that the rich cultivated what historian John Archer has called "a passion for beauty." An important ingredient of this passion was a desire for beautiful surroundings. The development of landscape design as an art form at that time resulted in "picturesque urban parks and romantically landscaped cemeteries." The passion for beauty led those of great means to create elegant and exclusive residential enclaves—private places and suburbs.

In 1871 America's foremost landscape architect, Frederick Law Olmsted, described a suburb as a community "with sylvan surroundings yet supplied with a considerable share of urban convenience." The urban upper class strove to attain this ideal—the creation of a community of neighbors who shared similar social backgrounds, industrial pursuits, incomes, cultural tastes, and ideals. These residential districts were placed in the most beautiful settings money could buy. In fact, they were urban oases.

Among the greatest contributions that post–Civil War wealth made to the city of St. Louis was the construction of magnificent homes beautifully displayed on quiet boulevards. The outstanding architecture of these homes and the elaborate, even opulent detail used to embellish them have left St. Louis a rich cultural legacy. As historian James Neal Primm reports in *Lion of the Valley*:

> In 1903 *National Magazine* ranked St. Louis first anywhere in this respect, saying that it outshone any combination of three cities in the world. Many homes were "veritable palaces in every particular of richness, appointment, and setting—even the size." Each was "surrounded by stretching green lawns, fresh and sparkling . . . diversified and enriched by luxuriant shrubs, flowers, and trees."

This resource can still be appreciated today in the premier private places called Westmoreland and Portland.

The creation of urban beauty depended on the generation of wealth by industry, and industrial production depended on the

There were still dirt roads in Westmoreland Place in 1900 when this photo was taken. The central parkway was first employed in St. Louis in Julius Pitzman's 1868 design for Benton Place.

railroads. In the late nineteenth century, St. Louis was already a key rail hub, connecting East with West. The principal railroads with track tributaries from St. Louis in 1887 were the Missouri Pacific; the St. Louis, Iron Mountain and Southern; the Ohio and Mississippi; the Wabash; and the Texas and St. Louis Railway Company, also known as the Cotton Belt line.

Hardware, dry goods, and groceries were vital to the expansion of America. As railroads forged deeper and deeper into frontier territory, they carried these goods to homesteaders and small towns on the edge of the wilderness. St. Louisans with dreams of building great fortunes saw the golden opportunities and made their city a bustling manufacturing center.

Among the leading St. Louis businesses in the 1880s was hardware wholesaling in a far-flung hinterland covering most of the West, the Middle West, and the South. Largest among the St. Louis hardware houses were the Simmons Hardware Company, the A. F. Shapleigh & Cantwell Hardware Company, and the Rubelmann Hardware Company. Henry Shaw was the first St. Louis merchant to deal exclusively in hardware. He amassed a quarter of a million dollars in the business between 1820 and 1840, which by real estate and commodity speculation he built into the large fortune that enabled him to give the magnificent Missouri Botanical Garden to St. Louis. The great wealth accumulated in the nuts-and-bolts hardware trade would be used by Edward C. Simmons, the founder of the company bearing his name, by his son Wallace D. Simmons, and by Alfred L. Shapleigh, son of A. F. Shapleigh, to build or buy palatial homes in St. Louis's most impressive private places—Westmoreland and Portland.

The dry-goods trade was also indispensable to the expansion of the nation. In 1887 St. Louis's largest and most successful dry-goods retail houses were Scruggs, Vandervoort & Barney, established in 1868; the William Barr Dry Goods Co., founded in 1849; and the J. H. Wear, Boogher & Co., which first opened its doors in 1867. In 1887 there were eight major St. Louis firms dealing exclusively in wholesaling and importing dry goods, twelve dry-goods commission houses, and more than three hundred retail dry-goods companies. According to the 1880 census, the dry-goods business in St. Louis grossed $28 million annually.

The wholesale dry-goods business produced a fraternity of St. Louisans whose profits propelled them into the highest echelon of society. Pioneer wholesale merchants Wayman Crow and Samuel C. Davis were followed by Murray Carleton, John T. Davis, Robert McKittrick Jones, Charles Stix, Walter McKittrick, Byron Nugent, and others. Many of these men

would soon plan to be neighbors in a still-to-be-created exclusive enclave at the city's western frontier.

The grocery trade was listed as part of the "dry-goods" business until the mid-nineteenth century, when it became a separately listed enterprise. In 1887 the Alkire Grocer Company, founded in 1852, was among the largest. The Brookmire & Ranken wholesale grocery was established in 1868. Grocer Benjamin W. Clark would use his fortune to build a home in the new exclusive neighborhood north of Forest Park.

In the late 1880s St. Louis was a leader in sugar refining, the largest inland coffee market, and a dairy center that grossed more than $1.5 million a year in butter and cheese. At the same time, the city exported an average of seventy-four thousand barrels of molasses, fifty thousand barrels of rice, and thirty-six thousand packages of tea per year.

St. Louis led Chicago as a wheat market in 1887. Wheat and grain fortunes would make neighbors of such families as

the Carters, Langenbergs, and Orthweins. At that time the Dozier-Weyl Cracker Co. of St. Louis was the largest manufacturer of soda crackers in the world. Lewis D. Dozier, son of the founder, Capt. James Dozier, would build a home in Westmoreland Place and become a neighbor of the leaders of the grocery, hardware, dry-goods, and grain industries.

Although the nation and the general population benefited greatly from the railroads, it soon became apparent that a few men were the chief beneficiaries of the growth of the rail system. It also became apparent that these rail barons wielded immense power. In fact, a government study conducted in 1887 concluded, "No man dared engage in any business in which transportation largely entered without first obtaining the permission of a railroad manager."

In St. Louis, Jay Gould and his representatives controlled the rail systems and wielded great power over other businesses. Many accusatory fingers were pointed at rail chieftains in

A weekend ride in the park was a popular pastime for the elite, such as this 1892 carriage excursion through Shaw's Garden.

1887 alleging bribes, kickbacks, and price-fixing, but relatively few charges were ever prosecuted. Railroad magnates often were able to appoint their own cronies to investigate allegations of wrongdoing. And it was common practice that the findings of investigators were decided before the probe began.

At that time there were nineteen railway lines in and out of the city, including the East St. Louis freight terminals. Over 215,000 loaded freight cars crossed the Eads Bridge in 1886, almost 30,000 more than the year before. Railroad executives such as W. K. Bixby, Carl Gray, William Bagnell, and William Guy would soon be able to retreat to their palatial Westmoreland and Portland mansions.

Well before 1887, barges had replaced steamboats in the river freight business and railroads dominated in overland freight and passenger travel. Mark Twain had observed a decade earlier that an era was ending. He found "half a dozen sound-asleep steamboats where I used to see a solid mile of wide awake ones!" Only four regular steamboat lines operated on the upper Mississippi in 1887, only two regular steamboat companies operated on the Missouri River, and only one packet line steamed the Illinois. But barge traffic increased in 1887 over 1886. Some 866,000 tons of goods were shipped that year.

The average upper-class St. Louisan was more likely to use a carriage than either the horsecars or cable cars in 1887, and there were fifty-two carriage-manufacturing companies in the city. One was owned by Lewis B. Tebbetts, who would soon move to the sanctuary of Portland Place. To keep the horsepower for those barouches, rockaways, buggies, trucks, and light wagons well shod, there were more than seventy blacksmith shops.

And for those St. Louisans who could not afford a carriage or who preferred to leave the family buggy parked in the carriage house when going downtown, seventeen streetcar companies provided the city's mass transportation in 1887. At first the steam-powered cable trains were decidedly unpopular. The temperamental cars screeched and careened, terrorizing horses all along their routes. But their benefits were slowly recognized. By 1887 it was possible to take almost any line from downtown St. Louis and connect with the Narrow Gauge Railroad at Grand and Olive for a trip all the way out to the suburban community of Florissant—a scenic journey of sixteen miles.

Banker Julius S. Walsh, a descendant of Pierre Laclede, the founder of St. Louis, was president of four of the seventeen car

Although many of the early residents of Westmoreland/Portland employed chauffeurs, the streetcar was a popular form of transportation for these residents.

lines. Steelmaker John Scullin was chief executive officer of three others. The families of both would build magnificent homes in the new private places near Forest Park.

St. Louis was growing at an incredible rate in the late 1880s. The homebuilding industry was booming. In 1887, 1,717 brick buildings were constructed in the city at an assessed value of $5,488,787. There were 519 nonresidential buildings erected that year at a valuation of $464,156. And St. Louisans expended $6,707,110 during the same period to improve their properties. Edward Sterling, who owned the Hydraulic Press Brick Company, father and son John and Robert Holmes, owners of a lumber company, and Louis Werner, whose company made wooden gutters, did a land-office business in 1887. They, too, would soon be neighbors in the new private enclave near Forest Park.

By 1887 St. Louis was moving out of the gaslit age and into the era of electricity. The city building commissioner, Louis Kledus, proposed converting all gaslights in city-owned buildings to electricity—and for a very good reason. The city could realize a substantial saving by making the conversion. Well-known restaurateur Tony Faust brought the first electric dynamo to St. Louis in 1878—just three years after Thomas Edison refined his "etheric force"—but St. Louisans would make the changeover from gas to electricity very slowly. There seemed to be general agreement with the woman who predicted to an

inquiring newspaper reporter that if the day came when all the buildings in the city were linked by electricity, "One clap of thunder would be apt to send the whole city to everlasting smash!" Nonetheless, electricity came to St. Louis, and fortunes made by electric power would make neighbors of the Breckinridge Jones and Henry Scott families.

The temperance movement was strong in the closing years of the nineteenth century and, by the late 1880s, "total abstinence" often included a scornful look at tobacco in addition to the call for prohibition of alcoholic beverages. But these two industries prospered in St. Louis nonetheless. The prominence of breweries in St. Louis in 1887 is well known. Some forty breweries produced more than 2 million barrels of beer each year for the thirsty patrons of more than one thousand taverns and beer gardens in the town. Yet the brewing business was not considered quite respectable by St. Louis society, and enormously wealthy German brewers were, on the whole, kept outside the gates of St. Louis's most exclusive private residential districts. Only two of the families who built houses in Westmoreland or Portland were associated with brewing: Elizabeth Schnaider was the widow of brewer and beer-garden owner Joseph Schnaider, and Anna Busch Faust was the daughter of Adolphus Busch.

Tobacco manufacturers were more readily accepted. Tobacco had its all-American roots in the upper South, including Missouri. At least a dozen tobacco companies operated in St. Louis in 1887, carrying on the industry that had begun seventy years earlier. The giant Liggett & Myers Tobacco Company was founded in the city in 1878 and in its heyday produced more plug tobacco at its headquarters at Thirteenth and St. Charles streets than any other manufacturer in the world. Other large tobacco firms located in St. Louis were the Catlin Tobacco Co., Dausman Tobacco Co., Drummond Co., and Price & Austin Tobacco Co. Catlin and Drummond were eventually swallowed up by the American Tobacco Co. There were also some four hundred cigar-manufacturing shops in St. Louis in 1887; the largest among them was the William A. Stickney Co.

Two of the tobacco czars would build mansions in Westmoreland Place—Daniel Catlin, Sr., and William Stickney. In addition, Catlin's son and namesake and the three daughters of tobacco tycoon John Liggett (Cora Liggett Fowler, Ella Liggett Wiggins, and Dorothy Liggett Kilpatrick) would each build a house in the Westmoreland-Portland district.

As in every other city, crime was a problem in St. Louis in 1887. By today's standards, the city's 1887 crime statistics do not appear alarming. Twenty-two murders, 211 burglaries, 33 robberies, 19 rapes, and 255 cases of assault with intent to kill were reported to the police. But there were other crimes seldom if ever seen today: 84 reports of highway robbery, 4 reports of rioting, 104 cases of taking a bath in a public place (usually a fountain), and 116 instances of "dumping filth on the street." Peace disturbances, public drunkenness, prostitution, and loitering also appear on the city's 1887 police blotter.

The offenses were of sufficient concern to the city's upper class that its members made every effort to insulate and isolate themselves from the threat of crime. Private residential enclaves were an attempt to ensure protection. St. Louis's wealthy citizens dug into the city's outskirts, erected protective fences and gates around their homes, utilized gaslights to their maximum, and hired private security guards. The streetcar companies, by charging relatively high fares to the Forest Park district, helped to keep the masses away from the exclusive West End.

Other problems in St. Louis in 1887 involved disease; in that year a diphtheria outbreak reached almost epidemic proportions. Residents were also on the lookout for flare-ups of scarlatina, measles, and Asiatic cholera.

Some of the city's health problems were caused by the heavy cover of industrial smoke. Mark Twain quipped that the dense smoke in St. Louis turned new furnishings into antiques almost overnight. But the stifling pall that enveloped the city was nothing to joke about. It debilitated and even killed thousands of St. Louisans. Soft Illinois coal produced thick smoke that spewed from factory stacks. Steamboats belched choking black smoke as they moved to and from the levee. Trains crisscrossing the city poured out more. And dark smoke billowed from almost every home chimney in town during the winter months.

Small wonder that at least 1,293 St. Louisans died of respiratory illnesses in 1887. These included membranous croup, whooping cough, bronchitis, and pneumonia. Many other deaths related to the inhalation of coal smoke were probably either misdiagnosed or unreported. The smoke nuisance was another reason that the city's upper-class citizens continued to move westward.

Why did City Hall not do anything about the killer smoke? Smoke meant industry and industry meant jobs and jobs meant paychecks. Thirty-two coal companies were located in the metropolitan area in 1887. Their owners—and the owners of the white-lead plants, railroads, brickyards, and steamboat lines that used the offending coal—were the same men who

controlled party politics and City Hall. They enjoyed the fellowship of the same private clubs, the secret handshakes of the same exclusive fraternal organizations, and living in the same posh residential neighborhoods. City Hall would not bite the hands that fed the city. Those who could afford to could find only one solution: move into the cleaner air farther west. Smoke would remain a serious problem in St. Louis until 1940.

Development of the area west of Grand Avenue was inevitable as the affluent moved to escape crime and grime. Early in the twentieth century Westmoreland Place resident Isaac Lionberger commented:

Progress has been attended by horrid waste. Every generation has been compelled to move three times. . . . If for a little while a pleasant neighborhood endures, composed of decent houses, it is soon besmirched by smoke and dust and dirt. Noise incessantly afflicts it and the roar of street cars disturbs its serenity. No forethought, no restrictions can prevail. Those who have the means move continually, leaving behind what they cannot endure.

The flight of the wealthy to avoid an encroaching city was not a new phenomenon in America. The nation's earliest suburban enclaves appeared in the 1840s. They flowered because of the attempt of affluent residents to escape the pollution, noise, crime, and disease of cities. Whether the fleeing upper class realized that the factories they had created and that had made their fortunes were responsible for the smoke, water pollution, and noise is moot. The poor housing that grew up around factories also contributed to the decline of the urban environment and bred crime—but such housing was all that underpaid employees could afford. In 1900 the average yearly income for a blue-collar worker in St. Louis was $485.

The idea of creating a safe enclave, a "private place" where residents could take on the responsibility for lighting, sewers, sidewalks, landscaping, security, and refuse collection in exchange for the right to privacy and to control over their neighbors was not a new one in 1887. By that time St. Louis developers had been experimenting with private places and restrictive residency for more than four decades. As architectural historian Charles Savage notes in his *Architecture of the Private Streets of St. Louis*, "Ironically, the private streets were introduced to provide [the] mercantile elite protection from the uncontrolled spread—blighting, noxious, and foreign—that their industry had generated. In the absence of any municipal initiative, the private streets evolved as a substitute for zoning."

Lucas Place was one of the earliest plush hideaways for St.

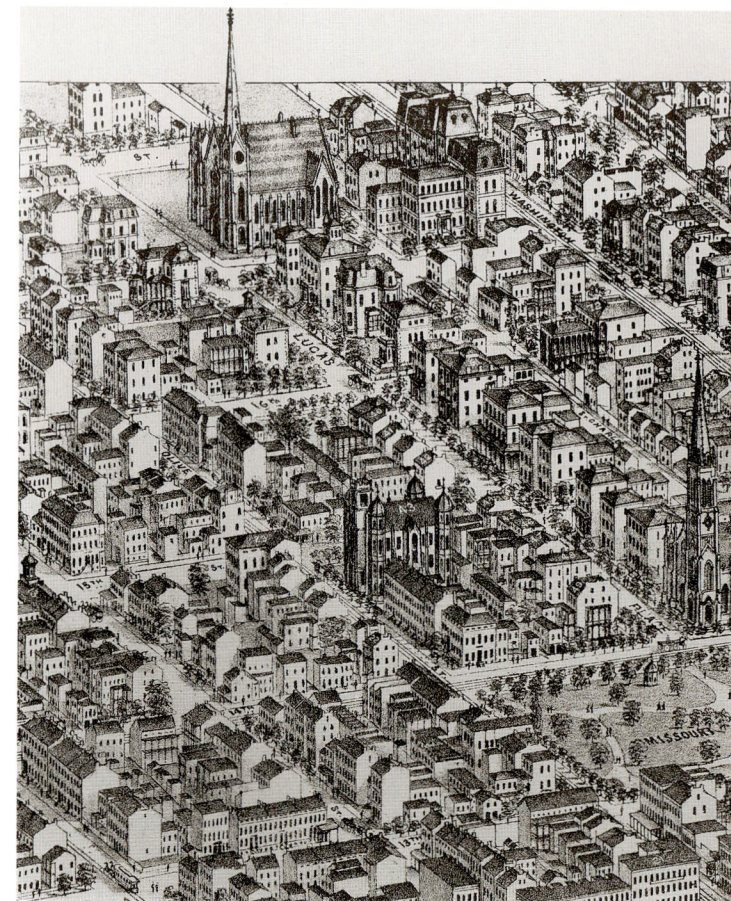

Lucas Place was an elegant private residential enclave created in 1851 by banker–land developer James H. Lucas.

Louis's upper class. In 1851 wealthy banker-landowner James H. Lucas invited his friends and family members to set up an exclusive encampment with him in what is now Locust Street between Fourteenth and Eighteenth. Lucas Place became the first private place in which the residents were given total responsibility for street maintenance. Lucas reasoned that the encroachments of the growing city could be made to bypass his enclave if he laid out a buffer corridor of green space between his private place and the city. There would be no public traffic near his home. While it is true that Missouri Park, as the green space came to be known, did effectively reroute pedestrian and carriage traffic, there was no way to shut out the noxious odors and smoke of manufacture.

Lucas's plan prohibited grocers, apothecaries, coffeehouses, dramshops, theaters, and circuses inside his private place but allowed his closed community to enjoy the cultural advantages of religion and education; thus his blueprint shows an allocation for Mary Institute, a girls' school, and for the First Presbyterian Church. But Lucas Place was too close to the industrial and transportation progression of the city to survive. James Lucas died in 1873; his sister, Anne L. Hunt, who was the doyenne of the exclusive enclave, died six years later. With their passing passed the superintendence of a grand and unique residential concept. In 1898 Locust Street was cut through Missouri Park and the park's privacy was destroyed. Some of the mansions soon became boardinghouses. Today the Campbell house, the Victorian mansion built in 1851 for James Hall and later lived in by fur trader Robert Campbell, stands as a lone reminder of the once gracious Lucas Place.

Just as James Lucas was developing his private residential area, attorney Charles Gibson was trying to set up a protected neighborhood around Lafayette Park. Gibson envisioned a plan for lasting exclusivity that was based on ringing the park with mansions of rare elegance. Gibson convinced the city aldermen to ban obnoxious business enterprises in the immediate environs of Lafayette Square. In 1852 the city agreed to landscape the park and to erect a wooden fence around it. Between 1855 and 1860 the city and Lafayette Square residents jointly raised $18,000 for further improvement to the park. In 1869 a $50,000 ornamental cast-iron fence replaced the wooden one. Gibson's residential enclave was looked on as a model community.

Lafayette Square reached its prime soon after the Civil War. Then unexpected events began to subvert its exclusivity. In 1876 the city extended its western boundary beyond Forest Park, encouraging well-to-do residents to move west, instead of south toward Lafayette Square, and a tide of immigrants moved into the Soulard neighborhood, close to Lafayette Park. When gaslights were introduced into the park, the working classes could use it at night to play baseball, a game then new and considered by the elite to be very rowdy. Before 1890 the best residents were moving out. In 1896 a killer tornado destroyed what was left of Lafayette Square and its elegance.

The house at the right was built by James Hall in 1851 and was purchased in 1854 by Robert Campbell. It is all that remains of the once majestic Lucas Place and is known today as the Campbell House.

Vandeventer Place, 1880. This view from Grand Avenue shows the east gate when the entrance was of ornamental wrought iron. Stone pillars and walls replaced the old gate sometime near the close of the nineteenth century.

The city's second private place with strong covenant restrictions was Benton Place. It was established on the north side of Lafayette Square in 1868 by Montgomery Blair, formerly postmaster general in Abraham Lincoln's cabinet and a noted lawyer and judge who had represented Dred Scott before the U.S. Supreme Court in 1857.

The Benton Place covenant gave a board of trustees full responsibility for street governance. This covenant was different from the homeowners' agreement drawn up for residents of neighboring Lafayette Square. The residents of the square were asked to share responsibility with the city for the upkeep of the streets that bordered the park. The Benton Place deed of trust empowered the trustees to levy fees, based on the size of each lot, to pay for all street repairs, lighting, center parkway maintenance, and sewers. The city was relieved of all responsibility for upkeep. To keep traffic away, Benton Place was designed as a cul-de-sac with an entrance gate that was wide enough to allow only one carriage at a time to leave or enter. Benton Place also introduced the center parkway to the St. Louis private place plat.

Vandeventer Place was St. Louis's next fashionable enclave. Established in 1870, it was the brainchild of Charles Peck, Napoleon Mullikin, and Joseph McCune. Its mansions were built on a scale never before seen in St. Louis, and it took the private place concept many steps beyond Lucas and Benton.

The covenant signed by Vandeventer Place homeowners prohibited any multifamily residency on the eighty-six lots. None of the buildings on the premises could be used for any purpose that might be considered a nuisance. The agreement also specified that the steps of each house had to be scrubbed at least twice a week and that each house had to have three sets of white lace curtains for each window. No home could be constructed for less than $10,000—equivalent to $180,000 in 1987 dollars. So affluent was the neighborhood that many of the carriage houses in the rear of the mansions were built for more than $10,000.

The planners of Vandeventer Place incorporated a landscaped central parkway as the core around which the houses would be built. This median park was much grander than the tiny strip in Benton Place. In addition, in a lesson learned from Lucas Place, the construction of churches, schools, or nonresidential buildings inside the gates was strictly prohibited. Imposing gates were constructed at the Grand Avenue entrance on the east and at Vandeventer on the west in 1894, a full twenty-two years after the first mansion was built. Bell Avenue was the northern boundary and Morgan (now Delmar) was the southern border. Signs were posted to let the outside world know that the place was private and that trespassing would not be allowed. Unfortunately for its future, Vandeventer Place provided no buffer zone between its backyards and the surrounding areas. Its restrictive gates were constructed too long after its establishment.

Founders Peck and Mullikin built the first mansions in Vandeventer Place and then the Panic of 1873 hit, an economic collapse that brought home construction to a halt. No new houses rose in Vandeventer Place until almost ten years after the panic.

There is some evidence that the developers of Vandeventer Place were willing to be accommodating in the early 1880s to encourage new home construction. An article in the December 5, 1884, *Globe-Democrat* noted that Dr. Henry Fisher had bought a lot with sixty feet of frontage on the north side of Vandeventer Place for the bargain price of $5,500. And the article announced Dr. Fisher's plans to build a $10,000 residence on the lot the following spring. Shortly after Dr. Fisher's home rose in 1885 and before the onset of the four-year depression that began in 1893, Vandeventer Place came into its own as a showplace community, even though the masses could only see the portions of the place that were visible from the periphery or from the backside. Vandeventer Place's stables were lined along its north and south boundaries.

But within four decades of its conspicuous founding, proud Vandeventer Place was already on the decline. In an August 21, 1916, *Post-Dispatch* article, tobacco tycoon Daniel Catlin is quoted as saying, "I live in the slums—Vandeventer Place." Several factors can be blamed for this decline. According to an 1895 article in the *St. Louis Republic*, Vandeventer Place was "too pretentiously exclusive for its own good. By its very seclusion, Vandeventer Place contributed to the eventual shabbiness of its own environment." When the electric streetcar clanged into St. Louis in 1890, bringing with it the shrieks of metal grinding on metal and hordes of noisy riders, Vandeventer Place could not maintain its isolation. At about the same time, Grand Avenue, the enclave's eastern border, was opened to commercial use. The city's privileged class began once again to look westward.

Although Benton Place, Lucas Place, Lafayette Square, and even the elegant Vandeventer Place had not been especially successful, Mayor David R. Francis (who lived in Vandeventer Place before moving to Maryland Avenue) at one time apparently considered turning Lindell Boulevard into a private avenue. In 1887 he told the municipal assembly, "In other cities such boulevards are maintained at the expense of the abutting property." The mayor concluded by suggesting that Lindell Boulevard property owners be given special consideration for maintaining the street. He recommended that if residents were required to pay for the maintenance of a street, "restrictions as to [its] use [should be] imposed and enforced." Even as the mayor proposed the idea of residents in affluent areas maintaining their streets in exchange for the right to regulate traffic in those streets, a newly formed syndicate called the Forest Park Improvement Association was busy preparing to acquire the land it would need to establish two private places just north of Forest Park.

Mayor Francis was a superb example of an enlightened politician who used all his resources—and those of his friends—to make his city a haven for the affluent and enterprising. He was known as progressive and forward-looking. The importance of St. Louis in national politics was underscored by the fact that the Democratic party chose St. Louis as the site of its 1888 convention.

Democratic President Grover Cleveland's 1887 State of the Union message focused on the necessity for reducing tariffs. Businessmen with local and national interests feared that Cleveland's foreign-trade program would open the gates to a flood of foreign competition. Others felt that tariff protection meant subsidizing business at the expense of the public.

Despite any negative opinions harbored by high-tariff Republican businessmen in St. Louis, Cleveland received a warm welcome when he came to visit in October 1887. He had been formally invited by Mayor Francis several times earlier. There were twenty thousand St. Louis signatures on the invitation that finally convinced him to come to town. Partisan politics were temporarily put aside as the red carpet was rolled out for President and Mrs. Cleveland. After all, the First Family is as close to royalty as this nation produces. Furthermore, Mayor Francis perceived quite accurately the benefits a presidential visit could provide for St. Louis, and for the personal political aspirations of the mayor and his cronies.

The presidential train arrived on October 2 shortly after midnight at the Fourteenth Street depot. The Clevelands found an enthusiastic welcoming party of dignitaries and gentry who rubbed sleepy eyes as the train chugged into the depot. Describing the group, a local newspaper observed, "There were the rich, the poor, the fashionable and the plain."

The Clevelands were taken by carriage to the home of Mayor Francis in Vandeventer Place. Security was rather lax. The small detachment of policemen assigned to the place's

In 1887, President and Mrs. Grover Cleveland visited St. Louis and met many private place residents. The land for Westmoreland/Portland was purchased that year.

entrances at Grand and Vandeventer avenues permitted pedestrian gawkers to enter for a peek at their president and first lady. Carriages were denied entrance, however.

After breakfast on October 3, the Clevelands set out for a busy four days of events. Their hosts planned well to be sure that the nation's First Couple saw the finest St. Louis had to offer. Their first outing was to a Sunday morning worship service at the Washington Avenue Presbyterian Church, a short carriage ride from the Francis mansion. The church was packed to capacity, floral arrangements bedecked the sanctuary, and the regular choir was augmented with extra singers.

The first big social event on the itinerary was a luncheon for Frances Cleveland at the mansion at Grand and Lucas of Mary F. Scanlan, the queen of lavish social affairs. She was a millionaire, thanks to a railroad's $2.14 million purchase of the Wiggins Ferry Company, of which she was the majority shareholder. And she was a member of the prominent old Christy family.

When the first lady arrived at the Scanlan mansion, she was greeted by a group of children from St. Vincent's Convent School, including Marie Scanlan, daughter of the hostess. Marie gave Mrs. Cleveland a bouquet of American Beauty roses and a poem written especially for her by St. Vincent

students. Then the guests lunched on twelve exquisitely prepared courses.

Mary Scanlan was a prototype of the St. Louis society to which the Clevelands were exposed. While the president was in St. Louis he would shake few hands that performed manual labor; Mayor Francis saw to it that most of the hands that pressed the president's were the soft hands that controlled the reins of the city. While the first lady lunched at the Scanlan mansion, her husband was off to the downtown Merchants' Exchange for an official welcome from civic, political, and business leaders. He would have difficulty there discerning Republican smiles and handshakes from Democratic greetings.

During their stay in St. Louis, the Clevelands enjoyed a public reception at Fairgrounds Park, a boat ride on the Mississippi River, a place of distinction in the annual Veiled Prophet parade, and a grand evening at the Veiled Prophet ball. Frances Cleveland was chosen the first matron of honor at the ball by the mysterious potentate from Khorassan. St. Louis was generally impressed with the beauty, charm, and graciousness of young Mrs. Cleveland. City fathers named a south St. Louis street in her honor—Folsom was her maiden name.

At a luncheon at the Fairgrounds clubhouse, the president chatted with Julius Pitzman, a former city engineer who had planned Benton and Vandeventer places. Pitzman may have told the president of his latest plan for two new private places that he would inaugurate within the year. It may also have been at this luncheon that the dashing young Isaac Lionberger impressed the president enough to be appointed assistant attorney general in the second Cleveland administration. Lionberger, who would build a house in one of the private places

Isaac Lionberger, the first owner of 37 Westmoreland, was quite an athlete and adventurer before he settled down to become an assistant U.S. attorney general and solicitor to the Department of the Interior under President Cleveland. At Princeton, Lionberger was captain of the football team and a gymnast, high jumper, and runner. In 1878, after leaving Princeton, he headed to Montana, where he worked as a cowboy for two years. In this photo Lionberger, shown on the left, poses with his cowboy companion, Will Sandford.

Pitzman was laying out, would also serve as solicitor to the Interior Department.

Certainly David R. Francis impressed the president. In 1896 Cleveland appointed him secretary of the interior. Francis, who was elected governor of Missouri just after his term as mayor expired in 1889, later engineered St. Louis's magnificent 1904 World's Fair and became U.S. ambassador to Russia in 1917. Francis's son Perry would build a house in Portland Place, the new Pitzman project being planned at the time of the presidential visit. Francis pulled off the successful presidential visit with the help of such fellow Democrats as Samuel Kennard, Judge Elmer Adams, Isaac Lionberger, and Claude Kilpatrick. These men would soon be charter homebuilders and neighbors in the two new private places being planned near Forest Park.

Grover Cleveland left St. Louis at midnight on October 5 with a host of new friends and a new respect for the progressive city he was leaving. The feeling was not entirely mutual. Working-class St. Louisans were not enthused by Cleveland's conservatism, and Civil War veterans hated his anti-pension stance. On one of his tours of the city, the president was struck in the face by a pie thrown by an irate Irish workingwoman.

In another issue much discussed in 1887, literate and cultured St. Louisans wondered if it would be *de rigueur* to cancel their subscriptions to the *Atlantic Monthly*. The magazine had dared to print a short story by Charles W. Chesnutt, a black man. In 1887 the issue of whether Missouri blacks could be educated in integrated schools came to a head when a white teacher in Grundy County refused to admit black children to her classroom. The parents sued the teacher on Fourteenth Amendment grounds, claiming the children's rights were violated. Missouri lawmakers did not wait for a ruling. The legislature passed a law in 1889 that ordered separate schools for students "of African descent."

Despite the prejudices expressed against Jews, blacks, Irish Catholics, Germans, and immigrants in general, St. Louis considered itself a cultured city in 1887. It was in that year that Henry Shaw officiated at the laying of the cornerstone for the new Mercantile Library building at Broadway and Locust. The library itself had been in existence since 1846 and claimed to be the first private lending library established west of the Mississippi River.

The list of the governing board of the Mercantile Library was a veritable Who's Who in St. Louis. Robert Brookings, who was a major benefactor of Washington University, was

The Lionbergers, Kennards, Mallinckrodts, Whitakers, Davises, Catlins, Allens, McMillans, Niedringhauses, Thornburghs, and Shapleighs were the early Westmoreland/Portland residents who supported the Mercantile Library with money and leadership.

president. The library's vice-president was Julius S. Walsh, head of Mississippi Valley Trust and president of several streetcar lines. His mother, Isabella DeMun, had recently sold some of her property under protest to the city for the establishment of Forest Park. The Mercantile's treasurer was Vandeventer Place resident John R. Lionberger, father of the ubiquitous Isaac Lionberger; Isaac would later move into a house he built adjacent to the park created from some of the Walsh property.

Among the Mercantile Library's directors were carpet magnate Samuel Kennard, Boatmen's Bank president Edwards Whitaker (who was also a vice-president of Bell Telephone and president of United Railways), and Mayor David Francis. One of two patrons who donated $10,000 to the library in 1887 was dry-goods tycoon John T. Davis, Sr. Tobacco czar Daniel Catlin gave the library $2,500. W. R. Allen, John R. Lionberger, William McMillan, F. G. Niedringhaus, W. F. Niedringhaus, H. Clay Pierce, W. H. Thornburgh, and Alfred Shapleigh each gave $1,000; Edward Mallinckrodt and David Francis each donated $500. And remembering the widow's mite—even if the widow was a millionaire—the library gratefully accepted the $100 donation of Mrs. Hudson Bridge. Seven of these leading citizens and their families were to be neighbors in Westmoreland and Portland places.

The St. Louis Symphony Orchestra, the second oldest symphony in the nation (the New York Philharmonic was the first), was already seven years old when construction was begun on the new Mercantile Library building. In fact, the St. Louis Choral Society, the forerunner of the orchestra, had performed its first concert on March 24, 1881, in the old Mercantile Library hall. The list of the orchestra's earliest patrons includes William K. Bixby, William Huse, Augustus B. Hart, Daniel Catlin, Claude Kilpatrick, Thomas West, and John T. Davis—all soon to be Westmoreland/Portland neighbors.

It is no coincidence that all of the preceding people were recognized in 1887 as among the movers and shakers of St. Louis. And it is not surprising that these pillars of the community, who shared an interest in literature and the arts, also shared a neighborhood, Westmoreland/Portland.

Many St. Louisans were more enthusiastic about baseball batting averages than about book-browsing or concert-going. St. Louis had two thriving baseball parks in 1887—the southside Red Stocking Park on Compton Avenue north of the Pacific Railroad tracks and the popular Sportsman's Park at Grand and Sullivan on the north side.

The St. Louis Browns had brought the city its first league championship in 1886, thanks to the unorthodox coaching style of Charlie Comiskey. Early in the 1887 season, the Browns were on an eleven-game winning streak when they were interrupted by a rain shower on May 11. The fans who sat on the damp benches at Sportsman's Park that day could not have known that while they were cheering a soggy home team on, a small group of local businessmen was consummating the real estate deal of the decade in complete secrecy. Developers were purchasing a tract of land near Forest Park in which they would establish St. Louis's two outstanding private places—Westmoreland and Portland.

The reading room of the downtown Mercantile Library as it looked in 1887 when Westmoreland/Portland residents Edwards Whitaker and Samuel Kennard served on the library's board of directors.

2. FOREST PARK AND THE FOREST PARK IMPROVEMENT ASSOCIATION

The visitor at Forest Park, as he saunters along the well-drained and neatly-graveled promenades, or about the park lake with its pleasant island orchestra, or rests in the grove in the shade of some one of its giant oaks, would find it difficult at best to re-create out of all the embellishments of those beautiful pleasure-grounds a true picture of the wild surroundings, the dangers, and the savage bewilderments of the primal site.

—J. Thomas Scharf, 1883

There would be no Portland Place or Westmoreland Place had there not been a Forest Park. There would be no Forest Park had there not been Hiram W. Leffingwell. And Hiram Leffingwell would not have been in St. Louis had there not been boundless opportunities for visionaries in the city.

Hiram Wheeler Leffingwell migrated to St. Louis from the East, as had most of the city's influential citizens at that time. He was born in 1809 on a farm in Hampden County, Massachusetts. After receiving a formal education in Pennsylvania, Leffingwell taught in Ohio and Pennsylvania, but he grew bored with teaching and answered the call to adventure in the West. He arrived in St. Louis in 1838, but a job with a wholesale grocery company took him to Rockford, Illinois, almost immediately. There he tried farming, failed, and turned to the study of law. He returned to St. Louis in 1843 and shortly thereafter was licensed to practice law. Following an appointment as deputy U.S. marshal, Leffingwell developed an interest in surveying and began speculating in real estate.

In 1849 Leffingwell envisioned a north-south distributor road to skirt the city. His dream eventually became Grand Avenue. In 1852 he was instrumental in planning the suburban community of Kirkwood. In order to realize these two projects, Leffingwell had to battle those of less vision and considerably less business savvy. When he took on his third project, he was ready to go for the long count.

Leffingwell wanted the city to have an immense municipal park—three thousand acres or more. Caroline Loughlin and Catherine Anderson state in *Forest Park*, "Leffingwell's 1870 plan was for the city to buy more land than was needed for the park, then sell the surrounding land as lots, allowing the city to reap the major profit for the taxpayers." The idea was avant-garde for St. Louis, but such a park had already been created in New York City. Designed by Frederick Law Olmsted, Central Park covered 840 acres that had been acquired by the city of New York in 1856.

In 1868, when Leffingwell began talking about his dream of a park, he was met with skepticism, ridicule, and legal obstacles. Anyone less determined than Leffingwell would have turned away. In 1870 he and his supporters reasoned that the best way to establish the huge park would be to have the Missouri General Assembly authorize the city to condemn a tract of land west of the city limits. Leffingwell had already set his sights on some rolling, heavily wooded acreage through which the then-beautiful River des Peres ran. It was the perfect site for a park, far away from industrial smoke, urban noise, and the frenetic pace of city living.

Leffingwell convinced Nicholas Bell, a freshman legislator from south St. Louis, to sponsor the park bill in the General Assembly, and the proposal was scaled down to 1,370 acres, still an enormous expanse. The backers of the park plan found support from county court judge Joseph O'Neil, who recognized that a city-owned park would be a great asset to the growth and development of St. Louis. The judge defended his stand against detractors by saying, "We are not thinking of your time and mine, but of generations yet to come."

Nicholas Bell successfully pushed the park bill through the legislature in March 1872. But constituent reaction was immediate and hostile. Opposition expressed by the owners of the tract in question was fierce. The principal owners of the land were Robert Forsyth, Thomas Skinker, Isabella DeMun, William Griswold, and Charles Pierre Chouteau and his sister Julia Maffitt—all members of powerful St. Louis families. They were angry that the state legislature thought it could condemn their property and pay them a pittance for it. Without doubt, their estimation of the value of their land increased in direct proportion to the attention it received.

Forest Park as it appeared in 1892 when the first mansions began to rise in Westmoreland and Portland. The two premier private places were advertised as extensions of the park.

The six principal landowners had done virtually nothing to improve the tract. More than one thousand acres lay in its natural state. The property was described in a municipal record as

a forest whose natural beauty had not been marred by the rude hand of the woodman. Nature had been lavish in her gifts . . . ; but only two antiquated dwellings with some dilapidated outhouses, and the huts of miners of the poorer class were to be found in its vast extent. Three neglected farms and two open but abandoned fields disfigured rather than adorned the forest.

Of all the property owners, Robert Forsyth probably had the greatest sentimental attachment to the land, as he was the only one who had actually lived there. In fact, the Forsyth home became The Cottage, a popular restaurant for bicycle riders in the 1890s. It was replaced by a larger building in 1893. Forsyth's son William recalled explorations in the vast forest around their home, when father and son hunted wild turkeys, ducks, and squirrels. He also remembered flocks of wild pigeons in such numbers that their weight caused large tree limbs to snap off like pipe stems.

Another of the principal owners of the disputed forest property also had good reason to be upset by the attempt to take over a portion of his property. Col. Thomas Skinker was a prominent Virginian who had come to St. Louis in 1847 in search of a climate that would suit his wife's fragile health. On a large tract of land just west of the dairy farm owned by the Cabanne family, he built a handsome brick southern colonial mansion. It was a few hundred feet west of the wide boulevard that bears the Skinker name today. (Skinker Boulevard intersects another street that commemorates one of the co-defendants in the litigation, Forsyth Boulevard.) The colonel called the impressive estate Ellenwood in honor of a daughter who had died in infancy. A street near the Skinker homestead is still called Ellenwood. The portion of land that the city wanted to take from Skinker was at the eastern sector of his tract and would form the western end of the proposed park.

The Skinkers were not pleased when the idea was first advanced of having sightseers and campers tramping through a recreational facility in their front yard. So it was a defiant Thomas Skinker who sought to defeat the park acquisition legislation as soon as it was introduced. It was only after Skinker was convinced by Leffingwell's argument that the park would enhance the value of his property rather than diminish it that Skinker dropped his case against the condemnation.

Louise Isabella Apoline Gratiot DeMun also fought to retain rights to her property. Descended from the Gratiots, one of St. Louis's first families, and the granddaughter of Pierre Laclede, Isabella had married the dashing and adventurous Jules DeMun in the spring of 1812. Born in Port-au-Prince, Haiti, and educated in Paris, the maverick DeMun had come to St. Louis in 1800. Seventeen years after DeMun joined the Chouteau fur-trading enterprise, he, Auguste Chouteau, Robert McKnight, and several other traders were arrested for selling merchandise and buying furs in Spanish Santa Fe. After turning over approximately thirty thousand dollars worth of illegally acquired furs and spending forty-eight days in the calaboose, the traders were released on the promise that they would stay closer to home.

In 1820 Jules took Isabella and their three young daughters to Cuba, where he had purchased a large coffee plantation. The family returned to St. Louis in 1831. A year after being elected St. Louis County recorder of deeds in 1842, Jules died, leaving his widow with the property he had acquired and the land she had inherited through her Gratiot lineage. Isabella DeMun was in her late seventies when the city threatened to condemn and seize some of her land for a park. She felt compelled to hold on to the property in the name of her distinguished family and in honor of her late husband.

William Griswold's attachment to the forest property was, perhaps, less sentimental than that of the other principal owners. He had not owned his segment long. Griswold had settled in St. Louis in 1871 after a long career as an executive first with the Terre Haute, Alton & St. Louis Railroad Company and later with the Ohio & Mississippi. A lawyer by training, Griswold and his wife, Maria, came to St. Louis to enjoy their retirement. Maria Griswold was related to John Carroll, the first Catholic archbishop in the United States, and to Roger Brooke Taney, the fourth chief justice of the United States.

The land the city sought from the Griswolds was then being used as a pasture for the cattle he bred as a hobby. But Griswold had a vested interest in the city's expansion beyond its western frontier—he was also an organizer of the St. Louis Transfer Company and was, for more than a quarter of a century, a member of its board of directors. When Griswold protested the takeover of his forest property, he may have done so as a matter of form and because he considered the purchase price too low. There was really no way he could lose on the deal. Even if the city paid a ridiculously low price for his property, he could benefit financially from the transit company that took people to the park. Griswold was later to clinch the best deal of all the property owners.

Robert Forsyth was the only one of the owners of Forest Park property to have actually lived on the land. The Forsyth farmhouse served as the Cottage Restaurant until it was replaced by a larger structure in 1893.

Recognizing the threat to their property, the property owners, headed by Charles Chouteau, decided to take the matter to court. Charles Pierre Chouteau was, at age fifty-three, the youngest litigant. He and his sister Julia represented the fourth generation of the venerable founding family of St. Louis and were also niece and nephew to Isabella DeMun. After graduation from the Civil and Military Institute of New York City, Chouteau had represented family interests in New York and London before returning to St. Louis. He was a pioneer in the iron industry in Missouri and a partner in the Chouteau, Harrison, and Vallé Rolling Mills. He had married his cousin Julia Anne Gratiot, and they had eight children.

Those who followed the course of the litigation might have thought the co-owners of the Forest Park property represented a wall of insurmountable power. But the Missouri legislature had had no regard for sentimentality or family connections when it called for the condemnation of their property and the establishment of a public park upon it.

Immediately after the legislature passed the park bill, Chouteau filed for *quo warranto* proceedings, demanding proof that the legislature had the authority to take such action. Circuit court judge Daniel Wagner issued a twenty-page opinion declaring the act unconstitutional. His decision was based not on emotional issues, which were the basis of most arguments against the park, but on the fact that the legislative act had also authorized a special tax for general purposes and was, therefore, void.

The litigation may have been too much for Robert Forsyth, who died eight months after the passage of the legislation and shortly after Judge Wagner's ruling. The defense of the Forsyth estate fell to his son William. Loving the countryside and hating the city, William had moved to Kirkwood—ironically another Leffingwell project.

The court action reversing the legislature's action did not dampen the efforts of Leffingwell and his supporters. Following the judge's ruling, park backers honed and polished their arguments. In addition to the idea that the masses needed a place of retreat from the noise and heat of the city, park supporters presented other arguments that had a basis in historical fact. One of the best, preserved in a municipal record, suggested that if the city park had not been established as a protectorate for the property under consideration,

The lowlands would, doubtless, sooner or later, have been devoted to large dairy establishments, pigsties, factories for glue, soap and other offensive things. Indeed, some of these, before the Park was acquired, had invaded the property: and experience in other localities of our city serves to show how rapidly nuisances multiply when they obtain a foothold on the borders of a stream and how speedily and thoroughly they destroy the value and uses of all surrounding and otherwise desirable property.

The former residents of such once-desirable enclaves as Benton Place, Lafayette Square, and Lucas Place could attest to the accuracy of that projection. Urban sprawl, with all its ugliness, had destroyed their beautiful homes and the surrounding area.

Advocates of the park plan offered another formidable argument. It was necessary for the city to acquire the forest land, they reasoned, because, as the city grew it would need another source of water. If the city purchased the park property well in advance of the need for more water, a reservoir could be constructed. The park's elevation of 180 feet above the Mississippi River made it a perfect location for such a reservoir.

Opponents of the park responded with grumbling about the property's distance from the hub of the city. Would the new park not become an exclusive recreational spot for the wealthy? The privileged class was the only class to have the livery to reach the western frontier. Taxpayers hostile to the park even suggested that the land might be put to better use as a site for truck gardens.

The tax argument was the strongest. If City Hall was responsible to all its citizens, roads would have to be constructed to enable everyone to reach the new park. And who would pay for the new roads? Taxpayers, of course. This complaint was taken to court by T. T. Gantt, Samuel Glover, and others. They warned taxpayers not to cut their own throats—or, more accurately, their own purses.

Park opponents also slung a bit of mud into the controversy. They denounced Hiram Leffingwell as more Shylock than saint, more shrewd businessman than altruistic visionary. It was a fact that Leffingwell owned land near the proposed park. His holdings would be worth much more if the park acted as a magnet to bring the citizenry within buying range. (Forest Park did not make Leffingwell a fortune; he moved to Florida, where he died in 1897.)

Despite the fray, Leffingwell's public-relations campaign paid off. Two years after the court reversal, the state legislature

rebounded with a modified bill. This time the proposal was introduced by a northside legislator, John I. Martin, and it was passed on March 25, 1874.

Opponents questioned the legality of the measure all the way to the Missouri Supreme Court, but the state's high court pronounced the modified legislation perfectly legal. The primary difference between the new law and the earlier effort was that a commission—the Forest Park Board of Commissioners—was set up to handle the condemnation and purchase of 1,372 acres for the park. Leffingwell was appointed one of the commissioners.

In order to give the owners a fair market price for their land, John G. Priest, Theophile Papin, and Charles Green were appointed to make an official assessment of its value. The three appraisers determined the property to be worth $799,995. A generous City Hall kicked in an extra $5 to round out the price tag to $800,000.

On June 24, 1876, Hiram Leffingwell, a host of local dignitaries, and an estimated forty thousand citizens gathered in the forest for the formal opening of the park. Gov. Charles Hardin and Mayor Henry Overstolz made speeches applauding the wisdom of the land acquisition. A statue was unveiled of Edward Bates, who had made a strong run for the presidency in 1860 and had been attorney general in Lincoln's cabinet. It was a gala occasion, even if it did take the throng a long time to get to the ceremonies and to return to their homes.

The former owners of the park could not appreciate the celebration. They had taken a financial drubbing. Only one of them, William Griswold, was able to recoup his losses. Thirteen years after the establishment of Forest Park, Griswold was approached by an organization called the Forest Park Improvement Association. The syndicate wanted to purchase seventy-eight acres of land adjacent to the park. The boundaries of the piece of property were Kingshighway on the east, Sarpy Carr Cabanne's farm on the north, Union Avenue on the west, and Forest Park on the south, as well as the St. Louis, Kansas City and Colorado Railroad Company tracks. The land belonged to Griswold, and he was using it for pasturage. But for the incredible sum of $400,000, Griswold decided his cattle could graze somewhere else.

On May 11, 1887, Notary Public Millard F. Watts witnessed the transaction in which William Griswold and his wife, Maria, were paid exactly half the sum all five Forest Park property owners had been paid for many times the acreage.

The "deal of the decade" became official when, at 10:53 on the morning of May 14, 1887, City Recorder of Deeds William A. Hobbs entered the terms of the sale in the official city annals.

The local business community almost unanimously declared the deal preposterous and inflationary. One newspaper account written eleven years after the sale reflected: "Failure was predicted by many well informed and sagacious business men when this enterprise was inaugurated, but results attested the fact that Mr. Capen and his associates had made a shrewd forecast of the future and had not overestimated the capacity of St. Louis people to appreciate or their ability to purchase beautiful homes."

In 1887 most St. Louisans lived east of Jefferson Avenue, which old-timers still called by its former name, Pratte Avenue. In 1876, voters had approved extension of the city limits beyond the western edge of Forest Park, but the far west end was seen by most people as unreasonably far away and perhaps even uninhabitable.

But others realized that the greenest pastures for attracting the wealthy lay in the sector west of Kingshighway. There was ample room for the establishment of new retreats for the upper class to the north and south of the central corridor, but these areas were being claimed by those of lesser pretensions.

To the north of the city's center was the section of town primarily inhabited by working-class German and Irish immigrants. Germans predominated in the city following the heavy influx of the 1850s. While the Germans occupied a residential section known as Bremen, the Irish congregated in the near northside section known as Kerry Patch. Many people in 1887 still remembered the bloody anti-Irish riots in the hot summer of 1854. And while there were respectable Irish names in St. Louis, like those of millionaires O'Fallon, Mullanphy, and Walsh, entry into the elite echelon was rare for anyone from the Irish working class.

The Soulard or Frenchtown district, south of downtown and just west of the river, was the home of a few Creole descendants and some black aristocrats, the latter presided over by a former slave, Pelagie Rutger. Through her marriage to the illegitimate son of a wealthy Dutchman, Madame Rutger had acquired a substantial block of land in the Frenchtown area. Within the shadow of the Rutger estate, other blacks lived in squalor.

By the late 1880s the German upper crust had turned to the south side. The Compton Hill residential area attracted many.

A key man in its development was Julius Pitzman, the civil engineer who is considered the father of the private place in America. The most important elements in Pitzman's concept of the private place were the control of traffic and the creation of a parklike setting. He used the cul-de-sac street plan, gated traffic barriers, a central parkway (which divided the street, giving it a suburban atmosphere), and uniform setback of houses from the curb. He also insisted on strict deed restrictions and control of the area by a board of governing trustees.

Born in Halberstadt, Germany, in 1837, Pitzman came to St. Louis in 1854 from the Hartz Mountain region. Unlike many German immigrants of that era, Pitzman came to take a specific job. His brother-in-law, C. E. Salomon, had offered him a position as an assistant in a thriving surveying and civil engineering company. In 1858, when Salomon beat out Ulysses S. Grant for the job of St. Louis county engineer, he turned over his successful business to Pitzman.

With the onset of the Civil War, duty called Pitzman to arms. He left the business and enlisted in the Union army, becoming an officer and mapmaker on General Sherman's staff. Ironically, he later joined General Grant's personal staff. While Pitzman was with General Grant near Vicksburg, he was seriously wounded.

Returning to St. Louis after the injury, Pitzman also returned to surveying. He developed a lucrative business by calling attention to the inaccuracies in government surveys. His penchant for precise survey detail made him much in demand, especially as a consultant to attorneys in property disputes. When Forest Park was established in 1876, Pitzman was the logical choice for the job of chief engineer to lay out the park. This assignment gave him a special interest in landscape design.

The first two private places laid out by Pitzman, Benton and Vandeventer, have already been mentioned. Although both places were being surrounded by urban sprawl by 1887, Pitzman was still the master surveyor and civil engineer and was approached by the syndicate of real estate developers that called itself the Forest Park Improvement Association. Despite criticism from the business community, the twelve members of the association sensed that they had pulled off a shrewd deal and were confident that Pitzman could use the best elements of his two earlier projects, discard their worst features, and create the grandest private place design yet.

The syndicate, incidentally, seemed to show little interest in

Surveyor-developer Julius Pitzman was commissioned by the Forest Park Improvement Association in 1887 to plat Westmoreland and Portland. Pitzman also planned most of St. Louis's other prestigious private places.

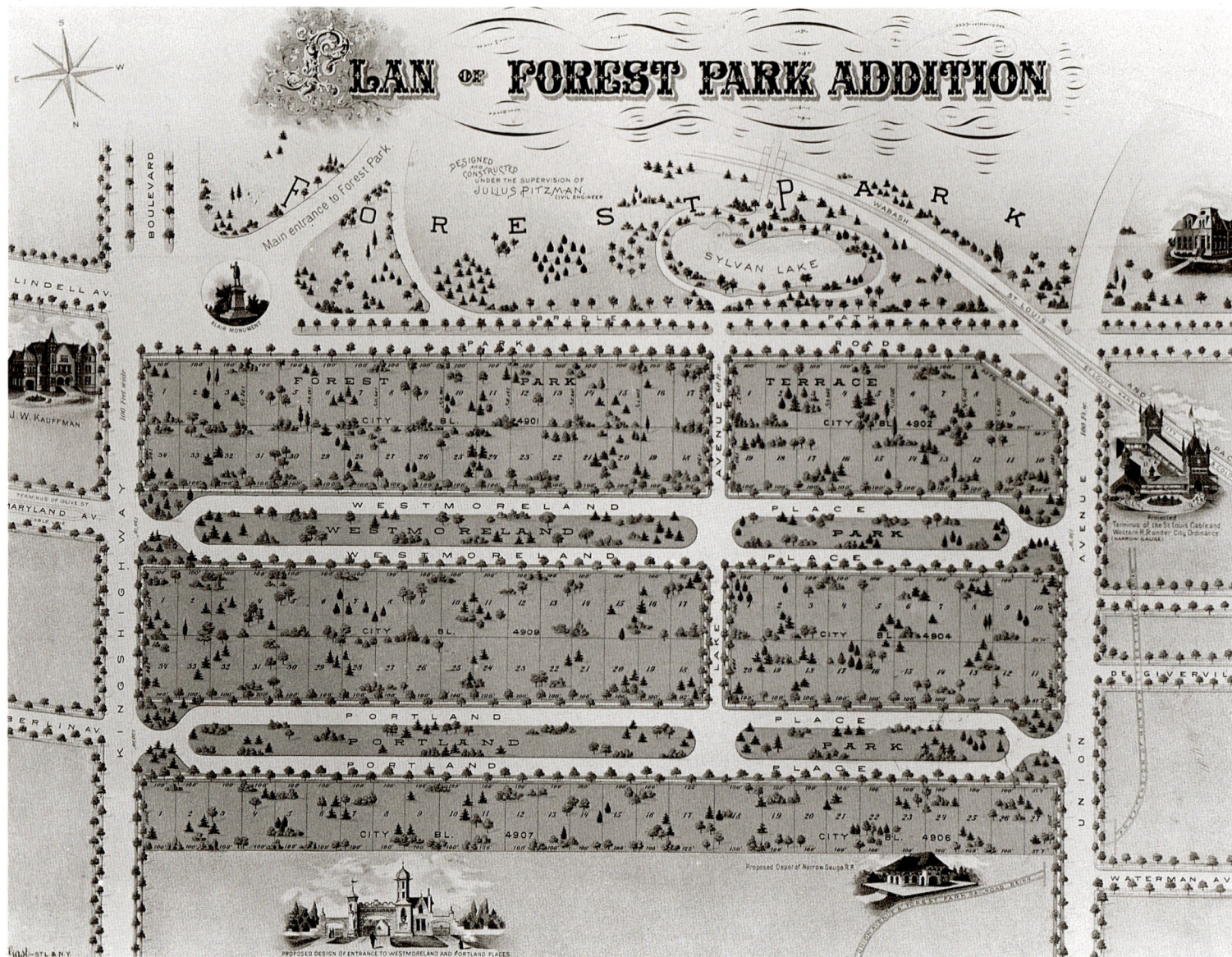

Julius Pitzman's 1887 prospectus map of the Forest Park Addition, which includes Westmoreland and Portland places.

away from jurisprudence when he moved to Chicago and bought the Great Northern Hotel. Later he started a roofing company. Laughlin was a good friend of Judge Elmer B. Adams and may have helped convince Adams to build his house at 25 Westmoreland in 1896. In fact, Laughlin named one of his sons Elmer Adams Laughlin.

On April 30, 1887, Laughlin sent a check for $145 to the secretary of state's office in Jefferson City in application for incorporation on behalf of the developers' association. In an exceptionally fast response, the incorporation was approved on May 2, 1887.

The syndicate ignored the naysayings of the business community and diligently set about creating what was called "the improvement of this property on a scale which had hardly been dreamed of in St. Louis prior to that time." Julius Pitzman went to work immediately. He had been given a handsome retainer and an offer to become a trustee of the new development, and he was afforded an opportunity to create a residential development without parallel.

Pitzman may have been attracted to the project by Henry Christian Haarstick, who was a member of the Forest Park Improvement Association, Pitzman's good friend, a fellow expatriate of Germany, and his colleague in the other project he was involved in at this time, Compton Heights (completed in 1889–1892). Haarstick's Mississippi Valley Transportation Company was the first to transport grain and flour from St. Louis to New Orleans by barge. By 1874 it had become the nation's largest barge line and the only one operating on the Mississippi River south of St. Louis. Two houses built by Haarstick for his two daughters on Forsyth Boulevard in Clayton are known today as University House and Whittemore House, both properties of Washington University.

In addition to Laughlin and Haarstick, the other members of the Forest Park Improvement Association were Alvah Mansur, William L. Huse, Edwards Whitaker, George D. Capen, William H. Thompson, Ethan Hitchcock, James B. Johnson, Dwight Tredway, Thomas J. McLemore, and Judson Thompson.

Alvah Mansur, president of the organization, had a strong track record as a successful businessman. At the time of the association's incorporation, Mansur was the chief executive

having Pitzman copy any aspects of the private place he had laid out in the year he received the Westmoreland/Portland commission. Cabanne Place, on the northwest outskirts of the city, had potential for uniqueness, but it did not attract a powerful enough backing or enough acreage for the grand statement the Forest Park Improvement Association wanted to make.

The Forest Park Improvement Association also needed a good lawyer with some political clout for the incorporation

procedure. They could find no better man for the job than ex-judge Henry D. Laughlin. At the time he applied for the association's incorporation, Laughlin was a member of the distinguished law firm of Martin, Laughlin, and Kern. However, he was beginning to turn his attention away from the active practice of law. A year after he put the Forest Park Improvement Association's legal affairs in order, he founded the National Hollow Brake Beam Company, which later became the Chicago Railway Equipment Company. Laughlin got even further officer of Deere, Mansur & Company, manufacturers of farm machinery. The surname of Mansur's former partner, Charles Deere, is synonymous with agricultural equipment. Charles was a brother of John Deere.

Mansur's other interests included directorship in the American Exchange Bank of St. Louis, the St. Louis Union Trust Company, and the Crystal Plate Glass Company. While Mansur did not elect to build a home in the new subdivision, he probably helped persuade his brother-in-law, Lewis B. Tebbetts, to buy a lot at 29 Portland. The house that rose there in 1891 provided a comfortable home for Mansur's sister, Ellen Mansur Tebbetts, and the four Tebbetts children. One of the two Tebbetts boys was named Alvah after his uncle.

William Huse was a friend of Mansur who also served on the board of the Crystal Plate Glass Company. Huse was one of only two members of the Forest Park Improvement Association who chose to build his house where he had invested his money. He was one of the first to start a house in the new development. But because he chose heavy Missouri granite instead of brick, the Huse home at 9 Westmoreland actually was the fifth to be completed. Huse had enjoyed the charm of a lovely mansion in Lafayette Square in the years before his

Henry Christian Haarstick was a prominent member of the Forest Park Improvement Association. He was also the key figure in the development of Compton Heights, giving the city of St. Louis the land that became Hawthorne and Longfellow avenues.

Although he never lived in Westmoreland or Portland, Alvah Mansur, as president of the Forest Park Improvement Association, was instrumental in the development of the two private places.

George D. Capen was another member of the Forest Park Improvement Association, and he was a key figure in the purchase of the Griswold tract on which Westmoreland and Portland were constructed.

William Huse, the man for whom 9 Westmoreland was built, was the grandson of Ethan Allen, the hero of Fort Ticonderoga. Huse was a familiar figure in the neighborhood as he took his daily constitutional.

westward migration. He must have believed that Westmoreland Place would provide his family with country comforts in an urban setting, just as Lafayette Square had provided before its decline.

Huse was president of the Huse & Loomis Ice and Transportation Company, which operated four steamboats and a fleet of twenty-four barges. It had two hundred and fifty regular employees and more than three thousand extra workmen during the ice-cutting season. Huse was also president of the Creve Coeur Ice Company, president of the Union Dairy, and a director of the Peru Plow & Wheel Company, the St. Louis Union Trust Company, and the Boatmen's Bank, as well as Crystal Plate Glass.

Edwards Whitaker was the other developer who chose to build a home in the new and exclusive section. Unlike Huse, who decided to build his house a few years after incorporation, Whitaker waited twelve years to build his home at 13 Westmoreland. He was a partner in the banking and brokerage firm of Matthews and Whitaker in 1887. He later became

president of Boatmen's Bank and of the St. Louis Clearing House Association.

An inveterate capitalist, Whitaker was also the first president of the United Railways Company, the consolidated transit company that put the first electric streetcars on the streets of St. Louis. Although he was a hard-nosed anti-union manager whose executive style was sometimes called unscrupulous, Whitaker once told a newspaper reporter that the secret of his business success was: "You can fool a lot of men by simply telling them the truth. Plenty of them won't believe you." When Whitaker died in 1926 at the age of seventy-seven, he left an estate worth more than $3 million.

Another association member, George Capen, shared Massachusetts as a birthplace with Alvah Mansur. Both men came from old New England families. Capen came to St. Louis in 1858 to seek his fortune when he was twenty years old. He first worked as a clerk in a hide and leather store and then used the money he had saved to start a fire and marine insurance company and a brokerage firm. He later organized the Mississippi Valley Transportation Company, which carried grain to New Orleans for export to Europe.

In the year of the incorporation of the Forest Park Improvement Association, Capen founded and became the first president of the Missouri Safe Deposit Company. Like Whitaker, Capen took a keen interest in street railroads, and he helped establish the Lindell Street Railway, a horse-car line. Capen was also a director of the Laclede Gaslight Company and acting manager of the Equitable Building. He is erroneously listed in some accounts as the president of the syndicate that purchased the Griswold tract. However, it is Alvah Mansur who is listed as president on the official incorporation papers. The confusion may have been caused by the fact that Capen was more active than Mansur in initiating the purchase of the land that eventually became Westmoreland and Portland places. Capen did not choose to build a house in the new development, but it is possible that he was able to persuade another Laclede Gas board member, Thomas West, to buy a lot in Westmoreland Place in 1891 and to build the house that became Number 11.

Association member William Thompson was one of the town's most powerful businessmen in 1887. At one time Thompson was president of thirteen corporations and a director of thirty-nine companies. From his seat as president of the Bank of Commerce, Thompson was at the center of many of the city's biggest business deals. Attesting to the respect held for Thompson's business savvy is the fact that he was appointed treasurer of the 1904 Louisiana Purchase Exposition. Next to fair president David R. Francis, Thompson wielded the most power in the running of the exposition. At the time of his death in 1905, Thompson's estate was valued at between $4 million and $5 million.

Thompson was content to remain in his comfortable home at 4487 Lindell, just four blocks east of Westmoreland and Portland. But, as president of the Bank of Commerce, he may have influenced other members of the business elite to relocate to the new enclave.

Both Mansur and Huse had a close association with their fellow developer Ethan A. Hitchcock. But Hitchcock, although he received national prominence as minister to Russia and secretary of the interior, was a strange bedfellow. He would become hated by the railroad men because, as interior secretary in the McKinley administration, he would sue the railroads to recover millions of acres of valuable coal country in Utah, Colorado, Wyoming, and Idaho for the government. In addition to taking on the railroads, Secretary Hitch-

Ethan A. Hitchcock was one of the twelve developers of Westmoreland/Portland but chose to remain in his Lucas Place home. He served as interior secretary in the McKinley administration.

cock would wage a battle against Standard Oil, which had acquired valuable oil leases in Oklahoma through what Hitchcock thought were less than honorable tactics. At the time of Theodore Roosevelt's nomination for president in 1904, the northwestern delegation threatened to bolt the Republican party unless Roosevelt dumped Hitchcock.

Hitchcock was president of the St. Louis Ore & Steel Company and was apparently happy with his handsome home in Lucas Place at the time of the development of the Westmoreland/Portland properties. But Hitchcock may have influenced his daughter, Sarah, to establish a home in Portland Place in 1912 with her husband, John Foster Shepley. Shepley's brother Arthur also built a handsome mansion in West-

moreland, in 1908. Sarah and John Shepley named a son Ethan after his distinguished grandfather. Ethan Allen Shepley became chancellor of Washington University.

After Hitchcock, James Brooks Johnson was the feistiest member of the Forest Park Improvement Association. Johnson had a penchant for filing sensational lawsuits. Several years after Westmoreland and Portland places were established, Johnson filed a personal-injury action against the St. Louis Transit Company. The streetcar company had successfully fended off thousands of such claims, and it initially appeared that Johnson did not have any chance of winning. When the St. Louis Transit Company merged with Edwards Whitaker's United Railways Company, Johnson's suit seemed even less likely to succeed. But in a surprising ruling in June 1920, the Missouri Supreme Court decided that the United Railways Company was, indeed, liable. Johnson then sued the stockholders, who had held on to their securities through the merger, and emerged victorious with an award of $41,106.

In another celebrated lawsuit, Johnson asked for an audit of the books of the Gerardi Hotel Company for a twenty-five-year period. Johnson's contention as a shareholder was that Joseph Gerardi, owner of the Westmoreland Hotel at Maryland and Taylor avenues, had misappropriated $400,000 in dividends over a number of years since 1895. At the time the suit was filed in 1922, Johnson claimed that one share of stock he had purchased for $50 in 1918, in proportion to Gerardi's stealing, was then worth $40,000 when compound interest was figured. The suit was still pending at the time of Johnson's death on September 14, 1923.

Contrary to the impression given by his penchant for filing sensational litigation, James Johnson was a respected businessman. He was president of the Anchor Warehouse Company and was at one time the vice-president of the Trinidad Asphalt Manufacturing Company. Johnson died at age eighty in his home at 5855 Cates Avenue, a short walking distance from the Westmoreland/Portland development he helped establish.

The other members of the Forest Park Improvement Association were less well known. Dwight Tredway was secretary of the Greeley-Burnham Grocery Company in 1887. He was a veteran of the Civil War and a pioneer grocer in St. Louis. Later he became president of the Cable and Western Railway Line. To help promote his streetcar company, Tredway also promoted the Kensington Garden at Raymond and Academy avenues. This oasis was one of the first summer gardens in the United States. Tredway was also a member of the executive committee that raised funds for the National Guard Armory, then located at 17th and Pine. Tredway did not purchase a lot in the new subdivision. He was content to watch the development from his home nearby at 5142 Washington.

In 1887 association member Thomas J. McLemore was a cashier in the prestigious wholesale and retail cotton processing firm of Allen, West & Company. He certainly was not in the same financial league as the other members of the Forest Park Improvement Association and may have been included for his bookkeeping and accounting skills. Two years later McLemore's star rose dramatically when his boss at the cotton company, Thomas H. West, was asked by E. C. Simmons, Capt. J. A. Scudder, Samuel Kennard, Daniel Catlin, and John T. Davis to head the first trust company west of Cleveland—the St. Louis Trust Company. West became a Westmoreland Place trustee and charter homebuilder.

Judson M. Thompson, no relation to fellow syndicate member William Thompson, was a railroad executive who must have had an interesting relationship with fellow association member and anti-railroad man Ethan Hitchcock.

The sale of lots in the new subdivision got off to a rather slow start, but by the end of 1897 twenty-nine houses had been erected. The lot purchase made by William K. Bixby on November 18, 1891, gives a good indication of the terms that the association required. On that date Bixby made the minimal deposit of $250 to secure Lot 7 of City Block 4907, having a front of one hundred feet and a depth of two hundred feet on the north side of Portland Place. Bixby was to pay a total of $12,500 for the lot, with $4,200 in cash and payments of $4,200 the following year and $4,100 the year thereafter. The interest rate was 6 percent per annum, payable semi-annually. The Bixby mansion was started almost a year to the day following the placement of the down payment on the lot.

When the officers of the Forest Park Improvement Association first decided to create an exclusive residential paradise, they were determined to avoid the mistakes that had contributed to the demise of earlier private place ventures in St. Louis. They had successfully snapped up the land near Forest Park, which a 1904 *House and Garden* article by Samuel L. Sherer noted ensured "the permanent preservation [of Westmoreland and Portland] as desirable residential districts." Following the acquisition of the land, they set out to create a governing document for each of the two private places that would be as invincible as the U.S. Constitution. These covenants were intended primarily to protect the area from outside nuisances and encroachments. They were designed to spell out the gov-

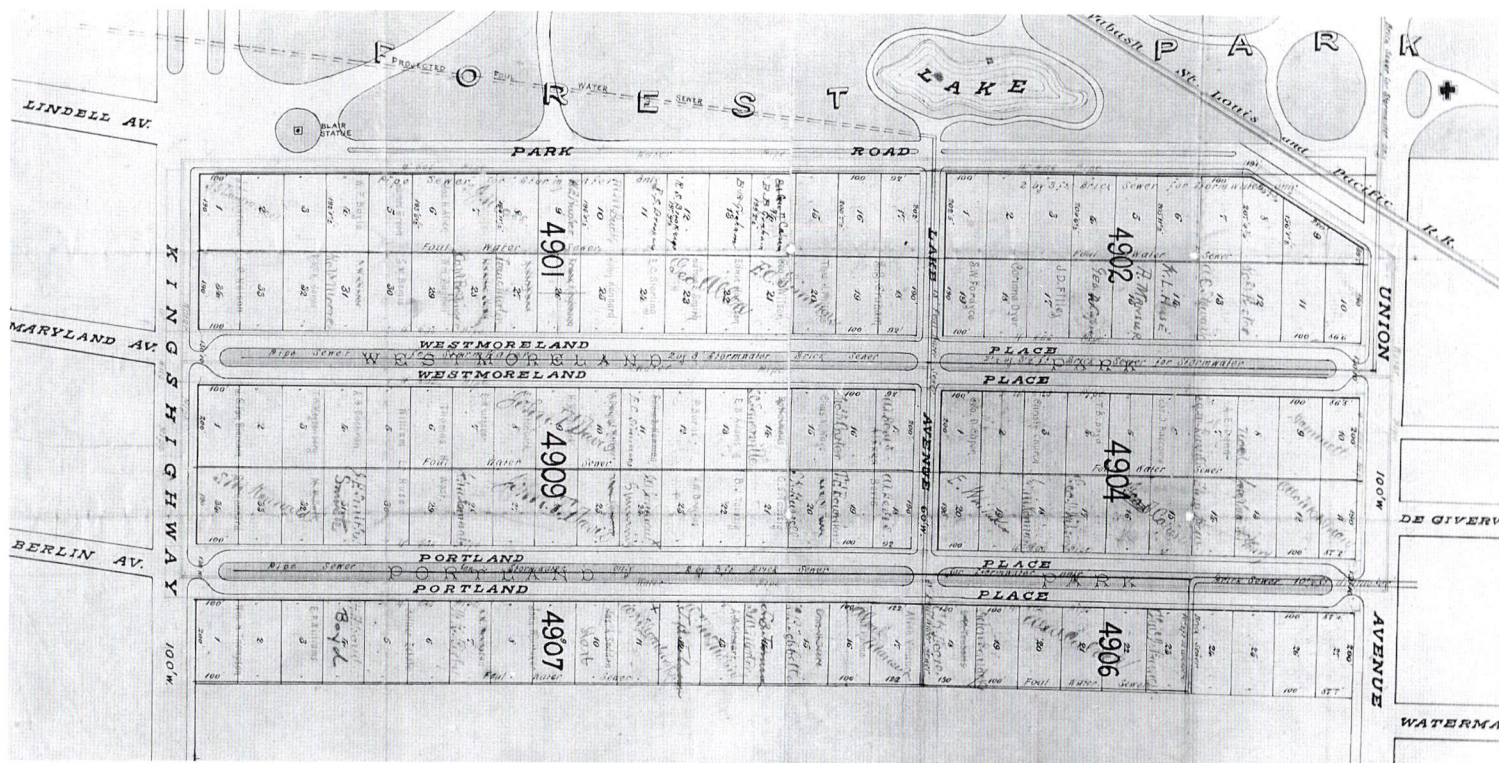

This 1888 Pitzman plat of Westmoreland/Portland shows the names of some of the charter landowners. Not all the original landowners actually built houses on the lots they purchased.

ernance of Westmoreland and Portland and to control the environment inside the district. On many points the founders sought tougher restrictions than those imposed by the city beyond their gates.

The architects of the Westmoreland/Portland concept probably used the covenant drawn up for Vandeventer Place as a model for their document. They took the best of the ideas conceived by Charles Peck, Napoleon Mullikin, and Joseph McCune and carefully discarded any ideas or regulations that were either patently ridiculous or virtually unenforceable. For example, a minimum construction cost for all the homes in the subdivision was prescribed, and the Vandeventer Place prohibition against using any building as a business establishment was copied. But it must have appeared unnecessary or even absurd to set forth in the covenant how many sets of lace curtains each household must have.

The deeds of trust of both Westmoreland and Portland obviously have the same authors. The language in the two

documents is, with few exceptions, identical. There are the same peculiarities of spelling—Forest Park appears as *Forrest Park*, and the street known today as Kingshighway is spelled *Kings Highway*. The language of each document is highly legalistic and typical of documents transferring rights to real property. There are dozens of references to the parties of the first and second parts, tracts, strips, parcels, plats, as well as whereases, therefores, heretos, whereofs, thereafters, thereupons, hereinafters, and even a few hereinaboves. For example, Clause C of Section One of both documents states:

> The said party of the first part has, and by these presents does create an easement of the duration, nature and extent hereinafter, in the clause stated and set forth, and subject to the provisions of this deed as relate thereto, in, over and upon the following described strip of parcel of ground (being a portion of the land embraced in said Map or Plat) that is to say:

The founders of Westmoreland and Portland were resolute in their attempt to incorporate the spirit of the words of Cicero

A view of Westmoreland Place circa 1900. The palatial mansions were a reflection of the wealth and power of the builders.

A view of Portland Place circa 1900. The statue of Ruckstuhl's *Mercure S'amuse* stands in the median parkway strip.

that later became the motto of the state of Missouri: *Salus populi suprema lex esto*, let the welfare of the people be the supreme law. A private place is not created unless the creators are interested in protecting the welfare of the homeowners, and the welfare of the residents of Westmoreland and Portland was not left to chance. The power of governance was placed firmly in the hands of an oligarchy, a board of trustees.

The Forest Park Improvement Association (the "party of the first part") appointed its first three trustees (the "parties of the second part") for each private place on November 6, 1888. For Westmoreland Place they were William L. Huse, Thomas H. West, and Edwards Whitaker. Their counterparts in Portland Place were Julius Pitzman, John Whitaker, and George D. Capen. While the trustees of Vandeventer Place had been required to be residents of the private place they served, that was not true of Westmoreland and Portland. None of the three original Portland Place trustees ever lived in Portland Place. The Forest Park Improvement Association evidently felt that sound business judgment and an appreciation for the syndicate's objectives were more essential to good trusteeship than residency.

No matter where they lived, the trustees were powerful figures in the management of the neighborhood. One factor that undergirded their power was that their appointments were for life. And if any trustee died, moved, declined to act, or became incompetent, the other trustees could call a meeting of the resident property owners and replace that trustee by voice vote or ballot. The original deed of trust for each private place states, "The owner or owners of said residence lots [are] entitled to only one vote for each of said lots owned by him or them." The authors of the deeds of trust were farsighted enough to put in black and white the procedure that would go into effect should one or two surviving trustees fail to fill a vacant position within sixty days after it occurred. According to the deed, the owner or owners of five resident lots could call a meeting of all residents to fill vacant trustee positions.

One of the weaknesses of the Vandeventer Place covenant was that all actions regarding the place required the unanimous approval of the eighty-six property owners. With the great mobility of its residents, whose business and recreational activities carried them across the nation and around the world, it was next to impossible to obtain a consensus in Vandeventer Place. This stipulation was not repeated in the original Westmoreland/Portland covenant.

The real power given the Westmoreland/Portland trustees is in Sections Four and Six. Section Four reads in part:

In exercising the rights, powers and privileges granted to them and in discharging the duties imposed upon them by the provisions of this Deed, the said Trustees may, from time to time, employ all such agents, servants and labor as they deem necessary; And may employ counsel and institute and prosecute such suits as they may deem necessary or advisable and defend suits brought against them, or either of them, in their character of Trustees.

And in Section Six the trustees are empowered to levy and collect annual maintenance assessments without the approval of the property owners so long as the fee does not exceed fifty cents per front foot.

But the trustees were also given more mundane duties. For example, they are responsible for the maintenance of the center parkway in each of the two private places. The parkways are to be "suitably covered with turf and planted with trees and shrubbery." The deeds of trust for both Portland and Westmoreland allow the trustees to exhibit their artistic tastes by adorning the parkways with "such decorations and works of Art as they deem suitable and expedient." Generally, the trustees are ordered by the indenture to "protect and preserve the said Park Place from encroachment, trespass, nuisance and injury."

The trustees are also responsible for maintaining the sidewalks and the tree lawns, which are to be kept in good condition. Since the city of St. Louis has no responsibility to provide street lighting in a private place, this was added to the trustees' list of duties. The wording of the trust indentures suggests foresight that may be deemed prophetic: "The Trustees shall make provision for lighting at night . . . by gas or electricity *or other means* [and] they shall pay the cost of making [and] maintaining such lighting." Westmoreland and Portland have already seen gas and electric lighting. Future trustees will not find their hands tied in pursuing whatever form of lighting might succeed electric power.

The Westmoreland/Portland trustees also have to be tax collectors. They are required to collect a reasonable annual fee to carry out refuse removal and the maintenance of sidewalks, sewers, lighting, and the parkways. The original indentures of both private places restricted the annual fees to "a sum not to exceed, in any one year, fifty cents for each front foot of each of said lots." Inflation has, of course, forced revision of the deeds of trust of both places. Currently, the assessments are recommended by the trustees and approved by a majority of the property owners at an annual meeting. In 1987, property owners in Westmoreland Place paid $4.60 per front foot plus $506 per residence for trash removal and security; residents of Portland Place paid $1,149 per residence.

If a property owner fails to pay any assessment, the deed of trust empowers the trustees to slap a lien on the resident's property. This attachment is to remain in effect until the fee is fully paid. In addition, the trustees of Westmoreland and Portland have the right to take any legal proceedings deemed necessary to collect assessments. The original deed goes even further. Any property owner taken to court to collect delinquent trustee fees was required to pay court costs and a twenty-five-dollar penalty. This penalty was removed by amendments to the original document.

The relationship between trustee and property and trustee and owner is clearly spelled out in Section Seven of the covenant of each place: "Each of the said residence lots and also the person or persons, from time to time owning same, shall forever stand and remain bound and chargeable to said Trustees . . . by any and all provisions of this Deed." In other words, the homeowners had to agree to accept the authority of the trustees in exercising the deed's provisions over their property.

To maintain uniformity in the house structures and the appearance of the Westmoreland/Portland properties, the covenants provide trustees with a set of commandments. Residents are warned:

I. Thou shalt not "at any time erect any building on said lots within forty (40) feet from the front line of said lot."

II. Thou shalt not "extend any tower, closed balcony or closed porch in front of such building line or steps or stone foundations for

Kingshighway, today a major thoroughfare, was still a dirt road when the east gate to Westmoreland Place was photographed circa 1900.

open porches or verandas, within twenty-eight (28) feet of the said place."

III. Thou shalt not "erect in front of such building lines any closed fence or wall separating lots."

IV. Thou shalt not "build more than one house upon any one of said lots."

V. Thou shalt not "erect any outhouse, stable or other subsidiary building on any of said lots within a distance of one hundred feet from the said place or within a distance of forty feet from Kings Highway or Lake Avenue or Union Avenue."

VI. Thou shalt not "erect any building or erection or obstruction of any character, except division fence, within ten feet of the rear line of any of said lots."

VII. Thou shalt not "erect any house on said lots at a cost of less than Seven Thousand Dollars (Westmoreland Place) or Six Thousand Dollars (Portland Place) unless the plans and specifications are approved by a majority of the Trustees."

VIII. Thou shalt not "use or permit any house or houses erected on said lots to be used, either directly or indirectly, for business of any description or for any purpose other than that of an exclusively private residence."

IX. Thou shalt not "make or permit any connections with the water pipes, sewers, gas pipes or mains located in said place or park or in Lake Avenue to be made except under the rules and regulations prescribed by the said City of St. Louis or by the Trustees."

X. Thou shalt not "convey, demise or otherwise dispose of any of said lots or any estate or interest therein, at any time hereafter, except as being subject to the covenants hereinabove."

While the officers of the Forest Park Improvement Association appear to have had an unflagging confidence in the private place concept, as evidenced by their acquisition of the Griswold tract and the sturdiness of the formal deeds of trust of both places, there is an interesting clause in each indenture that suggests that the association's members were not so certain that their creation would work. The trustees of each place were ordered to call a special meeting of the property owners "at the expiration of five years from the first day of March, one thousand eight hundred and eighty nine . . . the purpose of which said meeting shall be to decide whether the said Westmoreland/Portland Park and Place and said portion of said Lake Avenue . . . shall be dedicated to public use."

With the indentures filed in November 1888 and the trustees well established as governing bodies of the two places, the Forest Park Improvement Association held its last formal meeting on June 10, 1895. On June 18, with twenty-two houses built, association president Alvah Mansur appeared before a notary public to file papers to dissolve the syndicate. Mansur took an oath that the association had fully settled all its property, collected all its indebtedness, paid all its bills, and divided all its property equitably among the stockholders.

As quietly as it had been born, the Forest Park Improvement Association died. But this syndicate had created a unique jewel of a residential district, one that became an architectural hallmark for the entire nation.

3. THE TIES THAT BIND

My hold of the colonies is in the close affection which grows from commons names, from kindred blood, from similar privileges, and equal protection. These are ties which, though light as air, are as strong as links of iron.

—Edmund Burke (1775)

The pioneers who were bold enough to build mansions in the urban wilderness that was to become Westmoreland and Portland places had many things in common. Most of the homebuilders had at least some of the following characteristics: they were involved in the manufacture or distribution of hard goods; they were graduates of prestigious prep schools, colleges, and universities; they were usually Protestant; they often benefited from interrelated business networks; they were generally members of the same clubs and fraternal organizations; they had formerly lived in other private places or exclusive neighborhoods; they were Republicans or conservative (gold) Democrats; they were directors of corporations and institutions outside their primary business focus; they had survived financial panics and depressions; they had married into wealthy, influential, and highly respectable families; they were physically hearty enough to reach old age in defiance of the life-expectancy statistics of their era; and they were wealthy enough to leave estates totaling hundreds of thousands, even millions, of dollars.

While most of the founding homebuilders of Westmoreland/Portland were men, a number of widows built substantial homes as well. Most Westmoreland/Portland wives also belonged to organizations dedicated to improving the educational, cultural, and medical life of the city.

In many respects those who occupied the first homes in the Westmoreland/Portland neighborhood made up a large family of people whose life-styles were nearly identical; whose goals and aspirations were very similar; whose roots were neatly intertwined; whose business interests were interwoven; and whose material wealth was comparable. These "birds of a feather" flocked together to increase their security, enlarge their social contacts, and enhance their financial status.

Indeed, residents of Westmoreland/Portland formed a self-sufficient community that was able to operate in the business world without any contributions from outsiders. Although the following scenario is hypothetical, it is not unlikely.

If a Westmoreland/Portland homebuilder needed brick for the construction of a house, he or she could strike a deal with neighbor Edward Sterling, who was president of two brick-manufacturing companies. N. S. Chouteau Walsh also owned a successful brick refractory plant. So did the family of the late Louis Chauvenet.

Lumber used in the new house could be purchased for a good price after a chat at the club with William Bagnell or John Holmes. Homebuilders could, no doubt, get more than the standard discount on nails, screws, nuts, bolts, and any other needed hardware from Alfred Shapleigh's giant hardware company. Or they could do business with Shapleigh's neighbor Wallace Simmons, whose hardware company rivaled Shapleigh's in size and business volume. Claude Kennerly's Certain-Teed Products Corporation made roofing materials, so he could supply whatever was needed for the roof.

When paint was needed for a new house, it could be purchased from William Thornburgh's Platt and Thornburgh Paint Company. That same company could supply window-panes as well. And William Huse was a director of the Crystal Plate Glass Company, in case larger amounts of glass were needed.

Any iron needed for a house's structure or any wrought-iron decoration needed for the exterior could be provided at neighborly rates by the enclave's ironwork barons—George Allen,

The Cordelia and Edward C. Sterling house on the left (22 Westmoreland) was built in 1891. It was designed by Eames & Young. The Lillie and George L. Allen house next door to the west was built the following year and also designed by Eames & Young.

William Guy, Frank Johnson, or Theodore Meysenburg.

Stoves and ranges could be purchased from the two men whose companies made those commodities—Hudson Bridge, Jr., and William Culver. (Bridge and Beach Manufacturing Company was the first stove manufacturer in the Midwest.) Iceboxes and refrigerators were made by Louis Werner. Ice for the coolers could come from the river harvests of William Huse's giant Huse and Loomis Ice and Transportation Company. And once the mansion was ready for furnishing, neighbors could look to Samuel Kennard's company for carpeting.

After construction and furnishing were complete, Breckinridge Jones's Union Electric Light and Power Company was ready to install power lines. Telephones and intercoms could

Alfred Lee Shapleigh and his wife, Mina, built 6 Portland Place. In addition to running the Shapleigh Hardware Company founded by his father, the junior Shapleigh branched off into lead mining and banking interests.

be put in by telephone companies owned by either Eugene Nims or Breckinridge Jones.

Westmoreland/Portland residents went far beyond the neighborhood in their interrelated business dealings. It is not unlikely that wheat reaped in Kansas fields by Lewis Tebbetts's farm equipment was shipped to St. Louis on Carl Gray's Frisco Railroad in rail cars manufactured by the foundries of either William Bixby or William McMillan. It is possible that the tracks had been constructed by William Bagnell's company; that the wheat was turned into flour at the mill once owned by Harold Kauffman; that the flour was put in sacks made by John Filley's company; that the bags were sewn shut with twine made by Joseph Bascom's company; that the bags of flour were stored at a warehouse owned by Charles Wiggins— until the flour was needed at the bakeries of either Lewis Dozier or Leopold Freund. The entire transaction, from the wheat fields to the bakery shelves, could have been carried out

without a single element of it ever leaving the enterprises of the Westmoreland/Portland family.

Although competition was keen among St. Louis businessmen, there did not seem to be any intense rivalries in Westmoreland/Portland. The kingpins of the nation's two largest shoe manufacturing companies lived next door to each other. George Warren Brown, head of the mammoth Brown Shoe Company, bought the lot at 40 Portland, where his house rose in the spring of 1897. Oscar Johnson, one of the founders of the equally large Roberts-Johnson-Rand Shoe Company, constructed a house next door to Brown in the winter of 1905. Oscar's brother, Jackson, later moved into 25 Portland.

Hardware competitors Wallace Simmons and Alfred Shapleigh also lived in close proximity. Simmons bought the lot at 22 Portland in 1897. He sold that lot to Marion Lambert and subsequently bought and moved into 46 Westmoreland. His rival for the nation's hardware needs, Shapleigh, began construction on his house, 6 Portland, in July 1915. And to emphasize that fierce business competitiveness sometimes exists only on paper, William McMillan, president of the Missouri Car and Foundry Company, lived just down the street in Portland Place from the chairman of the board of the rival American Car and Foundry Company, William Bixby.

Why would competitors want to live so close to each other? One obvious rationale is that one could try to outdo the other in the scale and design of a mansion. Another reason might be that the competitors were in fact cronies. It is possible that each was making such a fortune that there was no need to harbor animosity for the other. Many brilliant business leaders enjoyed competition as a sport.

Nine lawyers were among the first homeowners in the neighborhood, and seven of them—Elmer Adams, Charles Nagel, Arthur Shepley, Isaac Lionberger, Alexander Cochran, Thomas McPheeters, and Daniel Catlin, Jr.—lived in close proximity in Westmoreland. Two bakers—Leopold Freund and Lewis Dozier—were neighbors in Westmoreland. Two residents with interests in brick manufacturing—Edward Sterling and Annie Chauvenet—lived next door to each other in Westmoreland. Brick baron N. S. Chouteau Walsh lived just a block over in Portland. Bankers Jacob C. Van Blarcom, Henry L. Newman, Charles P. Pettus, and Thomas H. West formed an enclave in Westmoreland and were just around the corner from Portland Place bankers Charles Wiggins, Breckinridge Jones, and John Shepley. Daniel Catlin, Jr., who family fortune was made in tobacco, and William Stickney, whose cigar company made him a fortune, lived across the parkway from each other

The Shapleigh Hardware Company at Fourth and Main as it appeared in 1890. Alfred Lee Shapleigh, the youngest son of the founder, lived at 6 Portland from 1915 until his death in 1945 and was active in the company for more than forty years.

The Simmons Hardware Company at Ninth and Washington Avenue as it appeared in 1889. Its founder, E. C. Simmons, became the second owner of the Newman house at 21 Westmoreland in 1893, and his son Wallace purchased 46 Westmoreland in 1916.

in Westmoreland. Westmoreland was also the home of dry-goods merchants Robert McKittrick Jones, Walter McKittrick, and Byron Nugent. Fellow dry-goods merchant Charles Stix lived in nearby Portland.

Housing patterns show that there was company togetherness as well as togetherness among competitors. After Simmons Hardware Company founder Edward C. Simmons purchased 21 Westmoreland, Mrs. Isaac Morton, widow of a Simmons Hardware vice-president, built a house at 43 Portland and Frank Johnson, a Simmons Company executive, built one at Number 47.

There is evidence that some of the early homebuilders used their money to regulate who their neighbors would be. Samuel Kennard, who built the twenty-five-room mansion that stood at 4 Portland, purchased three nearby lots before he moved into his home in 1892. He must have approved of Alfred Shapleigh because Kennard sold him the lot just west of his mansion in 1915. (The Kennard house was razed sixty-six years after it was built. Vacant for many years, it had become an eyesore.)

The neighborhood itself unquestionably brought people together for social occasions. Mrs. Norris H. Allen (Dorothea), who today lives in the home built by her grandfather William Huse, remembers, "Every night they would have whist games, all people from the block. It was sort of a club. They were all good friends—the husbands had the same type of business interests."

Many family bonds were solidified in Westmoreland/Portland. Brothers Edwin and George Steedman built houses next door to each other at 32 and 34 Westmoreland, respectively. A third brother, J. Harrison Steedman, lived briefly at Number 42. The Shepley brothers, Arthur and John, built houses at 50 Westmoreland and 53 Portland, respectively. Their sister, Louise, who was married to Isaac Lionberger, moved into 37 Westmoreland in 1906.

After both her parents died at the family mansion in Vandeventer Place, Mary Lionberger built 30 Westmoreland. She probably wanted to be closer to her brother Isaac, who lived at 37 Westmoreland, and to her nephew Clarkson Potter, who built a house at 42 Westmoreland. (Mary Lionberger bequeathed her considerable fortune to this nephew.)

Fathers and sons were neighbors in several early Westmoreland/Portland families. L. Ray Carter lived at 8 Portland, while his father, Thomas W. Carter, lived across the parkway at Number 5. Edward C. Simmons lived at 21 Westmoreland; his son, Wallace D., lived at Number 46. Wallace's son, Edward II, lived at 52 Westmoreland with his wife, Jean Ford Simmons, for more than thirty years. Jean Ford's sister, Elsie Ford Curby, and her husband, John, lived at 33 Westmoreland during the same time. Footwear magnate Oscar Johnson built 38 Portland. His brother, Jackson, was the second owner of 25 Portland. Andrew Johnson, Jackson's son, lived at 16 Portland. Andrew's sister Florence married Bradford Shinkle and lived at 48 and 35 Portland. Another sister, Helen, lived at 29 Portland with her husband, Lee Niedringhaus. The Shinkles, Rands, and Johnsons were related both by marriage and by the shoe-manufacturing business.

Joseph D. Bascom built a house at 45 Westmoreland, and his son, Charles, built one right behind it at 52 Portland. John A. Holmes constructed his house at 9 Portland, and his son, Robert, built his in the next block at Number 46.

John T. Davis, Sr., who had 17 Westmoreland built on three lots in 1893, also purchased the adjoining three lots of Portland, giving him the longest front footage on both places. His youngest son, Dwight Filley Davis, had his house erected on the Portland lots in 1911 with its back to the street. It showed its most ornate Georgian features to the Westmoreland property, where his mother and later his oldest brother, John T., Jr., lived. A third Davis brother, Samuel C., and his wife, Emma Whitaker Davis, moved into the house her parents

The E. C. Simmons family circa 1910. Simmons, shown here with the beard, established the giant Simmons Hardware Company. A number of Simmons family members have lived in Westmoreland/Portland.

Built in 1892, the imposing mansion at 25 Portland was designed for Eliza and William McMillan by Eames & Young. However, it was home to the McMillans for only a few years; William McMillan died in 1901 and Mrs. McMillan in 1915. The mansion's second owners, the Jackson Johnsons, moved in in 1915 and lived at Number 25 for forty-one years. The house is called the Jackson Johnson mansion to this day. The photographs on this and the following two pages, which were taken by Eugene Taylor and bound in leather for the Johnson family, have never before been published. These photographs not only give us a glimpse of the opulent living quarters for the masters of the mansion but also provide a rare look at the servants' living and working quarters.

The living room.

A second view of the living room.

The dining room.

This is the bedroom of the Johnsons' daughter, Ada, who was the 1920 Veiled Prophet Queen.

Mrs. Johnson's bedroom.

Mr. Johnson's bedroom.

The maids' dining room. The high chair to the right indicates that this may also have been where the grandchildren dined.

The butler's pantry.

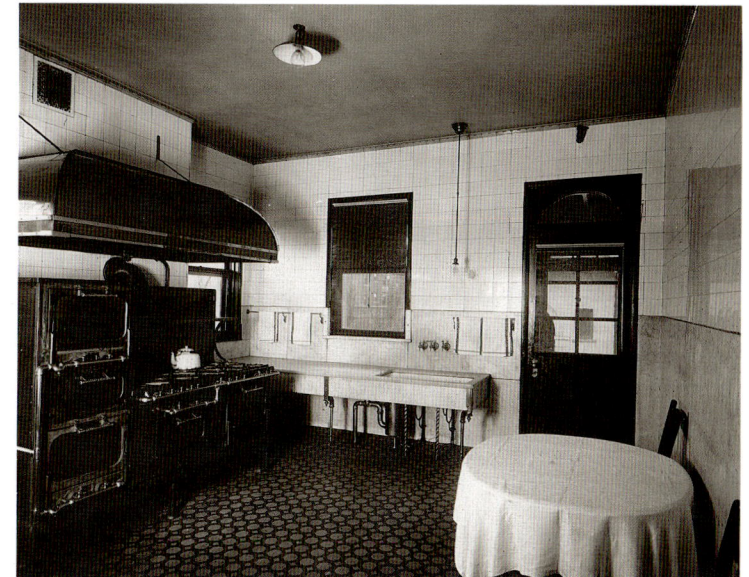

The kitchen.

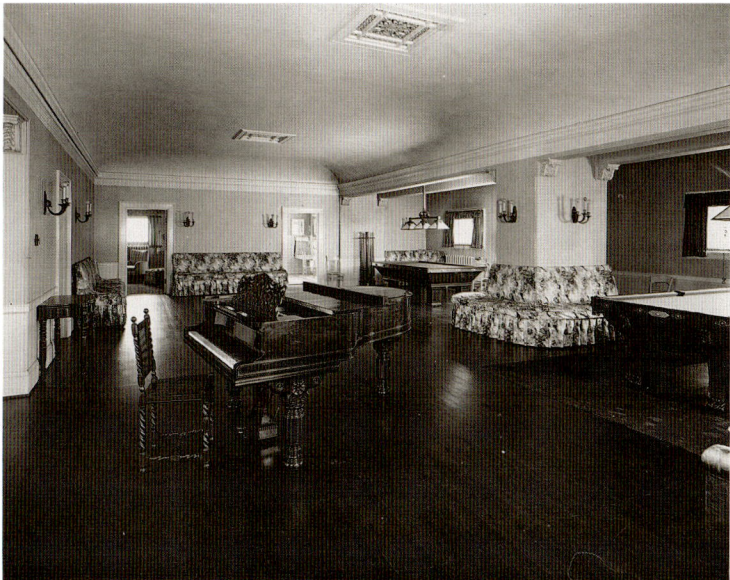

The billiard room.

The second floor hall.

The Jackson Johnsons' son, Andrew, and his wife, Helen, occupied a suite at the mansion before buying 16 Portland in 1927. This is the bathroom of those quarters.

Edwards and Sophia had built at 13 Westmoreland, forming a three-house Davis family compound surrounding a green expanse.

Dwight Davis was a national doubles tennis champion who donated the Davis Cup international tennis trophy in 1900. A red clay tennis court remains today on the east lot of 16 Portland. The recent history of Forest Park by Caroline Loughlin and Catherine Anderson extols Davis's role in establishing recreational facilities throughout the park. The park's tennis center is named in his honor. Davis later served as secretary of war in the Coolidge administration and as governor-general of the Philippines.

The tradition of family bonding in the places has continued with succeeding generations of owners. Behind Dr. John

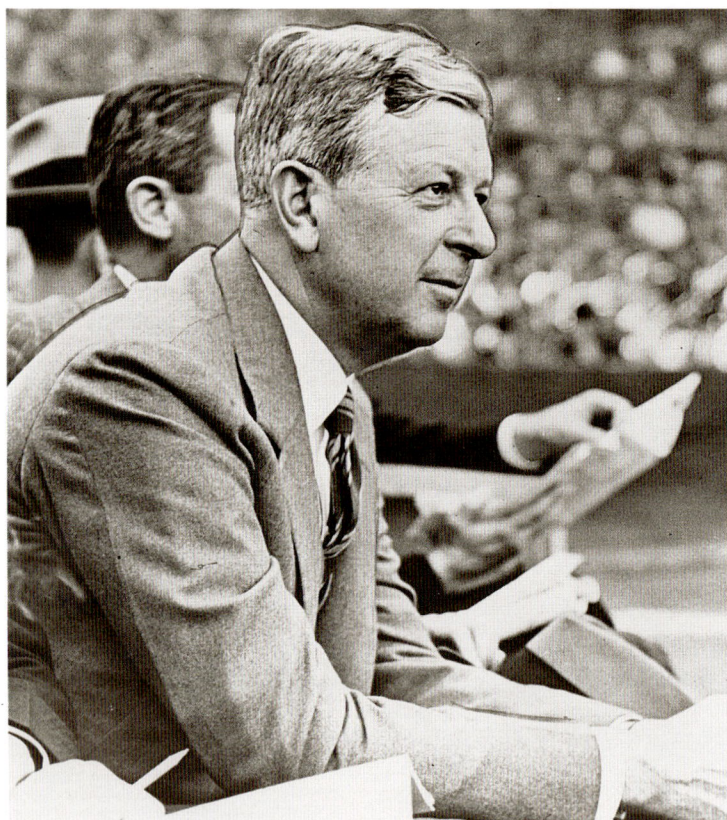

Dwight F. Davis, the builder of 16 Portland, gave the tennis world the Davis Cup. He served as secretary of war in the Coolidge administration and as governor-general of the Philippines in the Hoover administration. Davis is shown here at a 1928 World Series game.

Daake, a longtime owner of 48 Portland, lives his son James, at 47 Westmoreland. Another son, Thomas, is at 26 Portland. The houses at 33 Portland and 35 Westmoreland, built by two of the Liggett sisters, have been owned since the mid-1960s by Lucianna Gladney Ross and Katherine Gladney Wells (with her husband, Ben), the daughters of Frank Y. Gladney, one of the founders of Seven-Up.

The family with the largest representation over the years has been that of O. D. Filley, sixteenth mayor of St. Louis. His son, John D. Filley, two daughters, and eight grandchildren were among the early property owners. The second largest family represented was that of businessman and philanthropist William Cullen McBride of neighboring Washington Terrace. Three of McBride's four daughters resided in the places, as have five of his grandchildren and one great-grandchild. Two daughters of William Julius Polk, who lived at 28 Westmoreland from 1924 to 1939, made their homes in the places after their marriages.

Regardless of whether or not marriages are made in heaven, several were made in Westmoreland/Portland. Elizabeth Carter of 8 Portland married Wayman Allen, who resided at 26 Westmoreland. After the death of his first wife in 1918, Thomas McPheeters of 27 Westmoreland took Frances Filley of 40 Westmoreland as his bride. (She was the daughter of John D. Filley.) Five years after her husband, Selwyn, died of a heart attack at 41 Portland, Iva Dula Edgar married Kenneth Lemoine Green of 47 Westmoreland. Attorney Charles Nagel of 44 Westmoreland married Anne Shepley, sister of Arthur and John of 50 Westmoreland and 53 Portland, respectively.

The best example of neighborhood endogamy involves the Filleys, Wears, McPheeters, Burkhams, Langenbergs, Kauffmans, Moores, Whitakers, and Davises, who were all related by marriage. Other endogamous ties were forged by Marjorie Holland of 47 Westmoreland, who married Walter McKittrick of Number 54. Her sister, Amy, became Mrs. Clarkson Potter and moved from 47 Westmoreland to Number 42. Lewis B. Tebbetts married Ellen Mansur, the sister of Westmoreland/Portland developer Alvah Mansur, and moved to 29 Portland. Later marriages bonded the McBride, Orthwein, Mahaffey, Busch, and Love families in Westmoreland/Portland.

The camaraderie and social ties among the families were also created by the private city and country clubs to which they belonged. Most prestigious of the St. Louis clubs were the Noonday Club, the St. Louis Commercial Club, the University Club, the Mercantile Club, and the St. Louis Club. These clubs served as the focal point of the social circle of prominent

The Mercantile Club was the first club in St. Louis to offer facilities for women. This is the Ladies' Parlor.

St. Louisans. And the clubs' facilities served as the theater for more than social occasions. Important business deals could be made at the club, where handshakes sealed lucrative contracts. Financial tips were shared to increase personal fortunes. Political caucuses assembled in informal clusters to select candidates and plot platforms. Endogamous matches were made. And opportunities for recreation, physical education, and sports were also offered.

The club was an instrument by and through which the Westmoreland/Portland business czars could control their social environment. It was at the club that determinations could be made to govern the rungs of the social ladder as well as the climbers on those rungs. And an invitation could be extended over cocktails at the club to investigate the purchase of the vacant lot next door as the ideal spot for a new home.

Candidates for membership in any of the clubs had to be acceptable to all the members of that club. In the most prestigious clubs, one negative vote could exclude a hopeful applicant. Applicants could be denied admission on the basis of race, religion, occupation, political affiliation, education, gender, financial worth, and the number of years one's family had

The Mercantile Club at Seventh and Locust as it appeared in 1894. Westmoreland/Portland residents were prominent members of this exclusive downtown club.

held wealth. While some private clubs were established by and for the nouveaux riches, others offered admission to none but "old-line money."

This accepted practice of discrimination actually spawned new clubs. When Jews were denied admission to the St. Louis Club and the St. Louis Country Club, they formed their own private clubs and barred admission to gentiles. The first club in St. Louis founded for Jews was the Harmonie Club in 1857. By 1883 its membership roll had grown to 110 names. When it moved from Fourth and Market to Eighteenth and Olive, a contingent of its members who lived in south St. Louis formed a splinter organization called the Concordia Club. Later, Jews formed the downtown Columbian Club and the Westwood Country Club.

The St. Louis Jockey Club is the oldest private club in the city. It was founded in 1828 to promote the sport of horse racing. The running of the ponies was popular at that time, and the first races attracted large crowds of spectators and bettors at the Lucas track on the north side of the old St. Charles Rock Road. One of the club's incorporators under a later reorganization scheme was Julius S. Walsh, whose heirs were meshed into the Westmoreland/Portland family. The club's Cote Brilliante track, built at a cost of $70,000, opened to the public in 1877.

The University Club was organized by twenty college-educated men in January 1872. Its stated purpose was "to promote literature, science and art, and secure a closer union and cooperation of college and university men and graduates, with a view to a broader and higher culture." Thomas Allen, whose descendants were among the pioneer homebuilders of Portland/Westmoreland, was the club's first president.

For its first three years the University Club's members met at 911 Olive Street. Growth and prosperity took the club into new quarters at 1125 Washington, but when many of the members complained that the site was too far from the center of the city, the club was moved back downtown, to a building at Fifth and Olive.

The St. Louis Commercial Club was organized in 1880 and modeled after the Boston Commercial Club, which was the first of its kind in the nation. Despite its name, the club's stated purpose was to be a strictly social organization to bring businessmen together. E. C. Simmons, president of the hardware company that bore his family name and the owner of 21 Westmoreland, was on the Commercial Club's first executive committee.

In 1881 there was a call among St. Louis businessmen for a true "city club." As Scharf put it, "it began to be apparent that the existing club-houses were not situated at points convenient for the numerous business men who might otherwise be disposed to patronize their facilities, and a 'down-town' club was advocated." Thus the Mercantile Club was created. Among its incorporators were William McMillan and Samuel M. Kennard, both of Portland Place. Kennard was elected president in 1882; McMillan became the treasurer.

The Mercantile Club's first quarters were in the Sumner Building on Locust between Seventh and Eighth streets. Following an $18,000 renovation, the club's new quarters were dedicated in 1882. The Mercantile distinguished itself by being the first club in town to allow the wives of members to use its facilities. Membership was initially limited to four hundred men. That limit was reached within six months of the founding.

The St. Louis Club was organized in 1878. In that year the club purchased the old Finney mansion at 1532 Washington. Scharf relates that the building was "fitted up [as] one of the finest club-houses in the country, the building being spacious and conveniently arranged, and the grounds roomy and attractive. The appointments of the house were and continue to be of the most elaborate and elegant character." The club opened

The St. Louis Club, founded in 1878, as it appeared at Locust and Ewing in 1886. Many Westmoreland/Portland homebuilders were charter members of this exclusive club.

its doors to its more than three hundred members in September 1879. Four years later, John T. Davis was elected president and Daniel Catlin was made a director. Both later built mansions in Westmoreland Place.

The Racquet Club was organized in 1906 by a maverick group of young men who felt the older clubs were too stuffy and formal. A new club building was built at Kingshighway and Hortense Place so that, according to onetime club historian James C. Burkham, "coats could be removed at will and feet could be put on the tables without causing arched eyebrows or clucks of disapproval of the older generation." When the new Racquet Club building was dedicated in 1907, the Mercantile Club had 900 members; the St. Louis Club, 650; the Noonday Club, 420; the University Club, 390; the Country Club, 336; and the Glen Echo Club, 300. Of the 249 charter Racquet Club members, 43 were Westmoreland/Portland residents.

While it was difficult to gain membership in St. Louis's most exclusive clubs, it was even more difficult for a St. Louis resident to gain membership in an elite club outside the city. But several early Westmoreland/Portland residents managed it. Attorney Thomas McPheeters held membership in the Princeton Club of New York City and was also a member of the exclusive Cottage Club of Princeton, New Jersey. Banker Jacob Van Blarcom belonged to four New York clubs: the Union Club, Adirondack Club, Holland Society, and New York Club. Rail-car manufacturer William K. Bixby held membership in New York's exclusive Grolier Club. And banker Edwards Whitaker was a member of the Union Club, Manhattan Club, and Mid Day Club of New York. It was so important to belong to the right club that in newspaper obituaries the deceased's club affiliations were often listed before the names of the surviving family members.

It was important in top-level society to be seen at the right clubs and at the right parties and social functions. Not to be seen was not to have been invited. Not to have been invited meant either a social snub or a falling from social grace. But no resident of Westmoreland/Portland needed to worry about being dropped from the Blue Book.

This registry of St. Louis's prominent citizens included ten thousand names in 1887. It was a descendant of the St. Louis Directory, which David Banks Gould and an associate first published in 1872. Even before that, a printed census list was published in 1821. The term *Blue Book* was derived from an official report of the British Parliament issued in 1715, and the book was appropriately bound with a blue cover.

In the United States, the Blue Book became a register of socially prominent families. The Blue Books of Boston, Philadelphia, New York, and Washington, D.C., were much more discriminating than that produced in St. Louis. Entries into and dismissals from the former registers were tightly monitored by the old guard—the preeminent matriarch or patriarch of society or a committee whose scrutiny had the power to make or destroy individuals.

The St. Louis book compiled by Gould included names of "all the prominent householders" in the greater St. Louis area. The first St. Louis Blue Book was dedicated to E. C. Simmons, whose family figured prominently in the development of Westmoreland and Portland. The first edition included a shopping guide, "Hints on Etiquette," and seating charts for several local theaters.

The number of St. Louisans included in the Blue Book grew from ten thousand to fifteen thousand between 1885 and 1903—hardly an elite number. In 1903, two years after Gould's death, the Blue Book scandalized the blue bloods by listing for the first time apartment dwellers as well as homeowners.

The more important and more respected of the directories for St. Louis society was the Social Register. Published by the Social Register Association of New York, the Social Register appears to have been first issued in 1886. Eventually, separate listings were produced for more than a dozen cities—most of them on the east coast. A St. Louis Social Register appeared in 1886, making this city one of only three in the Midwest—with Chicago and Minneapolis—to have an exclusive listing of the elite in that year.

College and university ties were also bonds among early Westmoreland/Portland homeowners. Many were educated at prestigious institutions. Among the charter Westmoreland/Portland homebuilders there were at least seven Harvard graduates, seven Yale alumni, and four Princeton graduates.

Fourteen Westmoreland/Portland residents could talk over their college prep days. Charles Bascom, L. Ray Carter, Dwight Filley Davis, Edward Faust, Harold M. Kauffman, Robert H. Keiser, Claude Saugrain Kennerly, Walter McKittrick, Thomas McPheeters, Edward Mallinckrodt, Jr., Clarkson Potter, Charles Pettus, Edwin H. Steedman, and George Fox Steedman were all graduates of Smith Academy.

One of the most extensively educated men in the neighborhood was William Evans Guy, who built the house at 10 Portland. After attending both private and public schools in Cincinnati and Oxford, Ohio, Guy attended Kentucky Military Institute, Miami University, Princeton, the University of Heidelberg, the Freiberg School of Mines, and the College de France in Paris. He obtained a degree from Cincinnati Law School ten years after leaving the French school.

Honorable mention must be given to Alexander G. Cochran, builder of 7 Westmoreland, for his academic achievement. Cochran graduated from Columbia University Law School in 1866 and was admitted to the bar at age nineteen.

While the old college cheer could be heard at some neighborhood parties, there were several early Westmoreland/Portland homeowners whose former low incomes and family responsibilities had kept them from college. Oscar Johnson, for example, was an infant when his father died. Because his mother was left in near poverty, Oscar had to go to work full-time at the age of fourteen. He took a job as a general merchandise clerk in a store owned by his uncle, Oscar Rand. The fact that Johnson became the head of the gigantic International Shoe Company attested to his ability to learn on-the-job. Johnson's Portland Place neighbor, George Warren Brown, was born on a farm and received only a skimpy formal education, yet his and Johnson's shoe companies were at one time the two largest manufacturers of footwear in the world.

Formal education did not play a major role in William Wallace Culver's impressive success as a businessman. Born in 1835 to parents of meager means in Franklin County, Ohio, Culver attended a district school in the winter months and worked on a farm in the summers. He arrived in St. Louis at the age of twenty-six and could not find work. He returned to Springfield, Illinois, where he had earlier been employed as a carpenter. A year later Culver landed a job selling stoves from the back of a wagon, and he stayed on the road for six years. In 1860 he enrolled in a business course at Bryant and Stratton's Commercial College in Chicago.

Before long Culver started his own business selling stoves in Connersville, Indiana. By 1865 he had established Culver Brothers Company in Shawneetown, Illinois. He later went on to make a fortune selling stoves in the stores and plants he set up in Iowa, Missouri, and Kentucky. He moved his firm, Wrought Iron Range Company, to St. Louis in 1874. Culver retired from his company in 1903, shortly after selling the home he had built at 39 Portland. But his retirement did not last long. That same year he founded a company that manufactured asbestos and roofing materials.

George D. Barnard, the first owner of 35 Portland, was, out of necessity, a high school dropout. When his father died, fourteen-year-old Barnard was forced to find work. He began

The George D. Barnard Stationery Company at Eleventh and Washington was founded by the first resident of 35 Portland. The company was the largest manufacturer of blank books in the world.

become the head of the largest ice and transportation company in the Midwest.

Long before he became a top executive of the Bridge and Beach Manufacturing firm, twenty-one-year-old George Holland took a job with that company in 1868 making $25 a month. Carl Gray also started on the bottom rung. The man who would eventually become the general manager of the St. Louis and San Francisco Railroad started out as a telegraph operator in 1883 at the age of sixteen. Joseph Bascom started the road that would eventually lead him to the chairmanship of a prosperous rope-manufacturing company when he took a job as an errand boy for a retail clothing store. Bascom was only thirteen years old at the time.

Leopold Freund took over his father's baking business at the age of eighteen, but Moritz Freund's estate was valued at only $5,751.75 when he died in 1872. The Freunds' personal property was appraised at $83.65. Leopold, who built 53 Westmoreland, was able to turn the bakery into a highly successful company.

Other early Westmoreland/Portland residents made their entry into the business world at the top. After Samuel Kennard returned to St. Louis from military duty in the Civil War, his father took him into the family carpet business as a partner. He became president of the company upon his father's death. After brothers George and Edwin Steedman graduated from Harvard (in 1892 and 1895, respectively), their father bought them a graduation present that gave them a start in business: the Curtis & Company Manufacturing Company. The brothers learned about the manufacture of saws, sawmills, and pneumatic machinery from their own firm.

But such "silver-spoon" treatment did not automatically mean that the favored sons treated their companies as mere toys. Edward Mallinckrodt, Jr., for instance, who joined the chemical company founded by his father and two uncles, held an active interest in Mallinckrodt Chemical Company for sixty-four years, until he retired in 1965.

To reach the top, some Westmoreland/Portland homeowners displayed the kind of tenacity that is best exemplified by Jacob Craig Van Blarcom. After Van Blarcom came to St. Louis from New Jersey in 1866, he took a job with Peterson, Hawthorn and Company, a wholesale house for saddlery, hardware, and leather. When one of the company's traveling salesmen refused to go into the fever-stricken cities of the south, Van Blarcom volunteered for the job. At the age of twenty-one, he single-handedly put the firm in the black. Eventually he bought it. He was given the job of head accoun-

Edward Mallinckrodt, Jr., who built 16 Westmoreland, was active with his family's chemical company for sixty-four years. He is shown here receiving a 1952 American Chemical Society award from Society Chairperson Desiree S. Le Beau.

tant of the Bank of Commerce in 1879. When Van Blarcom died in 1908, he left an estate of more than $4 million.

Several of the Westmoreland/Portland pioneers had military service in the Civil War as a common bond. Veterans of both the Union and the Confederacy lived side by side a quarter of a century after Lee's formal surrender to Grant at Appomattox Court House.

Among those who saw active duty in the Union army was Charles Fach of Portland Place, who was a corporal in the Home Guards of the Missouri Militia. He served under Capt. E. Rice and spent his active duty in St. Louis. William Albert Stickney, later of Westmoreland Place, was working as a clerk in a Boston coffee, tea, and tobacco store in 1862 when he enlisted in the Sixth Massachusetts Volunteer Infantry. From there he moved to New York where he developed a greater interest in the cigar trade.

Henry Levi Newman served the Union army in a noncombat role. He ran a freighting operation for the government

clerking with a stationery manufacturing company. Six years after taking that job, Barnard and two friends opened the George D. Barnard Stationery Company. When he died in 1915, Barnard left an estate of more than $2 million. During his life he gave away at least that much to charities.

Several other residents started at the bottom of the ladder. Charles Stix got his first training as a stock boy in a Cincinnati dry-goods business after graduating from high school. Eugene Nims, a founder of Southwestern Bell Telephone Company, got his first taste of the real world at the age of seventeen as an employee of a lumberyard in Nebraska. An industrious young man, Robert McKittrick Jones worked for five years as an apprentice to a linen manufacturer in his native Belfast, Ireland, before becoming the head of the dry-goods firm that bore his name. William L. Huse took a job as a clerk in a Chicago grocery house at the age of seventeen and went on to during the war. Leopold Freund had what was perhaps the least dangerous job of the war. His bakery supplied bread for the troops stationed at Jefferson Barracks from the opening days of the war until the barracks' last day as a Civil War military installation.

As soon as the war broke out in 1861, Samuel Kennard joined Landis Battery, C.S.A., attached to Cockrell's Brigade. Kennard saw combat duty in and around Vicksburg in 1863, when that city fell to General Grant. Kennard was taken a prisoner of war and held until his release in a prisoner exchange. Kennard later became a lieutenant in the combined Landis and Guiboir batteries and commanded a section of that unit during the battle of Franklin, Tennessee, on October 30, 1864. Soon afterward Lieutenant Kennard became an aide-de-camp to Gen. Nathaniel B. Forrest, the founder of the Ku Klux Klan.

Kennard's neighbor across the back fence, Theodore A. Meysenburg, could have matched Kennard story for story. German immigrant Meysenburg fought on the Union side. When he first came to St. Louis at the age of sixteen, Meysenburg used the fine education he had received in Essen to land a job in the city engineer's office.

Like so many other German expatriates, Meysenburg left his job to enlist in the Third Missouri Volunteer Infantry as soon as arms were first drawn in the Civil War. When his term ended before the war did, Meysenburg did not hesitate to reenlist. He earned his stripes and was promoted to second lieutenant in the Benton Hussars. His superiors were impressed with him, and he was assigned as adjutant to Brig. Gen. Franz Sigel and was promoted to the rank of captain. This commission, signed by President Lincoln, was one of Meysenburg's most treasured possessions for the rest of his life.

While serving in the Army of the Potomac, Captain Meysenburg participated in the battles at Chancellorsville and Gettysburg. He might have recounted at least once to Sam Kennard the frightening experience of having his horse shot out from under him at Gettysburg. Unscathed and undaunted, Meysenburg pressed on to engage in the bitterly fought Shenandoah Valley campaign. His capabilities as a military officer were further recognized when he was promoted to lieutenant colonel. For the rest of his life, Meysenburg's name was prefixed with that earned title.

Thomas Henry West joined the Confederate army in 1863, when he was sixteen years old. Frank Nicholas Johnson served

Lewis B. Tebbetts and his wife, Ellen Mansur Tebbetts, built 29 Portland. He made his fortune in farm equipment and carriage manufacture. (His wife was a sister of Alvah Mansur, one of the developers of Westmoreland/Portland.)

three years in the Confederate army in the Virginia State Troops, Eatherd's Battery, the Stuart Horse Artillery, and the Army of Northern Virginia. Johnson remained an active member of the United Confederate Veterans for the rest of his life.

The bitter conflict between North and South brought Charles Nagel to St. Louis and ultimately to Westmoreland Place. When Nagel was fifteen years old, his father decided the family must leave Texas because of their pro-Union sympathies. He was probably surprised at the degree of pro-Confederate feeling that existed in St. Louis.

Oscar Johnson was a baby when his father, a Confederate soldier, was wounded in battle and died a short time later. Many years later, Oscar's wife, Irene, kept the embers of the southern cause alive. A native of Mississippi, Irene Johnson was the daughter of Confederate general Harvey W. Walter and a devout member of the United Daughters of the Confederacy.

David Coalter Gamble's father, Hamilton R. Gamble, became Missouri's provisional governor when the secessionist Claiborne F. Jackson was forced to flee Jefferson City in advance of Union troops. However, David Gamble, who was seventeen years old when the war started, avoided the conflict by not enlisting.

The Civil War was primarily a commercial concern for Lewis B. Tebbetts. As an executive of the Baltimore firm of Poole & Hunt, Tebbetts oversaw the construction of lighthouses and sold ammunition and engines for gunboats to the federal government. Nine years after the war ended, Tebbetts established an agricultural equipment business in St. Louis with Alvah Mansur and Charles Deere.

Another strong bond among Westmoreland/Portland residents was their religious affiliation. An overwhelming majority were Protestant, and most of those were Episcopalian. Very few Roman Catholics or Jews took up residence behind the gates of Westmoreland/Portland, although both were present in large numbers in the city. There were only three Catholics of record among the charter residents.

Charles Aaron Stix and Leopold Freund were the only Jewish Westmoreland/Portland homebuilders. The dearth of Jews suggests that some form of discrimination existed. It is known that a German-born Jew, Jacob Goldman, was denied entry to some of the exclusive private places in the city. Goldman, who made his fortune as a cotton merchant, was so stung by the discrimination that he founded his own private place in the shadow of Westmoreland/Portland. He named his new private subdivision Hortense Place in honor of a young daughter who had died in 1896.

St. Louis's top level of society discriminated against people on more issues than religion or race. Some occupations were considered unacceptable for entry into the highest social strata. Medicine or law, banking, real estate development, and the manufacture and distribution of hard goods and machinery were quite acceptable occupations, as were running a railroad, warehousing goods, or operating a flour mill. But even a millionaire could not find social acceptance if he had made his fortune as a restaurateur or beer brewer or in show business.

One brewer who felt frustration bordering on bitterness over exclusion from a private place was William Frederick Nolker. After he was denied entry, he built an enormous stone mansion at Lindell and Taylor avenues, now the residence of the Roman Catholic archbishop of St. Louis.

While there were dozens of beer barons in St. Louis in the 1880s, as was noted before, only two beer families made it through the gates of Westmoreland/Portland as charter residents. Elizabeth Schnaider built a house at 24 Portland. Edward and Anna Busch Faust were given the magnificent palace at 1 Portland by the bride's father as a wedding present. Adolphus Busch, with his $35 million fortune, could well afford to build an impressive mansion for his daughter and son-in-law. The construction cost of the seventeen-room Carthage limestone building in 1912 dollars was reported as $150,000.

Still, the Fausts were not readily accepted by all their neighbors. Some of the invitations to their open house were spurned, but eventually curiosity about the interior of their palace won out and the Fausts found slightly more acceptance. Perhaps it was a reaction to the discrimination that he had experienced that shaped Edward Faust's politics. Although he was not a Catholic, he rallied to the side of presidential aspirant Alfred E. Smith in 1928. Faust claimed that he was voting for Smith strictly because Smith's Catholic religion had been so widely assailed, but the fact that Smith opposed Prohibition may have influenced Faust's vote.

Several Westmoreland/Portland pioneers were of foreign birth. William McMillan, Byron Nugent, and William Bagnell were Canadian. Robert McKittrick Jones was born in Ireland. Leopold Freund was born in Austria. William Orthwein and Theodore Meysenburg were natives of Germany. And Louis Werner, the son of a wealthy family in Budapest, came to the United States shortly after the Civil War.

Many of the early residents spoke the same language when it came to politics. Most who declared their political preference were Republicans or conservative Democrats, but relatively few were at home in the political spotlight. The most powerful political influence exerted by Westmoreland/Portland residents was directed in subtle, behind-the-scenes ways. And most often that political influence was financial.

An exception was Breckinridge Jones. He was elected a member of the Thirty-second Missouri General Assembly as a Democrat and served as a legislator for thirty years. Although his primary interest was in banking—he was president of the Mississippi Valley Trust Company—Jones was known among his fellow lawmakers and his constituents as a capable legislator who liked to cut through the red tape that sometimes stifles legislation.

Lawyer Charles Nagel served one term as a member of the

Edward Faust was the son of the well-known restaurateur Tony Faust and the son-in-law of brewer Adolphus Busch. The mansion at 1 Portland was given to Edward and his bride, Anna, by her father as a wedding present.

Missouri legislature, 1881–1883. A Republican, Nagel also served as secretary of commerce under President Taft. Alexander Cochran served a term in the Forty-fourth Congress when he lived in Pennsylvania. And William L. Huse was elected mayor of Peru, Illinois, before he settled in St. Louis in 1861.

Nagel's brother-in-law, John F. Shepley, made a big splash when, during the William Jennings Bryan–William McKinley campaign of 1896, he announced he was abandoning the Democratic party because he was a "gold Democrat." Shepley switched to the Republican party to express his opposition to Bryan's free silver doctrine.

Isaac Lionberger appears to have been among the most politically vocal and active of early Westmoreland/Portland residents. He was expelled from the Missouri state Democratic convention in 1896 because of his outspoken views in support of a gold standard. Shepley and Lionberger had more in common than their politics. They practiced law together from 1886 to 1890. Their partnership was dissolved when Shepley took a position with St. Louis Union Trust. He later became chairman of the board of that financial institution.

Samuel Kennard was among the best known political power brokers of his era, but he preferred to remain behind-the-scenes. He masterminded the successful political career of David R. Francis, propelling Francis to the mayor's office at City Hall, to the governor's mansion in Jefferson City, and later to the post of interior secretary and diplomatic service as ambassador to Russia.

Another common bond among Westmoreland/Portland homebuilders was that so many of them lived longer lives than could be expected at that time, enjoying good health and exceptional stamina. Walter McKittrick, Isaac Lionberger, Charles Wiggins, and Claude Kennerly were nonagenarians. Edward Mallinckrodt, Alfred Shapleigh, Lemuel Carter, William Guy, George Carpenter, Allen West, Alexander Cochran, Eugene Nims, Edwin Steedman, Louis Werner, Lewis Tebbetts, and William Orthwein became octogenarians. Joseph Bascom, John Filley, George Allen, Edwards Whitaker, Thomas West, Harry Langenberg, Daniel Catlin, Sr., Henry Newman, Henry Siegrist, Hudson Bridge, John Fowler, Thomas McPheeters, Thomas Carter, William Culver, Claude Kilpatrick, John Holmes, Breckinridge Jones, John Shepley, and J. D. Perry Francis lived into their seventies.

Why were these barons of business, whose lives were filled with daily stress, rich food and drink, and relatively little physical exercise, able to live so long? It has been recognized since the early nineteenth century that there are wide differences in mortality by social class. No contemporaneous studies are available, but a study conducted by Jules F. Quint and Bianca Cody for the Metropolitan Life Insurance Company in the 1960s revealed that corporate executives live longer, on the average, than those in the general, nonprofessional population. The study concludes, "Age for age, eminent men enjoyed more favorable mortality." It further states that once a top business executive reaches the age of forty-five, his life expectancy is significantly higher than that of the general male population.

Another study conducted by Evelyn M. Kitagawa and P. M. Hauser at Harvard University was based on matching 340,000 death certificates with data on the 1960 census records. Kitagawa and Hauser noted that education and income were inversely related to mortality in the white population, with the differentials much smaller after age sixty-five than before.

An investigation at Cornell University Medical College by Dr. L. E. Hinkle, Jr., and associates, also points out the relationship between occupation, education, and health. The study of 270,000 people concluded that, contrary to popular theory, attaining the highest level of management does not increase the risk of coronary disease. It suggests that the same biological-social factors that propel people into attaining college degrees and high-pressure jobs also give them the mechanisms to survive stress.

The Metropolitan Life study states, "Many of those who attain high status are able to cope with and even thrive on stressful situations by harnessing tensions for productive use." In fact, work satisfaction plus public recognition may be an important ingredient of good health and longevity. Mental and physical fitness tend to go together. The Metropolitan Life study concludes that not only do college-educated males live longer than those not educated, but honor students also live longer than the general college-educated male population.

The men who built the homes in Westmoreland/Portland were obviously able to cope with stress. Many of them experienced financial reversals in the panics, depressions, and crashes of their era. It is certainly conceivable that they did thrive on challenges and saw them as opportunities for new economic adventures.

There were exceptions to the pattern of longevity, of course. John T. Davis was only forty-nine years old when he died of a kidney ailment, Bright's disease, in 1894. Bright's disease also cut Jacob Van Blarcom's life short. He died in 1908 at the age of fifty-nine. Oscar Johnson was fifty-three when he met death in 1916. George Holland was only fifty-five when he died of cancer in 1902. Charles Stix also succumbed to cancer at an early age, fifty-six. Robert Keiser was fifty-six when he died in Atlantic City in 1928. And heart disease ended William Thornburgh's life at the age of fifty-eight in 1901.

Many of the wives and widows of the Westmoreland/Portland merchant princes lived well into the golden years. For instance, Gertrude Catlin, widow of Daniel Catlin, Jr., lived to be ninety. Rebekah West survived her husband, Allen, by eleven years, dying at age eighty-one. Mary Lionberger, who never married, lived to be eighty. Hanna Freund saw her eighty-seventh birthday. Corinne Dyer, Annie Lee Chauvenet, Bertha Scott, Ellen Tebbetts, and Lucretia Meysenburg lived into their seventies. This is all the more remarkable considering that women of that generation were not allowed by Victorian standards to engage in any public physical exercise or vigorous recreation.

An interest in business, a competitive drive, and a desire for social standing tied neighbors together in Westmoreland/Portland. A Protestant background, an inclination toward conservative politics, and an appreciation of culture kept them together. Their ambitions led them to accumulate money; their feelings of responsibility to the community, their education, and their talents led them to want to share these acquisitions.

4. MONEY AND POWER

St. Louis is a closed corporation. Less than twenty men run it.
—Iseult Kuyk, 1919

The men who built Westmoreland/Portland were ambitious achievers—those who reached for the gold ring and then created a magnificent setting to display their attainments. The concentration of wealth and power among the first families in the neighborhood was impressive. What they did with their money and clout made an important contribution to St. Louis history. Sometimes it even made headlines.

After newspaper publisher Joseph Pulitzer's stinging defeat by Thomas Allen, president of the Iron Mountain Railroad, in the 1880 election for Congress, Pulitzer's *Post-Dispatch* began a campaign against the power circle in St. Louis. Pulitzer suspected Allen of using his wealth unethically, although he could never prove it.

The *Post-Dispatch* had an ally in its campaign—the *Mirror* of William Marion Reedy. Reedy, too, believed that a conspiracy of local business and political leaders was attempting to control the destiny of St. Louis. Reedy had grown up in the Irish section of town called Kerry Patch and knew well the problems of the underdog. Part of his appeal as a journalist was his ability to articulate the views of the working class. He stood ready to try to expose corruption and immorality among the rich. It was probably Reedy who coined the term *Big Cinch* to describe the closed circle of power brokers who controlled the economic and political development of St. Louis from the late nineteenth century until the first several decades of the twentieth.

Reedy may also have been "Iseult Kuyk," a pseudonymous observer who commented freely on the workings of the powerful. Writing in a little magazine called the *Iconoclast*, Kuyk

A view of Westmoreland Place circa 1900. Eighteen houses had been built in Westmoreland by this time.

leveled the following charges at the business-political clique that controlled the reins in St. Louis:

> They dare do anything. They control the banks, the trust companies, the street railroads, the gas works, the telephone franchises and the newspapers. They own everything in St. Louis worth owning. They are the local nobility. They can crush anyone who ventures to oppose their desires. They unite against the newcomer and crucify him. They control municipal legislation. They buy aldermen like cattle. The city is at their mercy. They are all religious and moral men; their crookedness is purely commercial and political.

Reedy's campaign against the elite was probably bankrolled by

a rather unusual benefactor—a Westmoreland Place resident. Scotch-Irish immigrant James Campbell, the second resident of 2 Westmoreland, despised his neighbors. Campbell had acquired his multi-million-dollar fortune in land speculation, railroad bonds, and street railways. But he never acquired a formal education or any of the social graces. He made his fortune in business deals with his neighbors but was never invited to attend their parties or to join their clubs.

Historian James Neal Primm observed in *Lion of the Valley*: "That the West End rich were masters of St. Louis seemed indisputable. They believed they were entitled to rule even when denying the fact; their detractors believed they conspired to rule; and most observers agreed." The founding fathers of Westmoreland and Portland and their successors formed a major part of the nucleus of power that shaped life in St. Louis, the Midwest, and, to some degree, the nation.

"They dare do anything."

Indeed, these men pulled off the grandest and most spectacular fair the world had seen when they produced and directed the Louisiana Purchase Exposition in 1904. Through hard work, political muscle, and personal wealth, they raised $45 million to put on a stupendous seven-month-long party. Nearly 20 million spectators had come to the fair by the time the lights went out. Without a doubt, the planning of this incomparable undertaking was a tie that bound the tight circle of the St. Louis elite closer together. The execution of the well-developed master plan for the fair gave exercise to the genius of the group. And the afterglow made this cadre of leaders dream new dreams of economic and political dominance.

Westmoreland/Portland residents were in the center of the circle that planned and executed the fair. Samuel Kennard was

The house at 2 Westmoreland was built in 1896 for Henry and Minnie Siegrist and was purchased six years later by James and Florence Campbell. Shown here are the "Moorish room" (above left), master bedroom (above right), and second-floor landing (below) as they looked during the residence of the Campbell family.

president of the Veiled Prophet organization when talk of a world's fair began to turn serious in 1891. George D. Barnard, who had made a fortune selling stationery and blank books, was on the original fair committee of two hundred, as was Charles A. Stix. W. K. Bixby, board chairman of American Car and Foundry, was a fair director and chairman of the fair's fine arts committee. Lumber millionaire John A. Holmes was also a director of the exposition, as was Isaac W. Morton, whose widow later moved to Portland Place. Tobacco-tycoon-turned-real-estate-baron Daniel Catlin, Jr., owned most of the land on which the fair's carnival was held.

Breckinridge Jones was not only an original member of the committee of fifteen that conceived the idea of the fair, he was also one of three men who accompanied David R. Francis to ask for President William McKinley's endorsement. And Jones was one of the lobbyists who threw a magnificent dinner party in Washington to muster congressional interest in the enterprise. When the fair was over, Jones accompanied Francis to Europe to deliver commemorative World's Fair medals to the crowned heads who had not attended. Jones had earned the honor of touring with Francis—he had devised a plan to raise $5 million for the fair.

While there can be no question that St. Louis benefited greatly from the 1904 World's Fair, Pulitzer, Reedy, and other critics warned that there was a selfish motive behind the beneficence of the fair's promoters. Detractors claimed the Louisi-

ana Purchase Exposition was set up to celebrate the business success of St. Louis's wealthy few. While many business enterprises did benefit from the fair, the nearly 20 million fairgoers and the thousands who found employment at the fair might contradict the contention that there were selfish motives behind the creation of the exposition.

In addition to living virtually next door to each other, fair planners also shared membership in the same exclusive clubs, and all but Barnard were directors of the city's leading banks and trust companies. In fact, Breckinridge Jones earned the appellation *father of the trust company* after he organized the National Association of Trust Companies in 1896.

Coming off their amazing success with the fair, some of the movers and shakers of the St. Louis business community dared to take on another project of unrivaled magnitude. They decided to build the tallest office building ever to be built in

Daniel K. Catlin, Jr., who built 41 Westmoreland, gave up his law practice to attend to the tobacco manufacturing and real estate interests initiated by his father, Daniel K. Catlin, Sr. In addition to his many cultural interests, he served on the board of the Carnegie Foundation for International Peace for seventeen years.

the city. The plan was to put all their railroad offices under one roof, with the William H. Barr dry-goods store (now Famous-Barr) on the lower floors. Even though the scope of the project produced a crop of Doubting Thomases and construction costs strained the available resources, the full-block twenty-one-story Railway Exchange Building slowly rose in 1908 to dominate the St. Louis skyline.

Among the men who dared to invest in this enterprise were the McKittrick brothers, Thomas and Walter. The venture came so close to ruining them that, in order to stay afloat financially, they had to sell their dry-goods business, including the William H. Barr retail store and their wholesale house, Hargadine & McKittrick. Walter McKittrick was not out of work long, thanks to his neighbors and fellow club members. After selling his company, he took successive executive positions with Ely & Walker Dry Goods Company and with Rice-Stix Dry Goods Company. The Rice-Stix firm was headed by

Breckinridge Jones and his wife, Frances, built 45 Portland. He was president of the Mississippi Valley Trust Company and in 1896 organized the National Association of Trust Companies.

McKittrick's Portland Place neighbor, Charles Stix. The other principals in the Railway Exchange Building project were Portland Place resident W. K. Bixby and his Westmoreland Place neighbor Thomas West.

"They control the banks, the trust companies . . ."

The first Westmoreland/Portland homebuilders constituted a "Who's Who in Banking and Trust." Even a partial listing of their banking and trust involvements indicates the extent to which the residents' financial holdings were interrelated:

Mississippi Valley Trust
  Breckinridge Jones, president and counsel
  William D. Orthwein, director
  Charles Wiggins, president

National Bank of Commerce
  Samuel Kennard, director
  John Holmes, director
  Lewis B. Tebbetts, director
  Jacob C. Van Blarcom, president

St. Louis Union Trust
  W. K. Bixby, director
  Daniel Catlin, Sr., founder, director
  Joseph Bascom, director
  John T. Davis, director
  John D. Filley, board chairman, director
  John Fowler, director
  William L. Huse, director
  Harry H. Langenberg, director
  John F. Shepley, board chairman
  Thomas H. West, president

Boatmen's Bank
  W. K. Bixby, director
  William L. Huse, director
  Byron Nugent, director
  Edwards Whitaker, president

State Bank
  Daniel Catlin, Sr., director
  John T. Davis, Sr., vice-president

First National Bank
  Joseph Bascom, director
  Harry H. Langenberg, director
  Thomas H. West, director

Mercantile Trust Company
  Daniel Catlin, Jr., director
  Lewis D. Dozier, director
  Walter McKittrick, director

Mercantile Commerce Trust Company
  Edward A. Faust, director

American Trust Company
  Charles P. Pettus, vice-president

Merchants Laclede National Bank
  Alfred L. Shapleigh, president

National Stockyards Bank
  Henry L. Newman, founder, president

Commonwealth Trust Company
  Lewis B. Tebbetts, vice-president

Joplin National Bank
  Henry L. Newman, founder, president

This partial listing graphically illustrates that the banking establishment in St. Louis was controlled by a small group of cronies who lived within a few blocks of each other, many of whom held directorships in more than one bank or trust company (current banking regulations prohibit officers from sitting on the boards of more than one financial institution). These neighborly ties allowed these men comfortable positions from which they could make deals that benefited their mutual interests. Residential bonds were strengthened by social bonds. For instance, membership in the Bogey Club, a country club founded in 1911, was initially made up almost entirely of officers of St. Louis Union Trust Company. And of the ten charter members, four were neighbors in Westmoreland/Portland: W. K. Bixby, Daniel Catlin, Jr., John D. Filley, and Thomas H. West. All these men were also members of the St. Louis Country Club and the Noonday Club.

Several Westmoreland/Portland stockholders controlled banking interests by the number of shares they kept in their families. For instance, at the turn of the century the Orthweins owned 334 shares of National Bank of Commerce stock; the McKittrick family owned 540 shares of stock in the same bank; the Luyties family had 590 shares; the Van Blarcoms owned 749 shares; the Tebbetts family held 1,140 shares; and the Holmes family owned 1,630 shares. The Bagnells, Bixbys, Bridges, Browns, Fausts, Kennards, Lionbergers, Mallinckrodts, Mortons, and Stixes, all of Westmoreland/Portland, also held a substantial portion of the bank's 49,740 shares. A two-hundred-unit block of stock was worth about $50,000 at that time.

St. Louis Union Trust might have more appropriately been called the Westmoreland/Portland Place Trust. At the turn of the century, ninety families controlled 32,592 shares in the trust company. Of those ninety, twenty-eight lived in either Westmoreland or Portland. These families controlled 15,056 shares—almost half the total. And of the sixty-four families who controlled 16,685 shares of Mississippi Valley Trust's total stock, thirteen Westmoreland/Portland families owned 4,486 shares.

Railroads were also a lucrative enterprise for a small number of investors who reaped handsome profits. When the Interstate Commerce Commission was finally given some power to enforce regulations after the turn of the century, it raised many questions about who profited most from the intricate inner workings of railroad transactions. Some railroads were organized strictly for the purpose of being bought out by larger railroads at a profit to the shareholders of the smaller line.

When a syndicate was set up to build the St. Louis, Brownsville and Mexico Railroad Company, which would connect Houston to Brownsville, Texas, it fell to St. Louis Union Trust to provide the financing. Not coincidentally, the officers of the lending institution controlled the lion's share of the railroad company.

A letter written in 1911 by Frisco board chairman W. K. Bixby confirms that deals among friends and neighbors were the order of the day. He says of a planned railroad enterprise, "What I want to do is to handle it through our friends in such a way that we can on fair terms let the Frisco take it over in the next year or two, as we have not at this time ready cash to put into the property."

The Brownsville Syndicate was indeed a society of friends. Westmoreland/Portland families figured prominently in the venture. Of the nearly $4 million raised to capitalize the railroad, $2.7 million came from Westmoreland/Portland pockets. A list of participants in the Brownsville Syndicate includes Joseph Bascom, W. K. Bixby, George Carpenter, Daniel Catlin, Jr., John Filley, William Guy, Robert McK. Jones, the I. W. Morton estate, Jeanette Morton, Eliza McMillan, Charles Pettus, Henry C. Scott, John F. Shepley, Thomas H. West, Edwards Whitaker, and Whitaker & Co.

Another example of how St. Louis's ruling class kept the reins of control tightly in their own hands can be found in a 1905 case involving the Wabash Railroad, which had fallen on bad financial times. Federal Judge Elmer B. Adams was charged with finding a receiver into whose hands he could place the ailing railroad. The judge did not look too far. He appointed his neighbor William K. Bixby as receiver. Bixby was not an attorney; he was the head of a company that made

Architect W. Albert Swasey designed 1 Westmoreland Place for the Jacob Van Blarcom family. It was built in 1894, and the conservatory shown to the left was added in 1900. Above is the main hallway of the Van Blarcom mansion. Van Blarcom made his fortune as a banker and left an estate of more than $4 million.

railroad cars. In addition to being neighbors, Adams and Bixby also both held memberships in the exclusive Commercial Club, the St. Louis Club, and the St. Louis Country Club. But so did most of their neighbors. Bixby owned shares in the National Bank of Commerce, and so did his honor the judge.

The National Bank of Commerce afforded its stockholders a cliff-hanging drama that went on for several years. Following the devastating Panic of 1907, the giant bank—the largest in the city—teetered on the brink of ruin. *Reedy's Mirror* reported on July 25, 1912, that $2.5 million in bad loans had had to be written off. The bank had made some poor investments that touched the pockets of its officers and shareholders.

But those who controlled the bank rallied to its defense. William Thompson, the man who was chief executive officer of the bank, had died. Others stepped forward to save face and a few necks. A caretaker committee was formed to shore up public confidence in the shaky bank. Among those appointed

to the group were W. K. Bixby and three others with ties to Westmoreland/Portland—Thomas McKittrick, Samuel Davis, and E. C. Simmons. Bixby was also a director of both St. Louis Union Trust and Boatmen's Bank. The Davis family held the second largest block of individual stock, 1,765 shares, in St. Louis Union Trust. Simmons and McKittrick also held large blocks of shares in the trust company.

"They control the gas works and telephone companies . . ."

In addition to serving as president of the powerful National Bank of Commerce in its heyday, Westmoreland Place resident Jacob Van Blarcom was influential in the city's utilities circle. He was one of the organizers of Missouri Electric Light and Power Company and Missouri Edison Company. This dual investment in electric power allowed Van Blarcom to leave his heirs an estate valued at more than $4 million.

Eugene Nims, who lived at 56 Portland Place, was primarily a lumberman when he settled in Perry, Oklahoma Territory, in 1893. But he developed a keen interest in utilities and pursued that interest with a passion. Before long, Nims had founded electric, water, and ice companies in the Cherokee Strip. He was able to do this easily because he was also a director of several Oklahoma banks. In 1914, when his electric company merged with Southwestern Bell, Nims became Bell's vice-president. Five years later, he moved into the chief executive's chair in St. Louis, serving as president of the company for eleven years.

German immigrant William Orthwein, for whom 15 Portland Place was built, was a leader in St. Louis's grain industry. In fact, at the time of his death in 1925, the grain company that bore his name was the oldest grain house in the city. Orthwein used the profits of his grain business to take over the reins of the Kinloch Telephone Company. Its growth and development

German immigrant William Orthwein and his wife, Emily, were the first residents of 15 Portland, where they lived for twenty-seven years.

were assured by the Mississippi Valley Trust Company, of which Orthwein was a director. Historian James Neal Primm refers to this kind of relationship between banks and utilities as "cozy."

Primm suggests "the interlocking relationships between the banks and the real estate and utilities firms made it virtually impossible to be an officer, director, or stockholder in the major financial houses without having benefitted from boodle." For example, John A. Holmes, the first owner of 9 Portland, was, like his neighbor Nims, originally a lumberman. But Holmes was also a director of the American Telephone and Telegraph Company and a director of the National Bank of Commerce.

The president of Mississippi Valley Trust Company, for which Orthwein served as director, was Breckinridge Jones, Orthwein's neighbor. Jones, who organized the National Association of Trust Companies, was, like Orthwein, a founder of the Kinloch Telephone Company. Jones was also a director of Union Electric Light and Power Company and served on the board of directors of the Laclede Gaslight Company. While there was nothing illegal about someone serving as president of a trust company and director of telephone, electric, and gas companies, an argument was made by critics like Reedy and the *Post-Dispatch* that such a person could create and maintain monopolies on essential services that would benefit a few already powerful men more than the community as a whole.

One of the most graphic illustrations of how the Westmoreland / Portland residents and the other West Enders stuck together can be seen in the 1900 transit company strike. Federal Judge Elmer Adams authorized his Westmoreland Place neighbor Edwards Whitaker, president of the St. Louis Transit Company and of Boatmen's Bank, to organize a *posse comitatus* of twenty-five hundred citizens to guard transit company property and interfere with horse-drawn buses run by striking transit workers.

The power and influence of the Big Cinch came under assault after the turn of the century. Rolla Wells, a Democrat and himself a powerful member of the business elite, was elected mayor in 1901, determined to eliminate corruption in city government and unseat Democratic party boss Edward Butler. Joseph Folk, the new city attorney, attacked not only corrupt city officials but also their partners in "boodle," the city's economic masters, going so far that he embarrassed Wells and the Democratic party. Wells was mayor for eight years; Folk was city attorney for four before his crusading efforts elevated him to the governor's office.

Ironically, Big Cinch support helped put Wells and Folk into

Judge Elmer B. Adams, builder of 25 Westmoreland, remained active in politics even after his appointment to the federal bench. He helped organize a posse to protect streetcar properties in the Transit Strike of 1900. Former President Taft led Adams's funeral procession in 1916.

power. Wells, president of the American Steel Foundry Company, was of the same silk fabric that put him into office, but his "new St. Louis" platform sought a squeaky-clean city government. Wells's father, Erastus, had inaugurated St. Louis's first mass transportation system in 1843 with a horse-drawn bus. The younger Wells reaped the financial benefits as heir to a fortune.

Folk, a native Tennessean, prosecuted the transit company owners and bankers who paid the bribes as well as the city legislators who took them, but the state Supreme Court rescued the major offenders. Folk gained national prominence,

Edwards Whitaker, the builder of 13 Westmoreland, was a powerful figure in St. Louis history. He was president of Boatmen's Bank, first president of the United Railways Company, and president of an investment firm. When he died in 1926, he left an estate of more than $3 million.

but after a protracted shudder, the members of the business elite adjusted to the fact that they would have to abandon bribery.

The only Westmoreland/Portland resident to be named in the Folk investigation was James Campbell. The Irish immigrant multimillionaire was accused of having used bribery to obtain lucrative street-lighting contracts. But Campbell could not be indicted because key witnesses evaded grand-jury subpoenas until the statutes of limitation had expired.

The two decades that followed the Folk investigations saw many alleged members of the Big Cinch give up their positions of power through death. The funeral hearse was frequently seen in Westmoreland and Portland during those years. Judge Adams, Samuel Kennard, and Daniel Catlin, Sr., all died in 1916. Carriage manufacturer Lewis Tebbetts, director of two banks, died in 1918. St. Louis Union Trust president Thomas

Henry West, who also served as director of a gas company, an electric company, a rail-car manufacturing company, a railroad, and another bank, died in 1926. That was the same year in which Edwards Whitaker died. Two years later the Westmoreland/Portland family buried one of its most powerful and influential members, Breckinridge Jones. With the passing of these seven men alone, St. Louis lost a powerful syndicate whose main trespass was that, with a tightly knit circle of friends and neighbors, they controlled the reins of the city in a less than democratic style.

If the Westmoreland/Portland coterie banded together in the development of business in St. Louis, they also did so in the development of the city's cultural and charitable institutions. While some millionaires are said to still have the first nickel they ever made, there is little evidence that the Westmoreland/ Portland pioneers were a tight-fisted bunch. To their credit, there are many examples of generous philanthropy among the homeowners in the two private places.

A number of educational institutions reaped the benefits of that philanthropy. Mrs. William L. Huse established the Mission Free School Home in 1905. She gave the building and the land in memory of her late husband. Under the auspices of the American Union Commission, Judge Elmer Adams went to Georgia to establish free schools for poor white children in Atlanta and Milledgeville. Breckinridge Jones lobbied successfully to have the head of an oil company whose wells were on Osage Indian land put up the money to compile a dictionary and encyclopedia to preserve the Osage language and culture.

Eliza McMillan, the widow of William Northrup McMillan, gave Washington University $300,000 to establish McMillan Hall for women students. She also purchased the Phillips School and presented it to the St. Louis Academy of Science and donated $100,000 to Mary Institute for new buildings. The Eye, Ear, Nose and Throat Clinic at Washington University also benefited from a $1 million bequest from Eliza McMillan.

The family of Westmoreland Place homebuilder Edward Mallinckrodt, Jr., will long be remembered for its philanthropy. Edward Mallinckrodt, Sr., gave $500,000 to Harvard University for a building to house the chemistry department. (The Mallinckrodts, father and son, were Harvard alumni.) In 1916 the senior Mallinckrodt gave $166,000 toward a fund matched by the Rockefeller Foundation for a research endowment to Washington University Medical School. This special endowment was for research in the relationship between hygiene and children's diseases. The father and son together

A native of Toronto, Canada, William Bagnell migrated to St. Louis in 1864. He was president of the Bagnell Timber Company, which was a manufacturer of railroad ties. He and his wife, Sallie, built 12 Westmoreland.

gave Washington University Medical School $250,000 to establish an institute of radiology. That department is still active and still bears the Mallinckrodt name.

The senior Mallinckrodt was extremely modest and even gave money anonymously. As president and member of St. Luke's Hospital's board of trustees, he made up that institution's deficit each year for many years, a fact very few people knew. The younger Mallinckrodt, an only son, continued the generous philanthropy of his father.

Dwight Filley Davis was a director of the St. Louis Tenement House Association and worked energetically to improve living conditions in the city's slums at the turn of the century. He also supported the development of public baths and public playgrounds and production of the fabulous Pageant and Masque in 1913. Railroad builder William Bagnell left real estate valued at $1 million to the Episcopal Orphan's Home and the Church of the Holy Communion. Shoe manufacturer George Warren Brown left the YMCA $300,000 for the erection of a large downtown building. In 1928 Joseph Bascom left

The house at 13 Portland was built by William Keeney Bixby and his wife, Lillian Tuttle Bixby. He was chairman of the board of the American Car & Foundry Co. The Bixbys moved from 13 Portland in 1904, and Bixby's son William H. purchased the house in 1923. At the left are two interior views of the house as it appeared during the time it was owned by William H. Bixby.

a $50,000 trust to be divided between St. Louis Children's Hospital and Washington University.

Westmoreland/Portland residents reached beyond their own community with their generosity. In 1906 Jacob Van Blarcom was treasurer of the committee that raised funds in St. Louis for victims of the San Francisco earthquake. During World War I, Charles Pettus left his secure banking position to head the department of canteen relief for the Southwestern Division of the American Red Cross. Frances Jones (the wife of Breckinridge) was a tireless worker and a director of the St. Louis chapter of the American Red Cross. Thomas H. West contributed $1,000 a month to the Red Cross during World War I, in addition to purchasing $400,000 in Liberty Bonds.

George and Mary Barnard were among the most generous of any of the Westmoreland/Portland philanthropists. Childless, the couple seemed to give charities the attention and support that other families gave to their offspring. The George D. Barnard Free Skin and Cancer Hospital was established in 1910 with a $200,000 donation from the Barnards. They also gave the ground and buildings for the hospital and a large three-story stone house east of the main building as a home for nurses. In 1913 Barnard gave $50,000 to erect a monument at New Bedford, Massachusetts, to commemorate the old sea life in the town where he had lived as a young boy. By conservative

estimates, the Barnards gave more than $2 million to their favorite charities.

The private place pioneers also supported the arts. When Charles Dickens came through the St. Louis area in 1842, he was not impressed with the level of the city's culture. He probably could not have imagined that a St. Louis resident would one day play an important role in the preservation of some of his works. William K. Bixby, chairman of the Committee on Fine Arts for the World's Fair, loved Dickens's prose and had the drive and the wherewithal to preserve some of the more obscure works of the great English novelist.

Bixby's connection with Dickens began in 1905 when J. H. Stonehouse, editor of the *Piccadilly Notes*, came to the United States to sell rare books and to locate a buyer for the Dickens-Dora letters. "Dora," David's wife in *David Copperfield*, was thought to be modeled on Maria Beadnell, a sweetheart of Dickens's youth. Stonehouse believed that Beadnell had had a great influence on Dickens, yet he could not interest leading New York booksellers or publishers in the letters.

Stonehouse had continued his search in Philadelphia, Baltimore, Washington, D.C., Chicago, and a host of smaller markets. He was just about to return to England without finding a home for the letters when he heard that W. K. Bixby might be interested. Immediately, Stonehouse had one of the

love letters copied and sent to St. Louis.

Shortly thereafter Stonehouse went to St. Louis himself. He recalled, according to *Piccadilly Notes*, "On calling at Mr. Bixby's office I was disappointed to find he was out of town; however, when his secretary added that he wished to see me, my spirits rose at once and I arranged to call again on Wednesday following."

On the appointed day Stonehouse found Bixby in his office and in a receptive mood. After listening to another letter, Bixby addressed the dealer: "I understand you want so much for the letters and manuscript of your book. If I buy them, am I at liberty to do what I like in the way of publishing the book?"

"Yes, that is so," Stonehouse replied.

"Very well, then," said Bixby. "I will buy the collection and give you a check right away."

After the particulars of the transaction were ironed out, Bixby wrote a check to Stonehouse for $35,000, and the Dickens papers became part of the vast Bixby collection of great works, including those of Shakespeare, Alfred Lord Tennyson, and Eugene Field. Bixby's Shakespeare folios were exhibited at the Central Public Library in St. Louis in 1911 to commemorate the tercentenary of the Bard's death in 1616. The works displayed included folios from 1623, 1632, 1644,

William K. Bixby was an active board member of a number of St. Louis organizations. In 1916, Bixby was photographed in a meeting at the Missouri Historical Society. From the left are Stella Drum, the society's librarian; Walter Douglas, the second vice-president; Elise Ware, the assistant librarian; Bixby, then first vice-president; and Nettie Beauregard, the society's archivist.

and 1685 and a first edition of Shakespeare's poems dated 1640. There was also a rare collection of books, prints, and drawings related to Shakespeare.

Part of the Bixby collection was auctioned at the American Art Association's Anderson Galleries in New York City in 1934. In the collection was the four-volume *History of the Reign of the Emperor Charles V* by William Robertson that had been owned by George Washington. Each volume had been signed by the nation's first president, and each had an excellent impression of his bookplate.

Bixby's Eugene Field collection was also sold at that auction. Among the works of the former St. Louisan who became known as "the children's poet" were several original manuscripts: "Echoes from the Sabine Farm," illustrated in watercolor and tempera; "With Trumpet and Drum"; "Little Book

of Profitable Tales"; "Little Book of Western Verse"; and "The Holy Cross." Also auctioned that day were the original manuscripts for twenty-three poems translated by Field from the works of Horace and autographed copies of his "Mrs. Billy Crane," "The Fisherman's Feast," "Jack Haverly," and "The Click of the Ice." In addition, the Bixby treasures sold that day included an original Robert Browning manuscript of twelve poems and his "Red Cotton Night Cap." And there was Lord Byron's autographed manuscript of the "Ode to Thomas Moore."

Bixby served on the boards of the St. Louis Public Library, the St. Louis Academy of Science, and the Bibliophile Society. He was a trustee of the Missouri Historical Society and a member of the governing board of the Massachusetts Historical Society. This devoted patron of the arts was often honored for his support. The Art Alliance gave a dinner in his honor at the Chase Hotel on December 8, 1924. Amherst College in Massachusetts granted him an honorary Master of Arts degree.

Bixby money established the Bixby Hall of Fine Arts at Washington University. He was one of the most important backers for the New York–to–Paris flight of Charles A. Lindbergh in 1927 and helped to open up the new field of aviation. Among the fourteen institutions named as beneficiaries in his will were the Missouri Historical Society, which received $50,000 and many invaluable manuscripts and books; the City Art Museum, which received securities with a face value of $80,000 and paintings worth $60,000; the St. Louis Artists Guild, which was willed $15,000 for a building fund, $2,000 for its endowment, and $3,000 for prizes over a fifteen-year period; and the Keats-Shelley Memorial in Rome.

It is no wonder that Bixby received praise as the ideal collector from the *New York Times*. In an editorial published on October 31, 1931, two months after his death, Bixby was cited as "one, who having done more than his share of the world's work, found zest in civic service and in cultivating his hobbies (of sharing his art treasures with others)."

Theodore Meysenburg was one of the most instrumental St. Louisans in establishing the city's current public library system and the City Art Museum.

Justina and Daniel K. Catlin, Sr., were also ardent art lovers. Catlin, whose personal wealth was estimated at $20 million, was a director of the City Art Museum. In 1917, a year after her husband's death, Justina Catlin decided to share some of the paintings she and her husband had collected during their forty-four-year marriage. In memory of her husband she

donated a collection of nineteenth-century French oil paintings then valued at $50,000.

Gertrude Hamlin Catlin, the daughter-in-law of the senior Catlins and the wife of Daniel, Jr., also made significant contributions to the enjoyment of art in St. Louis. She loaned and donated a number of paintings to the City Art Museum, among them two works by Gilbert Stuart, the noted eighteenth-century portraitist who gave the world the best-known image of George Washington.

Few personal art collections could rival that of Anna and Edward Faust. Their magnificent mansion at 1 Portland was the perfect setting for a grand gallery. The Italian Renaissance palace features rooms modeled after those in classic European palaces. The twin-curved stairway in the entry hall is modeled after a Medici staircase in Florence. A tapestry room is a reproduction of the great hall in the Davaezzi palace in Italy. And one of the mansion's ballrooms is lifted from the design of the Hall of Angels in the ducal palace in Urbino, Italy, built in 1465–1472 by Dalmatian architect Luciano da Laurana for Federigo da Montefeltro. The Fausts were generous enough to share their treasures with other art lovers. Numerous pieces from their collection were placed on loan to the City Art Museum, including Rubens's *Holy Family* and Murillo's *St. Joseph and Infant Child*.

Edward Faust served as vice-president of the City Art Museum board of directors and at one time was chairman of the St. Louis Municipal Art Commission. Anna Faust dabbled in another branch of the arts with limited success. Disgusted with the stereotyped movie plots of her day, she tried her hand at writing a screenplay for Hollywood production. The scenario was entitled "The House of Brandt." When Hollywood producers failed to beat a path to her doorway, an undaunted Anna Busch Faust published the script as a book. (It still failed to receive overwhelming acclaim.)

The Fausts also supported the St. Louis Symphony Orchestra. Because of Edward Faust's involvement on its executive committee, a string quintet from the orchestra provided music for his funeral services at 1 Portland on July 5, 1936.

Cora and John Fowler were also well known for their support of the St. Louis Symphony Orchestra. John Fowler served as president of the Symphony Society from 1916 until his death in 1924. Cora (Liggett) Fowler was named honorary president of the Symphony Society for 1927–1928. The orchestra was particularly grateful to her for a gift of $50,000 that kept it from going bankrupt and disbanding.

Other Westmoreland/Portland pioneers provided staunch

support and active leadership for the symphony. John T. Davis, Jr., was the fourth president of the Symphony Society, serving a term of two years beginning in 1897. Davis was succeeded in the post by his good friend and neighbor William N. McMillan. Davis's wife, Edith, in 1903 became the first woman to be elected president of the Symphony Society and served so effectively that she was elected to two terms of two years each. Oscar Johnson, Jr., whose parents, Oscar and Irene, built the mansion at 38 Portland, served the longest term of any Symphony Society president. Elected to the leadership in 1933, Johnson directed the affairs of the symphony until 1955.

Latter-day residents of Westmoreland Place, Ben and Katherine Gladney Wells, merit mention here for their backing of the orchestra's development in the last two decades. Ben Wells served as Symphony Society president from 1970 to 1978. Katherine Gladney Wells has long been a sponsor and benefactor of the orchestra and has been active in its public affairs. Her sister, Lucianna Gladney Ross of 33 Portland, restored the village of Kimmswick, south of St. Louis.

While Helen Durkee Bridge's contribution to the preservation of the arts was not a major one, she can be credited with an active contribution to their creation. The wife of Hudson E. Bridge, Jr., and mother of seven children (four of whom lived to adulthood), she devoted much of her time to painting in watercolors and oils at the family's summer home in Walpole, New Hampshire. She also developed a talent for painting on china. An active member of the St. Louis Artists Guild and a leading amateur photographer, Helen Bridge died in 1954 at the age of ninety-four, the last living member of her Mary Institute class of 1880.

A significant contribution to architectural knowledge was made by a Westmoreland Place homebuilder, George Fox Steedman. Steedman was not himself an architect. He was an industrialist who, with his brother Edwin H., owned the Curtis Manufacturing Company. The firm originally made saws and sawmill hardware but moved into the modern industrial age with the manufacture of pneumatic machinery, cranes, and air compressors.

George Steedman's heart was drawn to architecture. No doubt he had dreamed of becoming an architect, but he was locked into industry by his father's gift of a pneumatic machinery manufacturing company. In 1924 Steedman established a memorial to his brother by creating the James Harrison Steedman Fellowship in architecture at Washington University. The fellowship provides an annual grant to an outstanding student of architecture in line with Steedman's plan "to develop lead-

The grand foyer of the Faust mansion at 1 Portland Place. When the original owners, Edward and Anna Faust, lived here the walls were adorned with the works of such classic artists as Rubens and Murillo.

ers in the practice or teaching of architecture and particularly in the hope that it may promote architectural progress in St. Louis and its vicinity." The fellowship is governed jointly by the university and the St. Louis chapter of the American Institute of Architects.

Four years later Steedman made an even greater contribution. He established the Steedman Architectural Library at the St. Louis Public Library. The initial stock comprised more than six hundred titles in more than twelve hundred volumes from Steedman's personal collection. About 10 percent of these volumes are now rare.

Many of the books in the collection were purchased during the 1920s when Steedman and his good friend Louis LaBeaume went on a shopping expedition to Europe. La-Beaume, a distinguished St. Louis architect, had made a noteworthy contribution to the design of the Louisiana Purchase Exposition. He was also a president of the City Art Museum's board and a member of the National Academy of Design. As a partner in the firms of Mariner & LaBeaume and LaBeaume & Klein, he had had a hand in the design of twelve houses in Westmoreland and Portland. Like Steedman, LaBeaume had acquired his interest in architecture while a student at the Manual Training Institute run by Washington University.

The Steedman Architectural Library was officially opened in 1930. Among its priceless works are a four-volume set of original drawings by A. W. N. Pugin dating from 1833 and the valuable *Piranesi Opere*, which at one time belonged to the library of the British House of Commons. The Steedman collection also includes classic works by such architectural giants as Alberti, Palladio, Serlio, Vignola, and Vitruvius.

To ensure that his library would have the proper setting, Steedman hired the St. Louis architectural firm of Mauran, Russell & Crowell to make the design at a cost of $25,000. As Mauran, Russell & Garden, the firm had designed Steedman's Westmoreland Place home, as well as nine other houses in the neighborhood. Oscar Mulgardt was the principal architect in the creation of the sixteenth-century English library, complete with leaded-glass windows, carved oak furniture and paneling, and a handsome stone fireplace. The highly respected carpenter-craftsman Victor Berlendis was brought in to fashion the wood carvings and the decorative plaster ceiling.

Above the mantelpiece in the library is an inscription that is almost an understatement of its benefactor's goal: "This room and these books on architecture are the gift of George Fox Steedman and his wife, Carrie Howard. May students search these shelves for records of honest work and good design and so find inspiration for great achievement."

In order to maintain and increase the library's holdings, Steedman left an endowment of $10,000. Librarians must consult with the St. Louis chapter of the American Institute of Architects before any acquisitions can be made. The man who dreamed of architecture while building pneumatic cranes gave an incomparable gift to the city of St. Louis and to the art world with the establishment of the Steedman Library.

A great contribution to dance as an art form was made by a former resident of Westmoreland/Portland, Rebekah West Harkness, the daughter of Rebekah and Allen West. Her grandfather was Thomas H. West, one of the original trustees of Westmoreland and the founder of the St. Louis Union Trust Company.

The Wests of Westmoreland lived very comfortably. In addition to his inheritance, Allen Tarwater West was a successful broker with the G. H. Walker Company. He belonged to the right clubs—the Noonday, St. Louis Country, and Racquet. His wife, Rebekah, was related to the colorful evangelist Aimee Semple McPherson. One of Rebekah Harkness's daughters described her mother's family as "a very square, proper family, where you were just supposed to go to the country club, come out as a debutante, and get married."

Her Westmoreland/Portland contemporaries knew this tall, blonde firebrand as Betty West. One of her best childhood friends remembers Betty as "a happy girl; very upbeat. She liked to pull things over on her teachers, but all in fun . . . never anything malicious." Betty attended the Rossman School at Delmar and Belt and then went on to John Burroughs. Her parents next sent her to Fermata, an exclusive girls' school in South Carolina. Looking back on her life at the finishing school, Betty/Rebekah remembered it as having "offered a lot of fox hunting."

A conflict developed at 48 Westmoreland when young Betty asked her father's permission to become a dancer. Allen West would have none of the idea of his daughter going into "show business." Arthur B. Shepley, Jr., who lived next door to the Wests in the late 1920s and was a good friend of Betty's brother, Allen, remembers that Betty was ambitious: "When her father wouldn't let her pursue a career in dancing she took a very serious interest in figure skating. She'd take lessons at the old Winter Garden on DeBaliviere. Betty threw everything she had into learning to be a good skater. But that's how she approached everything she set her mind to . . . with a passion."

Rebekah West Harkness grew up at 48 Westmoreland. Her father's refusal to let her be a dancer only heightened her interest in dance. She was instrumental in founding the Harkness Ballet as well as the Joffrey and Alvin Ailey troupes.

She didn't seem to be terribly interested in playing the games the other girls were playing."

Betty's father did approve of her marriage to Dickson Pierce, who could trace his ancestry back to the family of the fourteenth president of the United States, Franklin Pierce, and was from a good, solid Vandeventer Place family. Betty herself said she married Dickson out of boredom: "I had nothing else to do."

The marriage was brief but produced two children, Allen, named for her father and brother, and Terry. After the divorce, Betty became bored with the restrictive environment of St. Louis. She packed up her two young children and went off to the big city—New York.

While working as a saleswoman in the fashionable Mainbocher Salon, Betty met millionaire William Hale Harkness. His family's fortune had skyrocketed after his grandfather helped finance the organization of John D. Rockefeller's Standard Oil of Ohio in 1870. Soon after they met, William and Betty were married. In addition to providing her with a regal life-style and a third child, Edith, Harkness introduced stability and order into Betty's chaotic life. Then Harkness suffered a massive heart attack in the summer of 1954. Some estimates put the Harkness estate at $500 million. More conservative estimates placed the inheritance Betty West Pierce Harkness received at $75 million.

Reviving the spunk that had brought her to New York, Betty set out to learn more about music and dance. She went to France, where she became a serious music student. She studied composition and theory with the legendary Nadia Boulanger. She composed several pieces but never achieved positive reviews of her work from music critics.

Four years after the death of her husband, Betty established the Rebekah Harkness Foundation to foster the art of dance. Her philanthropy funded Jerome Robbins's Ballet: USA, a tour of Africa by the Pearl Primus company, and the Jose Greco company. Money from the Harkness Foundation also established a series of free dance concerts in Central Park's Delacorte Theater and a season of modern-dance programs at Hunter College.

In 1961 Betty Harkness became familiar with the work of choreographer Robert Joffrey and became a patron of the Joffrey Ballet for the next two years. She often whisked the entire troupe to the Harkness retreat at Watch Hill, Rhode Island, inviting such then virtually unknown artists as Alvin Ailey, Gerald Arpino, Fernand Nault, and Brian McDonald to join Joffrey there. The choreographers were formally commissioned to execute some of their best creations in the Watch Hill setting.

Not satisfied with being merely a patron of ballet and modern dance, Betty Harkness made headlines in 1964 by dropping the Joffrey troupe and establishing her own dance company, the Harkness Ballet. To provide a home for her troupe, Betty purchased the four-story East Side mansion in New York City that has once been owned by Thomas J. Watson, the founder of IBM. Betty justified the opulence of the setting by saying, "I hope the beauty of Harkness House will persuade some of these people that ballet need not be dingy and that by their patronage they are contributing to the splendid and the glamorous."

Betty then spent $5 million renovating an old Broadway moviehouse, renamed Harkness Theater. While it enjoyed a few moments of glory, like many other dreams of Betty Harkness, this one crumbled too. The theater was torn down in 1976.

In 1970 for no apparent reason, Betty Harkness pulled the carpet from under her dance troupe while it was on tour in Monte Carlo. Apparently she felt she should be providing more than a checkbook for the operation and felt shut out as an artist. Then, after some serious problems with her children, she discovered that she had cancer. In 1982, after a long and painful bout with the disease, Rebekah West Harkness died at her Manhattan home at age sixty-seven.

The Westmoreland/Portland charter homebuilders and their descendants have made an indelible contribution to the arts, the culture, and the well-being of St. Louis, the nation, and the world. In spite of whatever aspersions were cast on the manner in which some of them made their fortunes, their contributions to the quality of life and their humanitarian concerns outweigh any iniquities.

5. LIFE IN WESTMORELAND/
PORTLAND: GROWING UP

Back, turn backward, O Time, in your flight,
Make me a child again, just for tonight.
—Elizabeth Akers Allen

Life in Westmoreland/Portland during the enclave's early years was similar to life everywhere in the United States—sweethearts married, babies were born, children attended school and discovered their talents, lasting friendships were formed, ambitions were realized, and inevitably people aged, struggled with infirmities, and died. These universal rites of passage were commemorated in Westmoreland/Portland with a definite protocol that was rarely violated.

Between the christening and the graveside benediction came the social debut, engagement announcement, bridal shower, wedding and reception, housewarming, and an endless round of teas, cocktail parties, suppers, and holiday celebrations. The receipt of a formal invitation to any party was a reconfirmation that one still held a proper place in the social order. Even attendance at a funeral gave a clear indication of the social standing of the deceased. Newspaper accounts of funerals often listed the names of mourners, wake-register signatories, and pallbearers.

Christenings for the babies of prominent St. Louisans were almost always formal social events. The gowns worn by both boy and girl babies were often heirlooms that reflected a family's heraldry. While christenings were sometimes private events for the closest family members only, invitations were often sent to other prominent families for a reception tea, brunch, or picnic—although all this activity was probably lost on the infant honoree.

Growing up in a private neighborhood was a special experi-

ence, especially in those halcyon days when birth in Westmoreland/Portland almost guaranteed a charmed and privileged existence. Westmoreland/Portland pioneers were generally prolific. In the eighty-nine homebuilder families in the two private places, 242 children were born. Only seven of those households were childless.

The largest of the pioneer families was the brood of Flora and David Gamble. Not all the eleven Gamble children—Mary, Hamilton, John, Flora, Maud, Edna, David Junior, Walter, Clarence, Ethel, and Allan—called 37 Portland home, for some had reached adulthood by the time the house was ready for occupancy in 1907. But no doubt they frequently gathered there for holidays and family celebrations.

Honors for the second-largest family must be shared by two clans—the builders of 26 Westmoreland and the first residents of 15 Portland. The George Allen family and the William D. Orthwein family each had eight offspring. The Hudson Bridge family at 23 Westmoreland had seven children, but three of them died very young. Lawrence, George, John, and Marion survived to adulthood.

The first generation of Westmoreland/Portland children left us a colorful chronicle of their lives in a newspaper produced, published, and promoted by some of the more enterprising boys. It was called the *Westmoreland Club News* and first rolled off the press in January 1918. Its young staff declared in the debut issue: "Of course we do not expect to compete with the *Literary Digest* and other magazines of that standard, but we will do our best, and though you will probably find mistakes in the various editions, we hope that you will take into consideration that this paper is entirely edited by boys, and that we are always doing what we can for the benefit of our subscribers." Despite the disclaimer, the newspaper was a slick and neatly edited publication. It usually had eight pages and

measured seven by eight inches.

The newspaper staff was headed by editor-in-chief Thomas Wright Pettus, son of Charles and Georgia Pettus of 33 Westmoreland. Issues of the newspaper indicate that young Tom was a stern and strict taskmaster who, even when asking for jokes to be submitted, took a no-nonsense approach to editing. He was ably assisted by Arthur Lionberger, who, like his father, Isaac, was a prolific and accomplished writer.

The Flora and David C. Gamble house at 37 Portland, shown on the left here, is a 1906 creation of Milligan & Wray. Next door is the George D. Barnard house designed in 1911 by Kivas Tully.

Hudson E. Bridge was president of the Bridge and Beach Manufacturing Company, a firm founded by his father. It was the first stove-
manufacturing company in the midwest. He and his wife, Helen,
built 23 Westmoreland.

turned out some distinguished pieces of prose and poetry from
his room at 37 Westmoreland.

McMillan Lewis, who lived in a neighboring private place,
was the newspaper's business manager. Jack Gordon, son of
Samuel and Katherine Gordon of 38 Westmoreland, was the
assistant business agent. These two business managers had
their work cut out for them. They were expected to sell subscriptions at the rate of eight copies for seventy-five cents. If a
subscriber wanted the papers delivered by mail, the cost was
eighty-five cents. Each individual copy cost ten cents. The
youthful business staff was also commissioned to sell commercial advertising space. The initial rates were two dollars for a
half-page, one dollar for a quarter-page, and seventy-five cents
for an eighth-page.

Despite the fact that many of the paper's subscribers—parents, other relatives, and neighbors—were millionaires, ads

were apparently difficult to place. In fact, one early editorial
noted: "We need ads and subscriptions badly. They are not
coming in as fast as they should. What's the matter with you
fellows? GET BUSY AND HUSTLE!"

Perhaps the newspaper's subscribers, especially the parents
of the staff, preferred that the enterprising young journalists be
just that—enterprising. Many fathers believed that publishing
a newspaper should be a way to learn the benefits and pitfalls
of free enterprise. However, such firms as Edward K. Love
Realty, the Elder Manufacturing Company, and Star Brand
Shoe Company did buy advertising in the *Westmoreland Club
News* regularly.

In its sixth edition (May 19, 1918), the newspaper boasted of
having seventy-five subscribers, ten commercial advertisers, a
lengthy write-up in the *Globe-Democrat*, copies filed in the
Missouri Historical Society, and even enough money in the
treasury to carry the paper through June of that year. But,
despite these successes, the *Club News* was having as much
difficulty in finding good jokes as it had had in snagging advertisers. One editorial complained:

The staff is having a very hard time finding first class jokes. For
the seventh issue we would like to devote one column to good jokes.
Also for the June issue we will need some. The only boys so far to
contribute to this department of the paper are: Shepley, R. Simmons, Swarts, Walker and O. Johnson. Try to have your name on
the list.

A small sampling of the humor printed in the *Club News*
shows that boys have not changed much since 1918.

Little Johnny (to guest): "That's Bessie's cup you're drinking out of."
Guest: "Ah, I feel honored. Who is Bessie? Your sister?"
Little Johnny: "Nope, she's our fox terrier."

*   *   *

"Have you forgotten us, waiter?"
"Oh, no, sir. You are the two fried smelts."

Many jokes had to do with the growing controversy over
whether there should be federal legislation banning the sale
and consumption of alcoholic beverages. The Eighteenth
Amendment to the Constitution was just two years away when
the *Westmoreland Club News* printed this joke:

Sales Clerk: "This vacuum bottle will keep anything hot or cold
for seventy-two hours."
Mr. Tipples: "Don't want it. If I have anything worth drinking I
don't want to keep it seventy-two hours."

But the primary purpose of the *Westmoreland Club News*

was to publish club news, not jokes. In those pre-television,
pre–video game days, there were numerous clubs to keep children busy. In 1918 a neighborhood stamp club, athletic club,
debating club, and gun club were organized by Westmoreland
Place boys. Membership in these clubs was eventually opened
to boys who lived in Portland Place as well. Rivalry between
the two places was generally good-natured and gentle. For
example, there was a lot of boasting among youthful residents
about which private place had the greener and better man-
icured lawns.

After a while, the four clubs began to admit boys from
nearby private places or exclusive streets. McMillan Lewis,
known to all his cronies as "Mac," lived in Hortense Place.
John Kennard Wallace and John Hayward joined the West-
moreland/Portland fellowship from Pershing. Freddie Swarts
came to the clubs from Waterman. Louie McKay was so popular he broke the social barriers of the era to gain membership
in the boys' clubs—he was the son of a Westmoreland Place
chauffeur. McKay, whose father worked for Maria Filley Davis
of Number 17, even became president of the Westmoreland
debating club.

Members of the stamp club met once a week to discuss the
availability of collectible stamps and to distribute approval
sheets. Noting that stamp collecting can get monotonous,
early in the club's existence members began preparing photographic features for the *Club News*. To make their philatelic
endeavors more interesting, the young collectors were urged
to buy liberty stamps to help the United States during World
War I.

The boys' athletic club held its first meeting on March 9,
1916. Its charter members were Arthur Gale, Oscar and Lee
Johnson of 38 Portland, McMillan Lewis, Charles and Tom
Pettus of 33 Westmoreland, and Richard Simmons. Oscar
Johnson was elected the first president. Four more boys were
"let in" later, according to the *Club News*, and Charlie Pettus
was voted an honorary member when he went off to boarding
school.

Membership in the athletic club seems to have been more
tightly guarded than admission to the other clubs. If ever there
was a club established and operated as a microcosmic replica-
tion of the exclusive clubs to which the senior Westmoreland/
Portland residents belonged, it was the Westmoreland Athletic
Club. There were some thirty laws governing membership in
the association. Like the Missouri Athletic Club, the Westmoreland club was set up to promote athletics—it held a

The *Westmoreland Club News,* first published in 1918, reflects the interests, concerns, and activities of the boys who later became St. Louis's business and civic leaders.

number of successful track meets and tennis tournaments. In addition, the youthful members threw occasional banquets. Since there was no official clubhouse, these banquets were held at the homes of various members.

Once a boy had gone through the close scrutiny that prefaced membership, he was required to pay dues of twenty-five cents a month. Members were assured in the *Club News* that the dues were "kept in the Savings and Trust Company, where the treasurer deposits [them] as soon as received from the members."

The debating club was the most academically oriented of the neighborhood's boys' clubs. The debaters took on some subjects that were perhaps weightier than many boys would choose to address. For the debate held on February 16, 1918, the subject was "Resolved, that the President of the United States should serve six years and be ineligible for re-election or that the President's term should remain the same." The judges voted that the boys who had taken the argument that the president's term should remain the same had presented the best case.

A few weeks before that debate, debating club members had tackled the question "Resolved, that National Prohibition should be adopted by the United States." Jack Gordon and Mac Lewis upheld the affirmative, while Louie McKay and Ned Simmons argued that Prohibition was a bad idea. Lewis's argument was judged best by the young listeners. An editorial in the *Westmoreland Club News* noted that Ned Simmons's speech was not very long and showed that "not much time had been put upon it." And while Jack Gordon was praised as having delivered an "exceedingly excellent" dissertation with points "clearly and forcibly made," Louie McKay's counterpoint was deemed weak because "he had plenty of material but failed to learn his speech very well, reading nearly all of it from paper." On January 12, 1919, these issue-oriented boys voted to write their U.S. senators urging them to oppose suffrage for women.

A great deal of serious attention was given to the debate club, but the lure of the great outdoors often won out over dedication to academic pursuits. The minutes from the club's last meeting before adjourning for the summer in 1918 noted, "The days are too good to stay inside." The club's twenty-one members were free to cast off heavy indoor thinking until the next meeting, scheduled for October.

The gun club was organized on December 30, 1917. Boys interested in learning the proper and safe use of firearms met every Saturday morning "about 11:45 o'clock" at 37 Westmoreland, the Isaac Lionberger home. The boys tried to dispense with all the old and new business palaver by noon, so they could adjourn to the Lionbergers' basement, where a full shooting range had been set up.

Parents who were nervous about their sons being wounded or worse during a gun club meeting were assured in the *Club News* that "every possible precaution is taken for the safety of the boys while shooting, and no carelessness will be tolerated by the club. Wires are stretched along the range to keep anyone from thoughtlessly entering the line of fire, while every effort is made to keep the members behind those who are shooting." Gun club members fired at Winchester targets fifty feet from the firing line in shifts of three boys. Each young man got a chance to fire at least fifteen shots each week. All scores were carefully recorded so that improvements could be duly noted. The shooting sessions generally lasted for forty-five minutes, and each boy was usually home in time for a one o'clock lunch.

There appears to have been a more than casual purpose behind the gun club's pursuit of keen marksmanship. A *Club News* article noted that it was a patriotic gesture for the boys to learn to shoot well because "someday should their country need them to fight for her, their knowledge on the subject may stand them to good avail, and help greatly in their future training." But gun club members also looked forward to using their shooting skills for hunting trips in the woods. Realtor Edward Love, whose son was treasurer of the club, enjoyed

The Westmoreland Athletic Club in 1917–1918. Top row: Holland Potter, Umie Niedringhaus, John Wallace, Shap Boyd, Dick Simmons, Mac Lewis, Jack Gordon; middle row: Charlie Schwab, Fred Swarts, Sonny Lionberger, Bob Bartlett, Tom Pettus, Ned Simmons, Bucket Hayward; front row: Bud Love, Oscar Johnson, Jr., Slew Johnson, Herbie Walker, Brownie Niedringhaus, Arthur Gale, Louie McKay.

taking the boys out to Dardenne in St. Charles County during the deer- and duck-hunting seasons.

The boys in the interrelated Lionberger and Shepley families, particularly Arthur "Bud" Shepley, Jr., knew of one incident in which a pistol may have saved the life of one of the family members. Isaac Lionberger was a firm believer that good health is the result of vigorous exercise and good nutrition. In fact, he was devoted to keeping the doctor away from the door at 37 Westmoreland. When his wife, Louise, became ill, he refused to allow her to receive professional medical attention.

When Arthur Shepley, Sr., heard that his sister, Louise Lionberger, was ill, he arrived at the home to inquire of his brother-in-law about her health. Lionberger assured Shepley that, although Louise was bed-ridden, she just needed rest and would soon be well. Shepley insisted on seeing his sister. Admitted to her bedroom, he found her to have an extremely

high fever. Shepley pleaded with Lionberger to call a doctor, but the latter refused.

Convinced that his pleas were falling on deaf ears, Shepley went back home, found the .45 caliber pistol he had used during the Spanish-American War, and returned to the Lionberger house, where he held Isaac at gunpoint until Dr. Fischel could be called to attend Louise. The Lionberger and Shepley boys and their cronies saw this story as an example of how a gun might be properly used by a knight in a chivalrous pursuit. This made the gun club even more popular with the boys.

Despite the emphasis on robust health, the boys in Westmoreland/Portland were not insensitive to illness. When "Bud" Shepley was unable to attend several debate club meetings because of illness, an article in the *Club News* noted that Bud was "a member who has missed very few meetings, and to whom the club owes a great deal for his enthusiasm." The salute went on to say that Bud "was greatly missed at the last

meeting. Bud has been quite ill for the last few weeks, and so to show that he had not been forgotten by the club it was decided to send him some flowers. We hope that Bud will soon be well and keep his spirit for next year."

Sixty-seven years after that warm tribute by his boyhood chums, Bud Shepley, at age seventy-nine, remembered the illness that had laid him low:

I had strep throat. They've got a cure for it nowadays, but there was nothing for it back then but a very painful cure. When the throat tissues got swollen, the doctor would lance the swollen areas and drain the pus. That hurt quite a lot. I had a very high fever and they almost gave up on me. I was in bed for about two months.

But to encourage my bravery, each time my swollen throat was lanced, my father would tell me that he would put a hundred dollars in my savings account as a reward.

Bud Shepley recovered just in time to head off, at age thirteen, for Groton, the exclusive boys' school in Massachusetts. As a member of the class of 1925, he became the first St. Louis graduate of that elite institution.

An informal club made up of Westmoreland/Portland boys in the decade following the turn of the century was called The Foresters. The boys in this club were led in sports activities twice a week after school by an athletic director. The major sports were baseball and football, played on the vacant lot where 20 Portland was later built. According to several men now in their golden years, the activities of the Westmoreland boys' clubs and the Foresters were anticipated with much eagerness after the school day.

School days were generally enjoyable for the first Westmoreland/Portland youngsters. Most of the girls attended Mary Institute. Founded in 1859 by Unitarian minister William Greenleaf Eliot, it is the oldest school for girls west of the Appalachians. Contrary to the name's implication, Mary Institute was and is nonsectarian. It was named for the founder's daughter, Mary Rhodes Eliot, who died at age seventeen.

One of the original guarantors of Mary Institute was Hudson E. Bridge, father of the builder of 23 Westmoreland. The elder Bridge was instrumental in helping the school secure its charter when it was established under the auspices of Washington University. The institution's first location was in Lucas Place. The mothers of some of the Westmoreland/Portland girls had attended "Mary I," and it was a foregone conclusion that their daughters would too.

Poet T. S. Eliot grew up next door to the school at the

Hundreds of Westmoreland/Portland girls have attended Mary Institute. The school was founded in 1859 by William Greenleaf Eliot, and its first location was in fashionable Lucas Place.

corner of Beaumont and Lucas Place in 1878. Late in his life, Eliot, a grandson of the founder, reminisced about Mary I:

Now I had four older sisters, all of whom attended Mary Institute; at least one cousin, I think, and other cousins who were here at one time or another who attended [the school]. So it should be obvious that but for the difference of sex, my brother and I would also have graduated from Mary Institute.

Bertha Drake Scott, who built 31 Westmoreland in 1914, three years after her husband's death, was a member of the Mary Institute class of 1884. She wrote of life there: "We dressed simply. Up to the age of sixteen every girl had a long braid down her back generally known as a 'pigtail.' At sixteen automatically all the hair went up, either coiled in a braid around the head or resting like a huge bun on the nape of the neck."

The early curriculum at the school featured such ponderous subjects as Hamilton's metaphysics, Horace, logic, Shlegel's

Dramatic Art and Literature, and the comparative physiology of vegetable life. A typical school day in the 1880s, according to Bertha Scott, was well regulated: "There were seven periods of 40 minutes and we began the day at nine and ended at two. One half period in the middle of the morning was given up to calisthenics, then conducted in as uninteresting a manner as it was possible to conduct it, thus rendering our only exercise a cordially hated interruption."

Mary Institute moved into the shadow of Westmoreland and Portland places in the fall of 1902. The selection of the new location, at Waterman and Lake avenues, may have been more than happenstance. Construction of the building was made possible through the donation of $100,000 by William McMillan, the first owner of 25 Portland. William and Eliza McMillan's daughter, named Mary, died just before Mary Institute moved nearby. The institute remained at Lake and Waterman for twenty-eight years, before moving to a forty-acre campus in suburban Ladue in 1930.

Some of the Westmoreland boys had to walk a little farther to school than the girls who went to Mary Institute. These boys attended Smith Academy, the companion school of Mary I. It was located at Union and Cabanne, about four blocks away. Like Mary I, Smith Academy was associated with Washington University; it was established in 1879 by a gift from James and Persis Smith. T. S. Eliot said of his education at Smith, "We were well taught and I was happy there."

In its best years, the school had an average enrollment of about four hundred boys. However, when it moved from its original location on 18th Street to the West End site at Union and Cabanne, it virtually cut off attendance from the south side and from residential districts east of Grand Avenue. Although it was not in vogue for wealthy children to attend public school, two West End public schools also gave Smith Academy sharp competition. The handsome and splendidly equipped Clark Elementary School rose within half a block of the academy in 1907, and the majestic Soldan High School followed in 1909 on Union just south of Clark. In addition, McKinley High School took many south-siders. In June 1917, Smith Academy closed because of a severely shrunken enrollment and consequent financial stress.

When Frank Hamsher, the principal of Smith, tendered his resignation, he noted:

When I first came to the Academy I was almost overwhelmed with the serious criticisms of the school. The systematic personal campaigns of the Eastern boarding schools in this city in recent years and particularly the propaganda for a country day school have been very strong adverse influences. The numerous small neighborhood primary schools with their obvious advantage of location have retarded the growth of our primary department.

Hamsher's announcement also outlined some changes to Washington University's Manual Training School. This school had been founded in 1879 by Calvin M. Woodward as a branch of the university's polytechnic department (now the engineering department). Its goals were to "educate the whole boy" and "to foster a higher appreciation of the value and

Mary Institute became a Westmoreland/Portland neighborhood school when it moved to Lake and Waterman in 1902. The move was made possible by a $100,000 gift from Portland Place residents William and Eliza McMillan.

dignity of intelligent labor, and the worth and respectability of laboring men."

In 1915 the Manual Training School had been formally combined with Smith Academy and had begun sharing its facilities. Despite the school's endowment in 1917 of $197,000, a Washington University report issued on March 27 of that year found:

> That the school is no longer needed is evident from the fact that in spite of the large number of scholarships provided through the endowment, the total attendance for the current year is fifty only, whereas in its earlier years it had an annual attendance of over 300. The public schools are splendidly equipped for doing this work and afford every facility which the Manual Training School, as originally planned, had in mind.

Ironically, the man who established the school, Calvin Woodward, had also campaigned to have manual training and pre-engineering courses included in the city's public schools. When his advice was heeded, the new public-school curriculum provided competition for Woodward's school.

The 1917 report also found that the operation of the prep school was costing Washington University about five thousand dollars a year over and above the tuitions and endowment. The study further found that the Manual Training School and the Engineering School were duplicating each other's efforts. To remedy the problem, it was decided that the Engineering School should absorb the Manual Training School. Thus, in 1917, under orders signed by Washington University head Robert Brookings, Smith Academy was abolished and the Manual Training School survived only as part of the Washington University Engineering School.

Memories of the days at Smith Academy and at the Manual Training School lingered for many decades. One of the largest reunions of the alumni of the two schools was held at the St. Louis Club in 1967. There were then 232 graduates of the Manual Training School still living and 72 graduates of Smith Academy. The featured speaker at the 1967 reunion was former Washington University chancellor Ethan A. H. Shepley, who had grown up at 53 Portland.

The decline and closure of Smith Academy and the Manual Training School, coupled with a growing dissatisfaction with the traditional forms of education, were directly responsible for the founding of several other private schools in St. Louis. The successor schools to Smith offered more liberal and more progressive approaches to education than St. Louis had ever seen.

According to *The History of Community School 1914–1979*, by Mary B. Reinhard, some enlightened parents in St. Louis were "disillusioned by the 'rigid, frigid, formal' system existing in the schools in 1914 in St. Louis and elsewhere in the country." Some of these parents were, said Reinhard, "brave enough to accept the challenge of starting a new progressive school in a city rooted in both social and educational conservatism."

That year a school patterned after the teachings of Madame Maria Montessori was established for thirty-five youngsters in the vestry rooms of Grace Methodist Church at Waterman and Skinker boulevards. The tuition was set at fifty dollars per child, and the church furnished the facilities, including utilities, at no charge. Later this fledgling school affiliated with Hosmer Hall and moved into a storefront at 6242-6244 Delmar. The relationship with Hosmer Hall seemed ideal because Hosmer had no kindergarten or first grade. But as the Reinhard history relates, the affiliation "was not satisfactory, as the founding mothers wished a freer and more flexible program than that being practiced at Hosmer."

So the parents huddled again and decided to pursue their quest for progressive education in a big way. They purchased a lot on DeMun Avenue in Clayton for about four thousand dollars, and on September 28, 1916, the Community School opened its doors. Nine mothers assisted the four teachers in the first classes. Grace Jones (the wife of Robert McKittrick Jones) of 6 Westmoreland supervised play at recess and taught dance to the first classes.

Enrolled in the first class was Mary Elizabeth Bascom, daughter of Charles and Ida Bascom of 52 Portland. The Catlins of 41 Westmoreland sent their sons, Daniel and Ivar. George Simpkins, grandson of the Filleys of 40 Westmoreland, was also in the first class. Later, the Wear and Fouke children of Westmoreland went to the new experimental school.

Many parents wanted their sons to have a "country day school" experience but did not want them to have that experience with girls. These parents founded Country Day School, which opened in the fall of 1917. The formal plan for the new school was hatched at a dinner held on March 27, 1917, at the Racquet Club. Charles Parsons Pettus, the builder of 33 Westmoreland, and Dwight F. Davis, the first resident of 16 Portland, were elected to the organizational committee. The influence of Westmoreland/Portland residents on this project increased significantly when Georgia Wright Pettus and Helen Brooks Davis were named to assist their husbands by spearheading a mothers' drive to raise capital for the new school.

The members of the organizational committee scoured suburbia looking for the proper site for their dream school. They

St. Louis Country Day School opened on September 29, 1917. Westmoreland/Portland residents Dwight Davis, Charles Pettus, Daniel Catlin, Jr., and George Niedringhaus served on the school's first board of directors.

had not had any luck and were about to give up when George W. Niedringhaus, who would purchase the Lewis Dozier home at 10 Westmoreland in 1920, suggested that the committee inspect the Julius Walsh estate on what was then Brown Road (now McDonnell Blvd.). The location received a quick nod of approval from the committee. The author of *St. Louis Country Day School, the First Fifty Years*, Gordon M. Browne, recounts that the Walsh estate was perfect for the country day school because "it could be reached from the city by streetcar in about fifty minutes, it had a large level field . . . and the stables and carriage house could easily be remodeled into shower and locker room and a passable gymnasium."

A board of trustees was set up, and once again the prominence of Westmoreland/Portland residents can be seen. Among those appointed to the board were Dwight Davis, Charles Pettus, Daniel K. Catlin, and George Niedringhaus. On September 29, 1917, St. Louis Country Day School officially opened. Forty-eight fifth-, sixth-, seventh-, and eighth-grade boys were enrolled in the first classes.

The school contracted with the Public Service Company to

run a special trolley to transport its students out to the distant country. Bud Shepley remembers walking the short distance every school day from his home on Westmoreland to the corner of Delmar and Kingshighway to catch the Country Day Special for the journey to the school's site near present-day Lambert Airport. Before long, a second car had to be hitched to the trolley to carry the urban youngsters to suburbia. Shepley recalls:

The school streetcar had to make a rather steep climb up Delmar from Kingshighway to Union. I believe the grade was even steeper than it is today. . . . Some of us boys decided to play one of those pranks that you can always count on young boys to play from time to time. We waited for the last local car to pass going west just before our school car appeared. We quickly went to work. . . . We took a couple of bars of soap and soaped down about 30 feet of track. Just as the "dinky," as it was called, came into sight we took our places innocently at the streetcar stop just as we had always done. When the car got to the soaped track it slid back. The motorman, who was probably surprised by the failure of the car to make the grade, backed her up and made another run. We boys stifled our giggles and watched in sheer delight. The motorman must have made ten unsuccessful runs before he got out and spread some sand kept in the car for ice patches. That worked. Of course, we didn't get to school on time. We were late—and we were happy.

Nonetheless, high-jinks and pranks were kept to a minimum on the streetcar. Some of the older boys were appointed monitors, and they kept order on the dinkies under penalty of being reported to the school authorities. The threat of extra homework or a note to parents was generally enough to encourage decorum. The trolley continued its run until 1949, when the Public Service Company canceled its contract to provide transportation to the school.

Contributions made by Westmoreland/Portland residents to the growth and development of Country Day continued through the years. Hobart Cale, whose family lived at 12 Westmoreland for a while, helped form the Alumni Association in 1923. Charles Parsons Pettus was the first secretary-treasurer of the school's board of trustees. When he was killed in a fall from a horse in 1923, Georgia Pettus gave the school enough money to build a library in her late husband's name. Elizabeth and Edward Mallinckrodt, Jr., the builders of 16 Westmoreland, remodeled the library in 1936 as a memorial to their son, Edward III, who had been killed in an airplane accident while a student at Harvard. Thomas K. Niedringhaus, cousin of one of the school's founders, was the first recipient of the Alumni Scholarship.

When the Country Day headmaster's house burned to the

This was one of the last classes held in the original Rossman School building on Delmar. The school opened its doors in the Westmoreland/Portland neighborhood in September 1917.

ground in the summer of 1947 following a gas explosion, a former Portland resident, Ethan A. H. Shepley, was called upon to lead the fund-raising campaign to replace the residence. The drive was a success. The $200,000 raised by Shepley's committee not only replaced the headmaster's house but also built three houses for faculty members.

When a decision was made in 1951 to move the school closer to the center of the school population by sharing facilities with Mary Institute, attorney Thomas S. McPheeters, Jr., of the class of 1929 handled all the legal work pursuant to the acquisition of a fifty-six-acre tract on Warson Road. McPheeters's father built 27 Westmoreland in 1931.

Another school can also trace its beginning to the demise of Smith Academy. Rossman School was founded by Mary Rossman and Helen Schwaner after the two borrowed $12,000 to buy an old mansion at 5438 Delmar. According to many accounts, the two veteran teachers bought unassembled furniture because it was cheaper than ready-made and worked many nights before opening day bolting the desks together.

A former student, Mrs. Samuel W. Mitchell, provided the

Post-Dispatch with a vivid picture of the two teachers in a March 13, 1967, article:

Miss Rossman looked very much like Gertrude Stein. She was stout and about 5 feet 5 inches tall, although I always thought of her as a mile high. She had a pince-nez and clipped, precise speech and you could always hear her coming down the hall in her sensible shoes. Miss Schwaner was tall, thin and very sweet and dear. If you were late she'd just mark you down and look sorrowful.

Miss Rossman contracted to teach you reading, writing and arithmetic for a set fee and that's exactly what she did. She believed that no child under 12 ever learned anything worthwhile after 11 in the morning. Art, music, science and sports she considered as babysitting. She was convinced that these things should be taught at home.

Stafford Lambert of 22 Portland remembered, "Miss Rossman ran a tight ship and taught us how to behave. We wore knickers and stockings and ties. We weren't allergic to getting dirty, but we didn't start the day that way. That was important. If you look like a bum, pretty soon you begin to act like one."

William R. Orthwein, Jr., whose grandparents built 15 Portland, recalls that, although it seemed odd, given Miss Rossman's strict rule, she thought it perfectly acceptable for boys to battle it out with their fists when they had disagreements. He related: "I had the first big fist fight of the year with Bill Boyd in the schoolyard. We weren't very big, but we were slugging it out 'til someone called Miss Rossman to stop us. But she said, 'This has been boiling up for a long time. Let them fight it out.'" Orthwein also had more pleasant memories of the school:

I remember it best for the quality and character of its teachers. And their interest and discipline—they used gold stars to teach you that rewards follow good performance. That's the American system.

Two days before graduation [in 1928] I came down with measles and couldn't get my diploma with my class. But the whole group, carrying a big American flag, marched across the street to our house in Beverly Place while I watched from a balcony. They sang me a song and wished me well. Then I rushed inside and bawled.

Rossman gave me a good solid foundation for everything I did later. That school made a perfectionist out of you. Afterwards you were unwilling to settle for second best.

Some Westmoreland/Portland children commuted to John Burroughs School after its founding in 1923. Mrs. Hugh McKittrick Jones, whose husband had grown up at 6 Westmoreland, was one of the school's founders. The founding parents wanted to establish a "country day" school for girls that was close to nature and free from the pollution that envel-

Mary Rossman co-founded Miss Rossman's School with Helen Schwaner. Miss Rossman is remembered by many Westmoreland/Portland residents as a stern disciplinarian whose softness showed only on occasion.

oped the city at that time. Then, after some of the parents visited coeducational institutions in the East, it was decided that Burroughs would be coed. Although Community School had run a successful coed program for kindergarten and the first and second grades before that time, the idea of having boys and girls go to the same school beyond the primary grades caused quite an uproar in the 1920s.

Post-Victorian standards still prevailed in the 1920s among the socially elite. Under no circumstances were young ladies and gentlemen entering puberty allowed to share their adolescent transitions in an academic environment. Members of the

Mary I class of 1924 remember the day that some Country Day boys on their spring vacation staged a romp in the hallways of Mary Institute. The police were called in to eject them.

Some of the more staid parents in Westmoreland and Portland who had attended separate-but-equal schools (probably Mary Institute and Smith Academy) elected not to have their children be a part of the new coeducational experiment at John Burroughs. Nonetheless, the school got off the ground as a coed institution in 1923. Girls outnumbered boys two to one in the first student body, which numbered seventy-five. Parents paid $500 a year tuition for each child enrolled.

Elsie Ford Curby remembers walking the short distance from her family home at 54 Westmoreland early each school day to the corner of Pershing and Union to catch the University streetcar. This trolley took the students for a transfer rendezvous with the Clayton 04, affectionately called the dinky, chartered by the school. It was a long ride out to John Burroughs for those who lived in the city's west end.

Each day's ride was an adventure. According to reminiscences compiled by Martin L. Parry, city youngsters, including those from Westmoreland/Portland, caught an eight o'clock streetcar that, as it wound its way to Clayton,

would have taken you past the County Courthouse and a scattering of shops, across open fields in the country, the rear end rolling to starboard and the front to port as it gathered speed, on past the little village of McKnight, until you were deposited beside a narrow blacktop country lane full of chuck holes. You had reached your destination at Price Road. As you climbed the footpath to the school, ahead lay the Director's house, a white frame building once a farmhouse.

When school was out for the summer, it was fashionable among St. Louis aristocrats to escape the oppressively hot city summer. Many families maintained a country estate. Carriages and trucks took the luggage to Delmar or Union Station for the train ride to the family's summer retreat. In many cases the husband and father stayed behind to handle business affairs while the rest of the family took off for cooler climes. He often had to sweat out most of the summer in his non-air-conditioned office and house until he could join his wife and children in the country for a few weeks at the end of August.

The annual retreat to the family's summer home was a particular joy for Westmoreland/Portland children. In a 1918 poem, young Arthur Lionberger, known as "Sonny" to his peers, summed up the thrill of fleeing the city with his brother and four sisters at the beginning of each summer vacation:

Cheer Up

Oh, the summer time is coming,
  And we'll soon be on our way
To a place of recreation,
  Where there's no more work but play.
Where we'll swim and sail and fish and row,
  Upon the waters of some bay;
Or hunt and ride and camp beside
  Some balmy woodlands far away.
Perhaps we'll be near a lake,
  And paddle a canoe;
Or come upon a mountain stream,
  And catch a trout or two.
We may travel to the tropics,
  Or may see the Northern Lights,
Or explore wild Arizona,
  Or enjoy New England's sights.
But no matter where we travel,
  Let us hark to Nature's call,
For our work is done till school's begun
  We're free until next fall!

Sonny Lionberger and his family usually summered at their retreat in Marion, Massachusetts. Sometimes they spent time at Dublin House, their aunt Mary Lionberger's summer home in New Hampshire. The George Barnard family looked forward to summers at their estate in Lake Geneva, Wisconsin. Judge Elmer Adams and his wife had a summer retreat in Woodstock, Vermont. The W. K. Bixbys went each summer to their vacation home at Lake George, New York. Selwyn and Iva Edgar and their two children also went to Lake George. The William Thornburghs hied to Biddleford Pool, Maine. The Jacob Van Blarcom family could be found at Little Moose Lake in the Adirondacks, and Mrs. Henry Scott took her four children to their delightful home-away-from-home in Rye Beach, New Hampshire. Katherine Dines (Mrs. Francis Lee Higginson), granddaughter of Mrs. George Allen, now lives in the Rye Beach house where Mrs. Allen spent her summers.

Summers away from St. Louis were generally relaxing times when cares could be cast aside. But George Conant, Jr., whose family summered in Maine, remembers the summer of 1936, when there was quite a bit of uneasiness among Westmoreland/Portland homeowners who had fled the city. The newspapers that arrived each day from St. Louis reported a rash of burglaries in their home neighborhood. The Conants scoured the news to find out if their home had been burglarized. Conant remembers:

We were greatly relieved not to find our home listed among those which had been hit. But we couldn't believe our eyes when we read one day that the burglar had been apprehended. What was incredible is that the guy had set up housekeeping in our carriage house as soon as we had left St. Louis. He had the perfect setup. The reason he was so successful in his looting was that while police were looking for someone coming in or out of the Westmoreland/Portland neighborhood, this guy was living right under the noses of the residents. He stored all the stolen stuff in our carriage house apartment. My family was tickled pink that the burglar had the graciousness not to knock off the host house.

For those children who stayed at home during the summer, there was a day camp called the Sebago Club. George Conant recalls:

All the kids from Westmoreland and Portland Place looked forward to going to the Sebago Club when school was out for the summer. It was near Warson or McKnight [roads] and run by a fellow named Matt Werner. Perhaps he also owned the club. I remember all the organized games we played there and I can never forget a huge wooden slide on the club grounds. We would get on throw rugs or mattresses to keep from getting splinters in our young bottoms. Those were great pre-teen days.

Childhood activities in the twenties and thirties were primarily segregated by sex. The neighborhood girls in and around Westmoreland/Portland had one of the earliest organized sports programs in town. It was run by an affable woman named Isabel Hull, a teacher in the St. Louis public school system. The girls called her by the name she preferred, *Mike*.

Emily Lewis Norcross (the wife of Hiram) remembers Mike as a fascinating woman:

We all loved her. She was of slim build and she always wore a stiff felt hat with a stiff brim. And she always wore a whistle around her neck. She'd use that to call us girls to order. She had what I guess you would call an "English outdoor face," if you know what I mean. But she had a rather heavy Southern accent. I'll always remember that she never got angry with us even when we were difficult. . . . To call her "Miss Hull" would have made her too much like one of our teachers at school.

Jean Wright Ford Simmons, whose family moved into 54 Westmoreland in 1920, remembers that Mike was a short, sturdy woman of athletic build and a dynamo of energy. "Everybody adored her," Jean Simmons remembers. "After school and on Saturdays, the neighborhood girls went to a mini-sports camp that Mike set up on a vacant lot, now the site of the Gatesworth Manor on Union Avenue. The parents of the young sports enthusiasts paid Mike a small fee for their daughters' participation in the activities."

Certain days were set aside during the week for certain age groups. On any given day there might have been as many as thirty girls eager to wind down from a day of scholastic regimentation. Although most of the activities on Mike's field were rather loosely organized, such as kickball, basketball, volleyball, and dodgeball, there were also organized activities, such as the Girl Scouts. In fact, the girls in Westmoreland/Portland belonged to Troop 2, the second oldest Girl Scout troop in St. Louis and one of the oldest in the nation. Among troop members were Jean Ford (Simmons), Almira Steedman (Bond), Medora Steedman (Bass), Martha Pettus (Burke), twins Elizabeth Carter (Allen) and Mary Carter (Walker), and Margaret Carter (Lady Clifden). When the Girl Scout troop did not have an outdoor meeting, their assemblies were held at members' homes on a rotating basis.

Mike's field was a multipurpose lot. A few neighborhood residents used it to cultivate World War I Victory gardens. These gardens formed the out-of-bounds and foul lines for the ballgames. When construction on the Gatesworth began, Mike moved her athletic field to the vacant lot in Westmoreland that later became the site of the Edwin Steedman family home.

Further recreational activities for the Westmoreland/Portland children and their neighborhood chums were provided by a unique arts-and-crafts program established by Westmoreland resident Mary Ruth Lionberger and her former Mary Institute art history teacher, Genevieve Lawler. Mary was the daughter of the Isaac Lionbergers. The two women called their art studio simply the "Workbench." The purpose of the Workbench was to provide space and tools for amateur artists—young and old—to relax from the stresses of daily life by creating crafts. A 1931 newspaper account praised Mary Lionberger for choosing to lead a life of gainful activity, noting: "She belongs to the Junior League and if she were so inclined, might dawdle away her time with the aimless, frivolous things that sometimes occupy young women in society."

The first home of the Workbench, which began operation in 1930, was in the Cabanne Arcade on Vernon Avenue at the Hodiamont streetcar tracks, just a few blocks from Westmoreland and Portland. The studio soon outgrew its quarters and in 1933 moved to three acres adjacent to the Sunset Hills Country Club on Lindbergh between Gravois and Watson roads. The site was nearly thirteen miles from the west gates of Westmoreland and Portland, but youngsters and oldsters flocked to the Workbench, despite the distance. There hob-

The Union Avenue entrance to Westmoreland Place was constructed in 1893 at a cost of $10,000. We can get a good idea of the extent to which the true costs of the Westmoreland/Portland homes were obfuscated when we compare the two-story brick home built for Corinne Dyer at 38 Westmoreland a year before this gate structure was built. The cost given for the Dyer home in 1892 was $18,000. The stable built by William L. Huse behind 9 Westmoreland in 1891 reportedly cost $5,000.

byists worked in wood, clay, leather, fabric, silver, and oil on canvas and china.

Mary Lionberger told a newspaper reporter:

It is the most interesting work I have ever done. Several years ago I decided that a life of idleness was one of punishment. I became interested in the arts and crafts at Mary Institute, where I met Miss Lawler, and when it was suggested that we go into business for ourselves, I jumped at the chance. I've never been happier.

And if you think that we haven't got a real job here, let me tell you that once we were here at six o'clock in the morning, we had china firing in the kiln and we had to watch it. Many times we are here at five in the morning and would stay until long after dark. It has ceased to be an experiment.

Friendships were an important ingredient of growing up in Westmoreland/Portland. George Conant, Jr., remembers that his boyhood buddies were almost inseparable. His closest chums were Andy Shinkle and Jack Johnson—heirs to the

International Shoe fortune—and Bill Niedringhaus, whose family had founded Granite City, Illinois, and held major steel interests there. Conant recalled life during the thirties:

Andy, Jack, and Bill weren't affected at all by the Depression. While they were getting new bikes during the height of the Depression, I remember going to a place on North Kingshighway with my father to buy a used bicycle. I was seven years old when the Depression really hit. I remember hearing that Dad's salary at SLIGO, Inc., had been cut and dividends diminished, but we were fairly oblivious to the deep anguish of those who were less fortunate than we. My family wasn't by any means in the same financial league with the Shinkles, Johnsons, and Niedringhauses, but we lived comfortably through the Depression.

Conant remembers one of his Westmoreland Place cronies as being rather eccentric.

George Mallinckrodt, an heir to the chemical company fortune, was a wizard . . . a genius, but he was also a little strange. It seemed that his whole being was aimed at one-upmanship. Not in any malicious way, mind you. It just seemed that George was happiest when he was using that master inventiveness of his to go us guys one better.

For example, when all of us got roller skates, George disappeared into his secret third floor lab at Number 16 and we didn't see him for days. He never allowed any of us into his lab and we knew that if we didn't see him for a few days he was working on some big project. As we were skating with delight one day up and down the streets of Portland and Westmoreland, here came George with skates connected to a back pack equipped with an automobile battery. He had wires run all up his trouser leg. And would you believe it? George had designed a pair of battery-powered roller skates! He had to top us with that big brain of his.

And then all the guys in Westmoreland and Portland got water pistols. There was a six-shot gun, a twelve-shot water pistol, and then a pistol that boasted the ability to give you twenty-five squirts. George disappeared into his lab again. We could almost guess what he was working on. In a few days he emerged once again. With rubber tubing, an eye-dropper and a Dr. Enos seltzer bottle, George Mallinckrodt had rigged up a water shooter that allowed him to squirt a quart's worth of spurts.

Conant went to boarding school in 1937 just outside Santa Fe, New Mexico. Nearby Los Alamos was the subsequent site of the Manhattan Project to develop the atomic bomb. Conant continues:

I will never be able to prove it, but to this day, I think George was working on that secret project. When I was home on leave from military service one summer, I mentioned just casually, in passing, to George that a once-rugged road into the hills near Santa Fe had been paved. Obviously startled, he asked me, "What do you know

about that road? How did you know about that road?" All summer long George would ask me what I knew about that road. It got to the point that when my doorbell rang, I feared it was going to be the FBI asking me about that darned road.

An activity enjoyed by both girls and boys in the 1920s and 1930s was driving through the private streets on flatbed motorized wagons called "red bugs." These wagons had the equivalent horsepower of a lawn mower. The motor was attached to a fifth wheel, and the vehicles were made to stop or go by raising or lowering this fifth wheel. The wagons were two-seaters, so there was room for a best friend to become one's copilot or to ride shotgun, depending on the imaginative mission of the ride. There were races along the streets almost every evening after school until the air filled with calls to supper. Residents of that era remember weekends in which red bugs seemed as numerous as today's Big Wheels and skateboards. George Conant recalls: "I believe it was right in the middle of the Depression that my chums got their new red bugs. Those were those little two-seater battery-powered cars that were so popular in those days. And expensive, too. I think I'm accurate when I say that a red bug cost $225 from Abercrombie's."

That Westmoreland/Portland youngsters enjoyed special privileges is best illustrated by a 1927 event following the triumphant return to St. Louis of Charles A. Lindbergh. "Lucky Lindy" had just completed his historic transatlantic flight in the *Spirit of St. Louis* and had come home to thank his financial backers, most of whom lived in the neighborhood around Westmoreland and Portland. Ernest Kirschten observes in *Catfish and Crystal*:

Tumultuous as Lindbergh's reception was in New York and in Washington, nowhere did people turn out to cheer him as they did in St. Louis. Everywhere every bit of available space—and there was a lot of it in Forest Park—was packed with people. Motorcycle police and mounted officers had constant trouble in clearing a quickly closing path for Lindbergh's car. There were the ticker tape, the confetti and the telephone directory pages, too, but there was something special about this demonstration which set it apart from so many others.

Historian James Neal Primm relates in *Lion of the Valley* that "during the grand homecoming at St. Louis, sloppy adoration reached a climax when at an alfresco banquet a society matron collected [Lindbergh's] corncobs and stuffed them in her purse."

Elsie Ford Curby was thirteen years old when she and a

When Charles Lindbergh visited St. Louis following his historic transatlantic flight, thousands of St. Louisans turned out to welcome him. A number of children from Westmoreland and Portland were among those who had the privilege of meeting the aviator in a more private setting.

number of other Westmoreland/Portland children were invited to a reception given for Lindbergh at the nearby Kingsbury Place home of Tom Dysart, one of Lindy's financial backers. She remembers that as soon as the big parade wound its way west on Lindell and turned north on Union, the chosen youngsters walked across the confetti-covered Union Avenue to the reception. They could hardly contain their excitement over meeting an internationally known hero. It was a privilege that millions of youngsters around the globe would have relished. In fact, there were millions of adults who would have given anything for the experience of being in the same room with the world's most celebrated flier.

According to Elsie Ford Curby, the glaring spotlight that had followed Lindbergh from Roosevelt Field, Long Island, across an ocean and back again was too much for him to accept comfortably. After having been pawed and clawed and applauded and lauded, the bashful Lindbergh stood in the middle of a room full of wide-eyed children and, as Curby recalls,

> was very, very unhappy to be doing it. He was so shy. He seemed to hate all the attention. He never smiled. And then somebody asked quite loudly: "Where's that famous Lindy smile?" Lindbergh just gritted his teeth and forced what appeared to be more grimace than smile onto his face. He quickly shook the hands of all the young people in the room and beat a hasty retreat. Before we knew it, he was gone.

It was a story that would be embellished at school, especially when told to the unfortunate classmates who were not invited to see Lindy.

The traditional progression of youngsters in Westmoreland/Portland and environs took them into dance instruction. Many girls in the neighborhood started with dance classes at Alice Martin's dance studio on Olive Street just west of Taylor Avenue, about five blocks from Westmoreland and Portland.

Martin taught ballet and interpretive dance in the style of Isadora Duncan, who continued to be the idol of many young dance students even after her accidental death in 1927. The girls of Westmoreland/Portland learned poise and carriage along with their basic dance lessons. Martin's studio remained a popular place until she married Harry Turner, a renegade member of a patrician St. Louis family who owned a speakeasy and published a magazine that raised many a highbrow eyebrow. Having involved herself in what was considered a scandalous liaison and thus fallen from grace, Martin shut-

tered her once-popular dance studio.

The most important step in learning dance was to go to Mahler's Academy of Dance. The Mahler studio was run by Jacob Mahler, a terpsichorean titan, despite his light, lithe build and despite the fact that he always wore velvet ballet slippers. When Jacob Mahler established his popular academy, he was carrying on a tradition started by his father, Albert, and by his first master, the eminent Monsieur Sarpy, to whom Jacob was apprenticed early in his career. Albert had begun teaching dance in a studio in the downtown Merchant's Exchange Building in 1860. M. Sarpy had conducted a dancing school that, with its French politesse and impeccable ballroom deportment, was credited by André Siegfried in *America Comes of Age* with "helping to 'explain' St. Louis." In 1906, Jacob Mahler moved his academy to Washington between Euclid and Kingshighway, providing a location that was more convenient for those in the nearby private places than Mahler's earlier ballroom on Olive Street east of Grand had been.

After-school classes for the young were held on Tuesday, Wednesday, Thursday, and Friday afternoons, graduating from beginners to advanced pupils. Friday evenings were special because those were the nights the "fortnightlies" were held. Jean Simmons remembers the afternoon classes:

> Each girl carried a flannel shoe bag with a drawstring. The bag carried a pair of dancing shoes . . . usually shiny, black patent leather shoes which were never worn on the street outside of Mahler's. Some of the girls who went to the classes with me to get ready for the fortnightlies were Mary Shepley, Ann "Sissy" West, Mary Lees Kennard, Christine Jones, and Cynthia "Cyn" Polk. . . . Mr. Mahler, a fascinating man, taught us such dances as the two-step and the fox-trot. But his very favorite dance was obviously the waltz, which we could never quite execute as gracefully as he. And I remember something else about Mr. Mahler's studio. He would sometimes be assisted by his daughter, who had the rather unusual name of Rosalyn Puffles.

William Julius Polk remembers: "Mr. Mahler was insistent that street shoes should not be worn in the ballroom, and he provided, in both girls' and boys' dressing rooms, tiers of drawers—each neatly labeled—in which dancing shoes could be stored."

The fortnightlies originated in the Vandeventer Place home of Mrs. John T. Davis, Jr., when she began to be concerned that the rapid and inevitable westward migration of St. Louis's elite families was going to make it hard for the children of

these families to meet each other. She described the fortnightlies as being "for our children to meet the children of our friends and their friends" (this motto was eventually engraved on every invitation to the fortnightlies). The gatherings began as a series of small dances, but about the time the Davises' son "Lion" went off to boarding school, they expanded to functions held at Mr. Mahler's ballroom, first on Olive Street and later on Washington Avenue. Youngsters were eligible for membership in the program at age fourteen and could continue through their junior year in high school.

Strict protocol was observed in the ballroom under the watchful eye of Mr. Mahler. After the children passed along the receiving line with palms extended—boys' palms up; girls' palms turned down—they were assisted in filling their dance cards by the chaperons. These vigilant adults always attempted to watch out for both the less popular girls and the more recalcitrant boys. Jean Simmons remembers:

> After our parents had dropped us off at the studio on those Friday nights we girls would walk through a receiving line of the four or five chaperons for the evening, and then we would be handed our dance cards. . . . Our hopes were that we would have every dance filled for the evening, but it was rather difficult to corral some of the young men who would sneak off as often as they could to go to the dressing room where rumor had it that some of them would try to steal a puff or two on a cigarette. But it was the job of the chaperon to round up the young boys who were absent without leave from the dance floor and literally force them to face the music and dance.

George Conant recalls:

> I remember Mrs. [William Julius] Polk, who was a chaperon at the fortnightly. She was a terror! We boys lived in fear and trembling of her, but we still tried as often as possible to slip away from the dances. Once when I had sneaked into the restroom to hide, I remember Mrs. Polk storming into the boys' room and yelling "George! You come out of there this instant!" The boys' restroom wasn't off-limits to her at all. She could breathe fire!

One of the dances the young students learned at Mahler's was a special creation of his called the "Ostend." In addition to teaching basic ballroom dancing, Mahler was respected for instructing youngsters in the social graces, which were expected of children invited to the fortnightly and which would be used when the youngsters became debutantes, escorts, or attendants at the Veiled Prophet balls. Curtsying, bowing, and making proper introductions, greetings, and leave-takings were taught. Mahler was considered such an expert at these matters of protocol that he was selected as master of ceremonies for thirty-five Veiled Prophet balls. Thirty-six Veiled Prophet queens emerged from his classes.

Other dance instructors were also available. George Conant remembers that when he was seven or eight years old, he and his buddies were expected to take dance lessons from a Mr. Trimp, whose studio was in the neighborhood. Then it was on to Madame Cassan's dance studio on Lindell, where boys and girls in the 1920s and 1930s were also taught social graces. Conant recalls, "Madame Cassan had a foreign accent of some sort. Madame attempted to make dancing fun for us, but the boys, in particular, hated it." Mrs. Cassan was Russian and had arrived in this country as a member of the Pavlov Ballet Company.

One of the most important rites of passage in the socialite world for young girls was the debutante or "coming-out" ceremony. A young lady was usually formally introduced to society after "finishing school" or "a year abroad" or the end of her first year in college. She "made her bow" at a formal affair often held at a favorite club. If her father was a member of the secret Veiled Prophet order, the young socialite's entrance into society was heralded at the annual Veiled Prophet ball.

This elegant ceremony began in 1878, when the first Veiled Prophet chose Susie Slayback (daughter of the ball's founder) as his queen. Each year since then a young lady has been chosen to reign over St. Louis society. The mysterious Veiled Prophet of Khorassan, whose identity is never revealed, also honors a bevy of young women who are chosen maids of honor at the elaborate white-tie ball. Being selected as the "Queen of Love and Beauty" has been the ultimate dream of young St. Louis society belles since Susie Slayback. Selection has always been based on a family's social prominence and financial contributions to the organization and to St. Louis.

A number of young women from Westmoreland/Portland have been chosen as Veiled Prophet queens. In 1901, Emily Catlin Wickham, granddaughter of the Daniel Catlins, Sr., was chosen the Veiled Prophet Queen of Love and Beauty. As Mrs. J. Clifford Rosengarten she later owned 20 Westmoreland. Jane Shapleigh, whose parents, Alfred and Mina, built 6 Portland Place, was given the honor in 1915. Ada Johnson, daughter of the Jackson Johnsons of 25 Portland, reigned as queen in 1920. Eleanor Simmons, daughter of Wallace and Jessamine Barstow Simmons of 46 Westmoreland, was selected queen in 1921. In 1926 Martha Love made her bow before the Veiled

Prophet and St. Louis society. Her parents were Edward and Laura Sproule Love, who moved into 44 Westmoreland that same year. Jean Ford became the Veiled Prophet's queen in 1929. Her parents, James and Jean, had moved into 54 Westmoreland in 1920. In 1933 Jane Johnson, daughter of the Andrew Johnsons of 16 Portland, served as queen. James and Ellen Filley Wear watched their daughter, Barbara, honored as the queen in 1941. The Wears lived in 40 Westmoreland, which had been built by Ellen Wear's parents, Frances and John Filley. In 1946, Anne Farrar Desloge, whose parents, the Joseph Desloges, owned 15 Portland, was the Veiled Prophet's choice. She was escorted to the ball by William Julius Polk, Jr., who grew up at 28 Westmoreland. Eleanor Simmons Koehler, who grew up in 46 Westmoreland and whose mother had been queen in 1921, was given the honor in 1950. In 1952, Sally Baker Shepley, daughter of the Ethan A. H. Shepleys and granddaughter of charter Portland residents the John F. Shepleys, was the Prophet's choice for queen. Laura Rand Orthwein, daughter of the William Orthweins, Jr., of 31 Westmoreland, was selected queen in 1959. Her mother had been queen in 1938 as Laura Hale Rand. Sally Ford Curby, daughter of the John E. Curbys of 33 Westmoreland, was introduced as the Veiled Prophet queen in 1960.

Jean Wright Ford Simmons remembers that special honor very clearly:

Those were the days when the Veiled Prophet ball was a big October event which signaled the official beginning of the social season. The ball was held at the old Coliseum on Washington at Jefferson. The parade always preceded the ball. My father told me as late in the summer as he possibly could that I had been selected. He knew I'd have fallen apart if he had told me at the beginning of the summer. I got the big news at the end of our family's summer vacation at Hyannis Port.

Of course everything had to be kept very secret. I couldn't tell any of my friends, and that's a big secret to keep. Some of my friends suspected that I would be named queen and they would tease me and try to get it out of me, but I didn't tell a soul. I was bound to secrecy.

One of the first things I had to do was order a gown for the ball. My gown was made at Vandervoorts by Mr. Harbison. He made many of the gowns for the Veiled Prophet queens and maids of honor down through the years. He always knew who the queen would be long before anybody else in the town. It was quite a bit of fun sneaking down to see Mr. Harbison for the fittings.

I remember we also had to sneak to Mr. Mahler's dance studio to learn how to bow correctly. Mr. Mahler's daughter, Mrs. Puffles, assisted in that part of my preparation for the big night.

All the girls who were named as queen could look forward to a

Jean Ford Simmons was chosen Veiled Prophet Queen in 1929. She learned of her selection at the end of the family's summer vacation in Hyannis Port and had to keep her secret until October.

special ride to the ball. A police escort always came to pick up the queen. And that's when many of your neighbors knew for the first time that a girl had been selected. I must admit I was disappointed by the escort that was assigned to pick up my family and me. A policeman on a motorcycle always seemed impressive to me. But it was raining rather hard . . . on my special night, so my escort was in a police car—and that just wasn't the same.

I understand the girls today take their gowns and dress after they get to the auditorium. But I wore my gown to the Coliseum and was ushered into a dressing room for last-minute things. My crown was really lovely.

While being named to this high honor was the ultimate dream of the Westmoreland/Portland girls and their neighborhood peers, Martha Love Symington, who was Veiled Prophet queen in 1926, remembers the experience as involving a lot of hard work, too.

We were on call to be available for civic functions for a full year after we were crowned. I spent a great deal of that year being introduced at this function and this affair and this event. Many of the parties were boring, but a Veiled Prophet queen has to develop a rather fixed smile and give the impression that she is having a wonderful time. I visited schools and hospitals and many other places as a goodwill ambassador for the city. I can't begin to tell you how often Mayor [Victor J.] Miller introduced me that year.

What was the highlight of Martha Love's busy year?

Without a doubt it was playing hostess to Queen Marie of Romania and her children, Prince Nicholas and Princess Ileana. The reception given for them by Mayor Miller was elegant, but rather stuffy. I could sense that Prince Nicholas, then about twenty-one years old, and Princess Ileana, who was seventeen, were having a miserable time. So I asked Her Majesty for permission to give a private party, a tea dance, at the St. Louis Country Club for her two children. She consented and I put in an urgent telephone call to Bert [Albert] Lambert [son of Maj. Albert Bond Lambert in nearby Hortense Place] to find all the boys who had cutaways.

I also gave Bert instructions that if any of the boys appeared to be awkward in the dances with the princess, he was to have one of the better dancers cut in. There were only about fourteen of us young people at the party. We had a delightful time. That evening I took the prince and princess to a debutante party for Julia Klipstein at her home in Brentmoor Park. The princess was attended by a lady-in-waiting, Madame Prokopiu, but had a marvelous time with the American "stag line."

One of the other fond memories I have of the royal visit was a horse show at the Coliseum. Queen Marie was seated in the box of honor and she was all decked out in her regal finest—including her crown. I sat next to Prince Nicholas, who impressed me with his knowledge of horses. He would pick out the winning horses in each category before the judges did, and I don't think he was wrong once in his judgment.

Martha Love Symington got the notice of her selection in a rather romantic setting. The year was 1926, and she was attending a boarding school in Florence, Italy. "I was thrilled and also scared," she recalls. "If only I could have shared my secret with my closest friends among the nineteen girls who attended the school." She continues:

My gown for the ball was really very short—just below my knees as was in vogue that year. It was designed by a Madame Frances in New York and was completely embroidered with little mirrors. My gown had a silver train underneath the official train, which was sixteen feet long. I must have gone to New York two or three times for secret fittings. One of the times I was being fitted by Madame Frances, we almost bumped into my cousin, Maude Streett. She was there to be fitted for the gown she would wear to the ball as retiring queen. Although she didn't know we were there, my mother found out she was there. So our secret remained closely guarded.

On the night of the grand ball, an escort of two policemen on motorcycles came to our home at 44 Westmoreland around 6:30 to take us to the Coliseum. My family and I packed into Mother's car for the ride. The police sirens screamed all the way downtown. It was thrilling! When we got to the Coliseum, I remember Mr. Mahler was there to take us through our dress rehearsal. It was quite a complicated parade on the stage before we would stand in the presence of the Veiled Prophet. Mr. Mahler, in his knee britches and with his precise European carriage, was a stickler for perfection in the ceremony. As we were lined up to practice our bows, it became obvious to all the girls who would make their entrance into society that night that I was going to be The One.

The Veiled Prophet ball and the debutante entrance into society were the most important events in the lives of the young women in Westmoreland and Portland places until their wedding days, marking the end of a childhood of warm memories for those who grew up in Westmoreland/Portland.

Martha Love Symington learned of her selection as Veiled Prophet Queen in 1926 while she was attending an exclusive girls' school in Florence, Italy. "I was thrilled and also scared," she remembers.

6. LIFE IN WESTMORELAND/PORTLAND: THE WEDDING FEAST TO THE WOEFUL FUNERAL

All things that we ordained festival,
Turn from their office to black funeral
Our instruments to melancholy bells,
    Our wedding cheer to a sad burial feast. . . .
          —Shakespeare

The life-styles of the Westmoreland/Portland residents made headlines in and beyond St. Louis. From the cradle to the grave, the early residents of these exclusive places were accorded little of the privacy that was the raison d'être for their neighborhoods. Headlines announced the births of the heirs and heiresses to Westmoreland/Portland fortunes, just as headlines in other cities detailed the entrances into the world of Mellons, Vanderbilts, Du Ponts, and Astors.

Although the wealth created by post–Civil War enterprises in St. Louis never reached the proportions of the fortunes of the eastern industrial families, the St. Louis fortunes were certainly respectable. When St. Louisans read in 1915 that Westmoreland homebuilder Daniel K. Catlin, Sr., received a personal property assessment that year of $44,756, the news guaranteed Catlin births, weddings, parties, and funerals a place in the headlines of that era. The $4 million estate of Catlin's neighbor Jacob Van Blarcom and the $3 million estate of neighbor Edwards Whitaker assured them and their peers in the exclusive residential enclave similar public attention.

The events that brought the Westmoreland/Portland residents out in their full sartorial splendor were well covered by the press. Even before photography was widely used, the high fashions of the Westmoreland/Portland women were captured in pen-and-ink sketches. Their clothes influenced the attire of women throughout St. Louis and the Midwest. Many of the clothes worn by the Westmoreland/Portland women were the

Fashion trends were often set by the early resident women of Westmoreland/Portland. Among the trendsetters was Mrs. E. D. Nims of 56 Portland. Mrs. Nims, whose maiden name was Lotawana Flateau, was an active patroness of music and was one of the sponsors in the thirties of a national college glee club competition.

works of European and eastern designers. In fact, Sarah Brant Colwell Jones of 45 Portland had a keen interest in preserving her apparel for posterity. She donated many articles of women's, children's, and baby's clothing to the Missouri Historical Society. None of the clothing was "off-the-rack"; the Jones wardrobe was fashioned by such internationally famous couturieres as Lady Duff Gordon and Bionnet, as well as by high-fashion designers in St. Louis. The generosity and foresight of Sarah Jones will enable future generations to see the apparel worn by the elite during the Golden Age at the turn of the century.

High fashions were particularly in evidence at society weddings. The weddings of Westmoreland and Portland residents were more than ritualistic nuptial unions. They were often mergers of elite families, cementing family enterprises and strengthening neighborhood ties. In addition, the actual ceremonies, as outlined with incredible detail in the society sections of newspapers, afforded readers of all stations of life the vicarious experience of being celebrants.

A classic example of grandeur and endogamy was the wedding of Almira Steedman, 32 Westmoreland, to Richard Baldwin, 23 Westmoreland. The ceremony, held at St. Peter's Episcopal Church on June 8, 1931, was conducted by the Rev. Dr. Edward Schofield Travers. The altar was profusely decorated with Easter lilies and cymbidium orchids. Clusters of ferns banking the chancel were interspersed with enormous vases of white roses.

Before the bride approached the altar, she was preceded by an elegant procession of ten bridesmaids. The groom's sister, Roccena Baldwin, was the maid of honor. The groom outdid the bride in the number of attendants. In addition to the best man, Edward M. Durham III, Richard Baldwin selected fourteen of his best friends to be ushers.

The pageantry of the Steedman-Baldwin ceremony con-

Another fashion trendsetter was Maude Moon Lee. She lived at 1 Westmoreland from the early 1920s until her death in the late 1950s. Maude Moon Lee was the only child of Lelia and John Moon. John Moon, who bought the mansion at 1 Westmoreland in 1921, started Moon Carriage Co. with his brother Joseph. The residents of Westmoreland and Portland were often in the public eye, and the clothes worn by the women set fashion trends throughout St. Louis and the Midwest.

tinued at the home of the parents of the bride, Mr. and Mrs. Edwin Harrison Steedman. An expansive canvas marquee had been built adjoining the house for the reception, and the area was lavishly decorated with spring flowers. Garden shrubbery formed the backdrop.

The bridal dinner was served next door in the dining room of the bride's uncle and aunt, Mr. and Mrs. George Fox Steedman, at 34 Westmoreland. There a U-shaped table was set to accommodate forty-two diners. Gleaming china and silverware were enhanced by clusters of lilies of the valley. A four-tiered wedding cake towered majestically in the center. After the reception, the bride and groom left for a honeymoon in Bermuda before spending the summer at the Steedman home.

Also in 1931, on February 4, Cynthia Polk and John Hayward were married at the home of her uncle, William Julius Polk, 28 Westmoreland. The bridesmaids and ushers included Jean Ford of 54 Westmoreland, Mary Shepley of 50 Westmoreland, Alicia Polk of 28 Westmoreland, Eleanor Church Johnson of 25 Westmoreland, Ellen Walsh Bates of 24 Portland, Tom Pettus of 33 Westmoreland, Dick Simmons of 21 Westmoreland, Lee Johnson of 38 Portland, and Erwin Niedringhaus of 10 Westmoreland.

Grand weddings involving Westmoreland/Portland residents were also staged outside St. Louis. One of the largest was the ceremony in which socialite Madeleine Taussig married Thomas McPheeters, who later built 27 Westmoreland. According to all accounts, the wedding, which was held in Jamestown, Rhode Island, at the summer home of the bride's grandparents, Mr. and Mrs. James Taussig, was the social event of the 1910 summer season among the "Shore-by-Hill" cottagers. The bride was given away by her uncle, St. Louis city comptroller Benjamin J. Taussig. Among the St. Louisans in attendance were Mr. and Mrs. Arthur Shepley of 50 Westmoreland and Edwine Thornburgh of 23 Portland. The newlyweds left for New York immediately after the ceremony and sailed for Europe, where they spent a six-week honeymoon. The marriage ended sadly with Madeleine's death eight years later. Thomas McPheeters later married Frances Filley.

The weddings of two sets of sisters, Alice and Janet Morton and Rebecca and Nellie Tebbetts, give a clear picture of the importance of weddings as ways to strengthen the bonds among members of St. Louis's ruling class. Alice and Janet were the daughters of Jeanette Filley and Isaac W. Morton. At the time of their weddings, the girls lived with their widowed mother and another sister, Helen, in Vandeventer Place. As a

Filley, their mother was already strongly enmeshed in the West-moreland/Portland family structure. Janet married into Portland, Alice into Westmoreland.

Janet married first. On November 5, 1906, she became the bride of Harold Kauffman, who was building 51 Portland Place for her. Kauffman was a prominent investment broker and an heir to a milling company fortune. The Morton-Kauffman wedding ceremony was one of the grandest and most elegant St. Louis had ever seen. In fact, the wedding was the last of the mammoth nuptial ceremonies performed in one of the city's most prominent churches, the Church of the Messiah at Locust and Garrison. Its sanctuary had been the scene of spectacular wedding ceremonies, including the breathtakingly elaborate marriage of Anna Busch to Edward Faust.

Accounts of the wedding on the society pages of the newspapers noted that the church was more elaborately decorated for this ceremony than it ever had been. One article states:

> The entire chancel and altar were massed with Boston ferns, an especially large size used, and these were studded with large, full-blown white peonies. Shower bouquets of peonies were tied upon the front pew ends and all available places such as the baptismal font, the choir appurtenances and the like were decorated with the fragrant spring flowers.

There were a dozen attendants in the wedding party. Among the groomsmen was Arthur Stickney, heir to a cigar fortune. His parents built a handsome home in Westmoreland Place two years after the wedding. Ralph McKittrick, many of whose relatives lived in Westmoreland and Portland, also attended the groom. Hugh McKittrick Jones, Ralph's cousin and the son of the Robert McKittrick Joneses of 6 Westmoreland, was an usher, as was James Holliday Wear, father of 1941 Veiled Prophet queen Barbara Wear.

Among Janet Morton's attendants were her two sisters, Alice and Helen. The bride also chose the groom's sister, Violet, and Ethel Gamble, whose parents had begun to build 37 Portland Place the same year as this memorable wedding. The bridesmaids entered the church's central aisle in pairs, wearing matching gowns in the popular princess style. The bodice and skirt of each were trimmed with pale blue satin daisies emphasized by a turquoise button in the center. The bridesmaids' hats were large and flaring, made of white chiffon and pale blue crinoline in a lacy braid, trimmed in satin, and highlighted with blue ostrich plumes. Each bridal attendant carried bouquets of pink sweet peas that cascaded to the hem of

Cynthia Polk and John Hayward were married on February 4, 1931. As with many of the Westmoreland/Portland weddings, the members of the wedding party were neighbors.

her skirt. The bride's mother wore white lace; the mother of the groom was attired in what a reporter called "a black net costume."

Janet Morton entered the church on the arm of her uncle, Westmoreland Place homebuilder John Dwight Filley. She wore an empire gown of satin messaline. The skirt was embroidered with *entredeux* openwork, and the bodice was trimmed in old point lace. Her voluminous tulle veil was attached to a coronet of orange blossoms; her bouquet was made of lilies of the valley. Around her neck the bride wore a magnificent diamond pendant fashioned in three sections. A large blue diamond was mounted in the center of the largest section. This pendant was a gift from the groom.

The guest list for the reception that followed the wedding was a copy of "Who's Who in 1906 St. Louis." Guests with surnames of Kilpatrick, Bascom, Jones, McKittrick, Catlin, Lionberger, Davis, Wear, Allen, West, Thornburgh, Nagel, Nugent, Kennerly, Mallinckrodt, and Simmons were, at the time of the wedding, neighbors—or would be shortly. And almost all the guests at the Morton-Kauffman wedding feast

were related by marriage.

By sharp contrast, the wedding two years later of Janet's sister Alice to successful grain merchant and Westmoreland resident Harry Hill Langenberg was a simple, low-key affair. The girls' mother, Mrs. Isaac Morton, had underwritten the cost of the magnificent Morton-Kauffman ceremony and obviously had no aversion to extravagance. There was no financial crunch in the Morton household—Mrs. Morton left an estate in 1933 of more than $1.3 million—so it can be assumed that the austerity of the Morton-Langenberg wedding was due to the bride and groom's preference.

Of this wedding one newspaper account reported: "The decorations at the Church of the Messiah were simple, being carried out entirely in palms and ferns." Alice came down the aisle on the arm of her mother's brother, John Dwight Filley, as her sister had. The gown she wore was probably her sister's wedding dress with some minor modifications. It even could have been the same dress worn by the bride's mother when she married Isaac Morton on June 19, 1877. A reporter at the Morton-Langenberg ceremony described the gown as

Theodore Link designed this house at 29 Portland for the Lewis B. Tebbetts family (1891–1892). The house was later modified.

The gown's crushed collar and girdle were finished with tiny chiffon rosettes. The tulle veil was attached to the bride's brown hair by pearl pins. Her bouquet was made up of white roses fringed by lilies of the valley.

In a departure from convention, the eight attendants were children, all related to the bridal couple. The little girls were dressed in white organdy dresses over pink silk slips with pink sashes, stockings, and shoes. The little boys were attired in black velvet Fauntleroy costumes with broad collars and deep lace cuffs. Carrying bands of pink satin ribbon, the children preceded the bridal couple into the library and formed an aisle through which the bride and groom passed.

Following the ceremony and reception, the newlyweds left for a honeymoon in the South. They returned to St. Louis to receive their friends at a party at the Beers Hotel the first Monday night of 1895.

When the Tebbetts-Breck marriage was barely six months old, events involving the bride's sister began to cause a considerable number of tongues to wag as residents in Westmoreland/Portland wondered: How could the sweet Rebecca Tebbetts become Mrs. Thomas A. Moore? There was even concern that disgrace could fall on the proud house of Tebbetts.

A newspaper account of the day reports that Rebecca Tebbetts "was as fair a maiden as ever shed lustre on West End Society or graced the handsome home of a successful St. Louis businessman." Apparently many people thought that Rebecca would not succeed as well as her sister Alice in finding a proper husband. One newspaper article that described her scandalous liaison reported, "At 8 o'clock last evening, Rebecca Tebbetts, spinster, ceased to exist, and Mrs. Thomas A. Moore was evolved from the storehouse of Hymen to fill the vacuum."

Tom Moore was considered a dashing, popular, and handsome young man. He rode into town from Chicago, where he worked for the Swift & Company meat-packing firm. Sent to St. Louis to handle business matters for his company, Tom met Rebecca through friends. According to their closest friends, her beauty, grace, and talents captured first Tom's eye—and then his heart.

Moore was quick to propose to Rebecca, but apparently his proposal stunned her. She was fond of Tom, but, as she confided to friends, she had doubts about his sincerity. Rebecca realized that her father would never consent to her giving her hand to a man who was not yet established. Lewis Tebbetts was then sixty-one years old. He had worked hard to establish a booming business. Tom Moore had no track record, no business trophies.

"trimmed with a great deal of fine old family lace." While her sister had chosen an abundant shower of lilies of the valley for her bridal bouquet, Alice selected white lilacs.

One of Alice's bridesmaids was her sister Helen. Another was her good friend Edna Gamble, another of the eleven children of Flora and David Gamble. The prolific Gambles furnished many more weddings with brides, grooms, and attendants. The groom chose as one of his groomsmen Charles Bascom, the first owner of 52 Portland, whose aunt had married Giles Filley.

Following the brief wedding ceremony, the bridal party and a small number of guests went to the Vandeventer Place home of the bride's mother for a two-hour reception. After a trip to the East Coast, Alice and Harry sailed from New York aboard the steamship Cedric for a honeymoon in Europe.

The second set of sisters with intriguing stories of love and marriage is Rebecca and Nellie Tebbetts, the heiresses to the farm-equipment fortune of Lewis and Ellen Mansur Tebbetts. Nellie Mansur Tebbetts became Mrs. Robert Breck on December 18, 1894. The Tebbetts mansion on Portland Place was

only a few years old when Nellie and Robert said their "I do's." On the night of the wedding, the Tebbetts residence was sparkling. The interior of 29 Portland became a garden of smilax and LaFrance roses, the bride's favorite flowers. The library, which was the setting for the ceremony, was decorated with palms and potted plants, which were massed to form a tall pyramid. Pink roses filled great vases throughout the room, and some peeked through delicate ferns banking the mantel. The adjoining salon, where the reception for several hundred guests was held, was graced with a canopy of smilax interwoven with roses.

At seven o'clock that wintry evening, Nellie and Robert stood together in the library in front of the Rev. Dr. Jesse Bowman Young and made their vows. The ceremony was witnessed by members of the immediate family only. The bride, who was described on the society page as "a stately and handsome girl," wore a gown of ivory satin that fell in folds to the bottom of a rounded train. Its waist was high and made of accordion-pleated white chiffon. The bodice was close-fitting and short, and the sleeves were fashioned in a butterfly shape.

Despite Rebecca's reluctance, Tom's tenacity prevailed. Following his earnest proposal, Rebecca consented to a secret engagement. Only the couple's closest friends were informed. Shortly after promises were made, Swift recalled Tom to Chicago. He pressed Rebecca to marry him right away. She did not want to cause her parents heartache by creating a scandal, but eventually she consented to a secret marriage.

Before Rebecca could have a change of heart, Moore and a friend obtained a marriage license and arranged an appointment with Rev. R. C. Cave. The ceremony would be performed in the parlor of a nonsectarian church. At the appointed hour a few close friends arrived to serve as witnesses. Immediately following the brief and informal ceremony, young Tom kissed the bride and, vowing to return for her in a few days, raced off to Union Station to catch a late train for Chicago.

The abandoned bride, as a society-page reporter put it, "went home, made confession and received absolution." But the story of the unconventional wedding became the talk of the town. The marriage did not last long. Shortly after that spring night in 1895, the newlyweds were divorced as abruptly as they were married. Later, Rebecca Tebbetts Moore married Lloyd Richart, the secretary and general factotum to Robert Lee Hedges, president of the St. Louis Browns.

Young society maidens and their mothers could dream of seeing the title *baroness*, *countess*, *duchess*, or even *princess* preface their names. According to Joseph J. Thorndike, Jr., who chronicled the life-styles of America's aristocracy:

> The ultimate glory that an American heiress could bring her family—or so some mothers thought—was to marry into the European nobility. In the decades before European aristocracy fell upon hard times, some of the very richest American ladies acquired titles of nobility for their marriageable daughters. Fortunately, as this ambition became more general it coincided with the beginnings of a severe pinch on European—and especially British—noble incomes.

The first daughter of Westmoreland/Portland to become a member of the English peerage was Margaret Carter, whose husband, Victor Agar-Robartes, was the Eighth and last Viscount Clifden. Margaret's parents, May and Lemuel Ray Carter of 8 Portland, were probably also pleased at the choices made by their other two daughters. Mary Carter became Mrs. George Herbert Walker of Connecticut, and Elizabeth Carter married a neighbor, Wayman McCreery Allen, whose family built 26 Westmoreland.

Edwine Thornburgh of 23 Portland captured headlines when she became engaged to Sir Wilfred Peek, Third Baronet Peek of Rousdon, Devon. The two were wed in an elaborate

and colorful ceremony at First Presbyterian Church in St. Louis on May 7, 1913. The bride, dressed in heavy satin, wore a beautiful diamond and pearl pendant, a gift from the groom. Peek also gave Edwine a magnificent traveling case with gold fittings. Among her other gifts was a diamond tiara given her by Sir Wilfred's family. The groom's brother officers of the Royal First Devon Yeomanry sent a massive silver bowl. Sir Wilfred's aunt and uncle, the Viscount and Viscountess Midleton, sent two beautiful silver entrée dishes. And the Lord Bishop of Glasgow sent a picnic basket.

Edwine's father, William Henry Thornburgh, had been president of the very successful Platt and Thornburgh Paint Company when he died in 1901. Her stepfather, William C. Stribling, had retired as the head of the Tennent and Stribling Shoe Company. Her sister Marjorie married John Holliday, first cousin to Ida Bascom and to James Holliday Wear.

"Marrying well" was a goal of which no Westmoreland/Portland resident has ever been ashamed. Many times a marriage resulted in social advancement for the groom as well as for the bride. Thus, Edward Faust married into the $100 million Busch brewery empire. And John Fowler gained consider-

William L. Huse, on the far left, came to St. Louis in 1861 after youthful experiences as a grocery clerk and steamer pilot. After coming to St. Louis, he organized the Huse and Loomis Ice and Transportation Company. Carpet manufacturer Samuel M. Kennard and his wife, Annie, built the original 4 Portland. A Confederate hero in the Civil War, Kennard became one of St. Louis's most powerful leaders in Democratic politics.

ably by marrying Cora Liggett, daughter of tobacco tycoon John E. Liggett.

When Mary Frederick and Joseph D. Bascom married, they united two very successful families. He had established a profitable wire-rope manufacturing company in 1876, a year before the wedding. She was the daughter of George Frederick, who made a fortune building storage warehouses. He also was one of the first entrepreneurs to harvest ice from the upper Mississippi River for use in St. Louis during its torrid summers.

Daniel Catlin, Sr., was called the "Astor of St. Louis" long before he died in 1916. Most likely he was a millionaire before he married Justina Kayser in 1872, but her prominence rivaled his. Justina was the daughter of Henry Kayser, a former city engineer who had worked with Robert E. Lee on Mississippi channel improvement projects in the late 1830s.

Marrying well did not necessarily mean marrying money. It was at least as important to marry into a distinguished blue-blood family. For example, Emma Richmond married Judge Elmer Bragg Adams, who was not a wealthy man. Judge Adams's estate of slightly more than $100,000 was quite small in comparison to the sums left by his Westmoreland/Portland neighbors. But she did marry a man whose father was Jarvis Adams, a rigorous Puritan and a lineal descendant of John Adams, second president of the United States.

Robert Hough Keiser married into a branch of the venerable Chouteau family. Furthermore, Julia Keiser's father was a Maffitt and her mother had been a Skinker. One's position in the St. Louis social registry was guaranteed if one could boast of being a member of the Chouteau-Maffitt-Skinker line.

Martha E. Brown probably had no difficulty at all convincing family and friends that she was marrying a gentleman of good family when William L. Huse asked for her hand. He could trace his ancestry on his mother's side to Ethan Allen, the dashing American hero who had routed the British at Fort Ticonderoga on May 10, 1775.

The 1893 wedding of Sarah Hitchcock to John Foster Shepley brought about the bonding of two distinguished St. Louis families. She was the daughter of Ethan Allen Hitchcock, who was to become minister to Russia and secretary of the interior in the cabinets of presidents McKinley and Theodore Roosevelt. He was the grandson of Ethan Shepley, first chief justice of the supreme court of Maine and first U.S. senator from Maine. Sarah and John Shepley built 53 Portland.

There are scores of other examples of marrying well among the first families of Westmoreland/Portland. Obviously social dictates and pressures helped determine one's choice of a spouse—and whether one married for money, social prestige, or love.

Just as these early settlers of Westmoreland/Portland observed the proper execution of all other rites of passage in life, they also followed the correct procedure at the end of life. They were formally eulogized and laid to rest in similar style and in traditional settings. Even the simplest funeral service for a Westmoreland/Portland pioneer became a regal affair. Some funerals were close to being spectacles.

For almost three decades after the turn of the twentieth century it was still traditional for funeral services to be held in the home of the deceased, even if the deceased had been an active church member. Samuel M. Kennard was a member of St. John's Methodist Church, yet last rites for him were held at his home at 4 Portland, where he died on December 8, 1916. Kennard was certainly one of the most prominent and influential men of his day. He had been a Confederate Army hero, chairman of the board of the J. Kennard & Sons carpet com-

pany, an organizer of the old Agricultural and Mechanical Fair, president of the first Autumnal Festivities Association, which devised the Veiled Prophet ball, and vice-president of the Louisiana Purchase Exposition Company. He was prominently identified with the Missouri Masonic Order, first president of the Mercantile Club and of the Businessmen's League, a director of the National Bank of Commerce and the Commonwealth Trust Company, and a Barnes Hospital trustee.

Kennard had stipulated that no church service be held for his funeral, but his immense power could not be minimized. His survivors and those who appreciated his service to the community held a memorial in the Barnes Hospital rotunda two days after his death. Officiating at the ceremony were Methodist Bishop E. R. Hendrix and Dr. J. W. Lee, hospital chaplain. But by the time of the memorial ceremony, Kennard had already been buried. His remains were taken straight

from his home to the family burial vault in Bellefontaine Cemetery.

Funeral services for financier and art patron W. K. Bixby were also conducted from his home, at 26 Portland. Bixby died of a heart attack in 1931. He had been quite active in the First Congregational Church, and the church pastor, Dr. W. C. Timmons, conducted the service. Bixby's four sons and two sons-in-law were the actual pallbearers. In addition, 180 honorary pallbearers were named, including Westmoreland/Portland neighbors Charles Bascom, L. Ray Carter, Robert McK. Jones, H. H. Langenberg, Edward Faust, Claude Kennerly, Isaac Lionberger, Eugene Nims, Hudson Bridge, George Carpenter, Daniel Catlin, Jr., John T. Davis, Jr., Edward Mallinckrodt, Jr., A. L. Shapleigh, Louis Werner, and Charles Wiggins. The fact that these men were named as official mourners attests to the great fraternal bond that made Westmoreland/Portland residents a family.

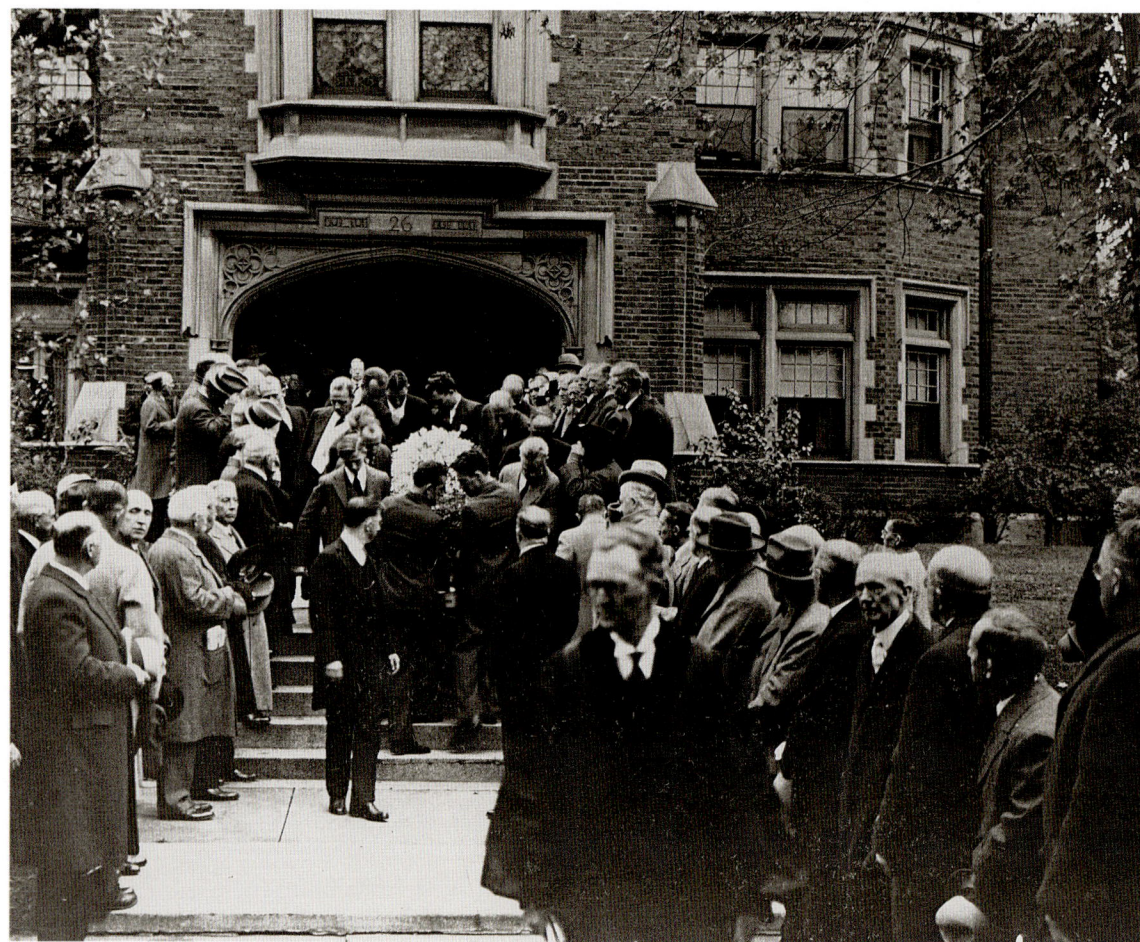

Funeral services for William K. Bixby were conducted from his home at 26 Portland in 1931. Bixby was eulogized in the *New York Times* for his contribution to the preservation of classic art.

William K. Bixby built 13 Portland and later moved to 26 Portland. He was chairman of the board of the American Car and Foundry Company and an avid collector of art and classic literature.

Bixby had requested a simple funeral service at which only two hymns, "Abide With Me" and "One Sweetly Solemn Thought," would be sung. Out of respect to his memory, the east wing of the Jefferson Memorial, housing the Missouri Historical Society, was closed the day of the funeral. The City Art Museum, where Bixby was chairman of the board of control, closed at noon. As another memorial to Bixby's philanthropy, the art school at Washington University also closed its doors for the day.

One of the largest funerals ever seen in St. Louis was held for Charles Stix, president of Stix, Baer & Fuller Company and its Grand Leader department store and the first owner of 26 Portland. Stix died at his home on September 6, 1916, following a long battle with stomach cancer. An estimated 3,000 people viewed the body as it lay in state at the home immediately after his death. At the funeral service at Temple Israel at Kingshighway and Washington, more than 2,500 people packed into the auditorium, which had a seating capacity of 1,500. Newspaper accounts reported that an additional 3,000 mourners surged in the streets around the temple.

Stix had named eighty-four honorary pallbearers, including Archbishop John Glennon. Mayor Henry Kiel, also an honorary pallbearer, said of Stix, "He unselfishly gave his energy and time to all political and civic movements that were calculated to build up the community and never permitted his business interests to guide him when the public weal was the issue."

The funeral cortege included more than one hundred automobiles and extended for more than a mile. Three automobiles and a large truck carried the hundreds of floral designs sent by businesses, social organizations, and friends to Mount Sinai Cemetery. As a further tribute, the Grand Leader store was closed for the day, and even the rival Famous-Barr, Scruggs, Vandervoort, & Barney, and Nugent department stores were closed for a half-hour during the funeral rites.

Another elaborate funeral was held for pioneer lumberman Louis Werner, who died at the age of eighty-six at his home, 36 Westmoreland. In addition to the major role he played in the development of the yellow-pine lumbering industry, Werner was a director of both the Mississippi Valley Trust Company and the Boatmen's National Bank. He was also the founder of a sawmill company and a stave-manufacturing plant in Shreveport, Louisiana, both of which bore his name.

A man of Werner's stature in the community deserved a funeral and interment of considerable pomp. The funeral mass was celebrated at a packed St. Louis Cathedral; the burial was at Calvary Cemetery. Of the eighty-nine honorary pallbearers chosen, several were Werner's Westmoreland/Portland neighbors, including Edward Mallinckrodt, Jr., Robert McK. Jones, Edward Faust, Charles Bascom, Isaac Lionberger, William D. Orthwein, Hudson Bridge, and Lewis Dozier. August A. Busch was also one of the honorary pallbearers.

Werner, although he had one of the largest funerals in St. Louis history, was not buried near most of his neighbors. Calvary Cemetery was Roman Catholic, and there were few Catholics among the private-place homebuilders. The Protestant Bellefontaine Cemetery, on the other hand, is the burial site for seventy-five of the eighty-nine Westmoreland/Portland

Charles A. Stix, the charter resident of 26 Portland, was the founder of the Stix, Baer & Fuller department store. He was also a director of the 1904 Louisiana Purchase Exposition.

pioneer homebuilders and their families. In fact, entire lanes of the fourteen miles of roadway inside Bellefontaine appear to be extensions of the four blocks of Westmoreland/Portland.

The funeral service for Breckinridge Jones four years before the death of Werner was an impressive show of respect and praise. Jones died at his home at 45 Portland in 1928 at the age of seventy-two. The cause of his death was blood poisoning from a throat infection.

Many years earlier tragedy had plunged 45 Portland Place into darkness. On August 13, 1904, less than a year after the mansion was built, the Breckinridge Jones family visited the World's Fair grounds, as hundreds of thousands of others had done. Jones, his wife, Frances, their daughter, Mary, and Jones's niece accepted a carriage ride from Oscar Chouteau. At about five o'clock that evening, the carriage neared the southwest corner of the Boer War exhibit. Jones was on the box with Chouteau, who was driving, when the carriage started down a steep incline. Suddenly the carriage struck a large obstruction with enough impact to throw the driver from his seat.

As he fell, Chouteau kept the reins in his hand, but the jolt frightened the horses. They began a wild run, and Chouteau lost his hold on the reins. Jones was able to jump from the carriage but tried in vain to grab hold of the bit. He then tried desperately to clutch one of the traces but failed again. The horses and the carriage with Frances Jones and the two girls plummeted down the hill to the bridge that spanned the intramural railroad tracks—eighteen feet down a steep embankment.

One of the horses tried to draw the carriage over the bridge, but the other, a spirited bay, pulled toward the embankment. The carriage took a violent swerve, and Frances Jones and the girls were thrown down the embankment. The girls were thrown clear, but the carriage rolled over on top of Frances Jones. Two of the Boer soldiers ran down the hill and, by sitting on the heads of the prostrate, struggling horses, kept them quiet until Frances could be pulled from under the carriage.

Dr. William Smith, the surgeon at the Boer camp, was quick to attend the injured woman, who was taken on a stretcher to the tent of a Captain Blakesly. As thorough an examination as possible under the circumstances was made. It was determined that Mrs. Jones had at least two broken ribs and was suffering from a concussion. Dr. Smith was certain that the broken ribs had caused severe internal hemorrhaging.

More physicians were summoned to the scene. Dr. L. H. Laivley, medical director of the fair, arrived, followed by Dr. J. G. Moore, chief of the fair's emergency hospital. All three doctors worked to keep the unconscious woman from slipping away, but Frances Miller Reid Jones died about an hour after the accident without ever having regained full consciousness. Her body was taken to the family home in Portland Place by ambulance. The bereaved family leaned on next-door neighbor Frank Johnson to make the funeral arrangements and answer the inquiries from the press.

The two other Jones children, Reid and Breckinridge, Jr., were summoned from a visit to their grandparents' home in Kentucky for the burial. Frances Jones was forty-four years old when she was killed. Newspaper accounts recorded that Breckinridge Jones was nearly destroyed emotionally by the accident.

Six years later, in 1910, Jones married widow Sarah Brant Colwell in a quiet ceremony. Sarah Jones lived until 1928, dying only two months before her husband. Seven years after

Jones's death, his mansion was torn down. Family members were no longer willing to pay taxes on the unoccupied building. The three-story, sixteen-room house, with its three large halls, five baths, and three-car garage, had begun to deteriorate. For tax purposes, the house had been assessed at $15,600 just before it met its demise.

Prominent banker Charles Parsons Pettus was another Westmoreland/Portland resident who died as a result of an accident. In June 1923 Pettus was on his way to see his son, Thomas, graduate from Lawrenceville School in New Jersey when he stopped to visit his brother-in-law, Thruston Wright, in Pittsburgh. On a visit to the Rolling Rock Country Club on the private estate of R. S. Mellon, president of the Mellon National Bank of Pittsburgh, Pettus went for a ride on a horse owned by Wright.

Pettus was an expert horseman, so there was some alarm when the horse galloped into the stable yards without him. Several hours after a search party was dispatched, two farm boys found Pettus unconscious on a country road. His skull had been fractured when he fell from the horse. The forty-six-year-old Pettus was rushed to a hospital where doctors worked feverishly to remove pieces of skull from his brain. Pettus never regained consciousness and died about an hour later.

Pettus was eulogized in a *Post-Dispatch* obituary on June 23, 1923, the day after his death, as "a gentleman in the finer and deeper meaning of the word—a man of education and honor, high principles, courtesy, and kindness." Stella Cartwright, who later married Charles Parsons Pettus, Jr., was a Rossman School classmate of Mary Pettus. She recalls the mournful figure of the Pettuses' youngest child appearing at the school completely swathed in black crepe on her first day back to classes following her father's burial.

To add to the Pettus family's grief, Charles Pettus's widow, Georgia, reputed to be a brilliant pianist who loved to host social gatherings at her home, died suddenly of a massive cerebral hemorrhage in 1934. The fifty-three-year-old woman was entertaining friends at her home when she was stricken. She left five children.

Several of the Westmoreland/Portland pioneer homebuilders died of pneumonia, including Thomas McPheeters, Blakesley Collins, Mrs. Joseph Schnaider, John Holmes, and Harold Kauffman. A few of the original homebuilders died of that traditional euphemism for cancer—*a long illness*. Among them were Theodore Meysenburg and Claude Kilpatrick.

David Gamble's death is a classic example of a physician not healing himself. Although he was a distinguished professor

of otology at Washington University Medical School, and although he had been warned that cigar smoking was not compatible with his heart condition, Gamble refused to give up tobacco. He died of "acute dilatation of the heart" and was actually puffing on a cigar when he was stricken.

Judge Elmer Adams's death was attributed to overwork. He was stricken with paralysis two weeks before he died in 1916. Judge Adams is credited with coining the phrase "the man higher up." While charging a grand jury in an investigation of naturalization frauds, he instructed the panel to "look not only for the little man who is made a tool, but for the man higher up." His funeral procession was led by his close friend, former president William Howard Taft.

A few deaths among St. Louis wealthy families were the results not of accident or illness but of design. Life took on a black pall for Henry Scott after his brother, Arthur, accidentally shot and killed himself in 1894. Despite his success as chief executive officer of the Laclede Power Company, the Missouri and Illinois Coal Company, the National Light and Power Company of Fort Worth, the Texas Light and Power Company of Waco, the natural gas utility in Wichita, Kansas, and the Citizen Railroad of Waco, Scott sank into a deep depression. His chronic blues were aggravated by an attack of appendicitis and a severe case of influenza. The physical illnesses heightened his emotional distress, and Scott found it almost impossible to sleep. Finally, on January 13, 1911, Scott spent the entire night wide awake. The next day he raised a gun to his head and died instantly from a self-inflicted wound. Just before his suicide, Scott confided to his wife, Bertha, that he felt he was no longer in control of his life. In 1912, his widow built 31 Westmoreland.

While Henry Scott's death was, without question, caused by his own hand, Jeanette Filley Morton never admitted that her husband's mysterious death was anything but an accident. The incident was never discussed publicly by Mrs. Morton or by her three daughters, Alice, Helen, and Janet. Eleven years after the tragedy, Mrs. Morton moved into the newly built 43 Portland Place.

Isaac W. Morton was a man who was proud of his ancestry. His American lineage could be traced to Nathaniel Morton, secretary and historian of Plymouth Colony. Morton led an active life in St. Louis. He was one of the planners of the 1904 Louisiana Purchase Exposition, a member of the board of Washington University, a director of St. Louis Union Trust, a director of the mammoth Simmons Hardware Company, and the president of the Mercantile Library Association.

One crisp day in October 1903 Morton went to the Cuivre Hunting and Fishing Club to spend some time away from the rigors of his business life. The next morning he was found dead at the club with a bullet wound to the head. The community was shocked. An inquest was quickly held. The verdict came just as quickly: Death by accident. The coroner's report noted, "A revolver was found tightly grasped in the dead man's right hand."

Morton had directed in his will that his wife conduct his funeral in the simplest manner possible. The brief service was held in the family home at 49 Vandeventer Place. Although he had specified that there be as little public mourning as possible, all classes at Washington University were canceled on the day of the funeral and the service was attended by more than two hundred prominent St. Louis businessmen.

Clara Ballentine Hart's death in 1918 was the result of an incredible mixup. Her husband, Augustus, had died two years earlier of uremic poisoning, and Clara had decided to keep their home at 19 Portland. She loved travel and, like all of St. Louis's wealthy residents, fled the city's blistering summers.

In 1918 Clara Hart was spending the summer at the fashionable Brown Palace Hotel in Denver. Her doctor had prescribed the vacation and the location. He had also prescribed some medication to help her sleep. However, when she sent the prescription to be filled, she sent the wrong slip of paper, one that contained an order for strychnine. Mistaking the white powder for the medication, Clara Hart took a large dose of the poison. She died within an hour. She was sixty-two years old.

As impressive and prominent as were the lives and deaths of the wealthy, the handsome tombs, crypts, and headstones that mark their graves are just as impressive. Among the more intriguing markers is the monument to Portland Place homebuilder Herman Luyties. According to reliable accounts, Luyties made a trip to Italy in the early 1900s and met a beautiful and alluring young woman who worked as a model for an Italian sculptor. For Luyties it was love at first sight. At once he asked the young woman to marry him. She declined. (Luyties was still married to May Carlin Luyties at the time. Records show that he was not divorced from her until June 1912.)

With his dream of marriage to the lovely model shattered, Luyties, according to stories that buzzed through St. Louis society, asked the sculptor to render a likeness of the woman who had captured his heart. A twelve-foot-high marble statue resulted. It was shipped to the Luyties home at 36 Portland, where it was kept in the foyer until it began to sink through the

The Bellefontaine Cemetery grave marker for Portland Place resident Herman Luyties is encased in granite and glass. It was fashioned in the likeness of a sculptor's model Luyties met in Italy in the early 1900s.

wooden floor. Luyties had the statue moved to Bellefontaine Cemetery, where it was mounted in granite. Because of a cemetery rule, the marble figure had to be enclosed in glass. The stunning monument to Luyties's love—and to his death at the age of fifty in 1921—has come to be known simply as "the girl in the shadow box."

The hexagonal mausoleum for the remains of Portland Place resident George Warren Brown was designed in 1928 by the Mauran, Russell & Crowell architectural firm. It is the most imposing mausoleum in Bellefontaine Cemetery.

Another member of the Westmoreland/Portland family earned the posthumous distinction of having one of the shortest stays on record at Bellefontaine Cemetery. When Jacob Craig Van Blarcom, multimillionaire banker and builder of 1 Westmoreland, died in 1908 of Bright's disease, his remains were placed in the receiving tomb at Bellefontaine. The body remained in the storage morgue for only a month. Then for reasons that have become obscured by time, the body was moved to another cemetery.

When they died, the first residents of Westmoreland/Portland left fortunes that attest to their business acumen and shrewd investments. A listing of the estate values of some of the pioneers indicates their worth: Edward C. Simmons, $14 million; Jacob Van Blarcom, over $4 million; William McMillan, $4 million; Edwards Whitaker, $3 million; Daniel Catlin, Jr., nearly $3 million; William Bagnell, $2.5 million; George Barnard, over $2 million; Emma (Mrs. John) Copelin, $1.5 million; Bertha (Mrs. Henry) Scott, $1.4 million; Mrs. Isaac Morton, nearly $1.4 million; William W. Culver, over $1 million; Joseph Bascom, Mrs. Augustus Hart, and Mrs. Claude Kilpatrick, $1 million each.

It should be noted that these estates were amassed and bequeathed in those halcyon, pre-income tax days, when a dollar was worth much more than it is today. In addition, some of these figures do not reflect the true worth of a total estate. As with the purposely deflated construction costs that show up frequently on City Hall records, the well-to-do residents of these two private streets appear to have been quite adept at concealing sizable chunks of their assets from public and press scrutiny.

With regard to the estates of the earliest Westmoreland/Portland residents, it was often true that where there was a will, there was a way to contest it. A grandchild of lumber baron William Bagnell filed suit in 1928 to protest the terms of his grandfather's will. The would-be heir was the child of divorced parents and felt slighted by being left out of the bequest.

One of the nastiest probate court battles involved the $16 million estate left by Westmoreland homeowner James Campbell. The suit filed in October 1914 claimed that Lois Ann Campbell Burkham, heiress to the fortune, was not actually the daughter of James Campbell. Disgruntled Campbell relatives also alleged that the witnesses to the will were officers of the Mercantile Trust Company. Since Mercantile Trust was named as executor of the will, the plaintiffs argued that the officers could not have been impartial witnesses. To add more

The hexagonal mausoleum housing the remains of Portland Place resident and footwear magnate George Warren Brown was designed in 1928 by the Architectural firm of Mauran, Russell & Crowell. The firm created a number of houses in Westmoreland and Portland.

fuel to their claim that Campbell had actually died intestate, his relatives charged that Saint Louis University, a principal beneficiary of the estate, had unduly influenced the dying man. The suit alleged that Jesuit priests, who had visited Campbell during his last hours, had persuaded him that "the salvation of his soul depended largely upon the distribution of his property to religious and charitable uses."

While the plaintiffs promised to furnish proof that Lois Campbell Burkham was not legally Campbell's daughter, based on questions surrounding his marriage to Florence

Campbell, attorneys for Mercantile Trust produced proof to the contrary. They exhibited a record of James Campbell's marriage to Florence in New York and found a record of Lois's baptism at St. Patrick's Cathedral officially signed by Archbishop Michael Augustine Corrigan. To the charges that Campbell was not of sound mind and had fallen victim to pressure tactics used by Jesuits, Mercantile Trust lawyers appealed to all who knew him to attest to the soundness of Campbell's mind at the time of his death. They cited the fact that just a short time after the execution of his will, Campbell had put together one of the biggest financial deals of his active business career.

Lois Campbell Burkham must have known that the suit was without foundation. When reporters tracked her down for her response to the news of the suit, they found her at a baseball game. Finding the contest on the field more interesting than the contest in circuit court, Lois Burkham had no comment for the press.

Still another suit regarding an estate was filed in June 1933 by the sons and daughters of William K. Bixby. Two years after Bixby's death the heirs filed to recover a $50,000 loan made to old family friends. Plaintiffs William H., Donald C., and Harold M. Bixby, Ruth Bixby Stevens, and Emma Bixby Jordan claimed in their petition that they had loaned the money to Lucie McMillan, daughter-in-law of their Portland Place neighbor, William N. McMillan. The Bixbys told the court that the money had been loaned in 1927 to settle claims against McMillan's estate on behalf of W. K. Bixby, who was trustee of McMillan's father's estate. If this sounds confusing, suffice it to say that the preceding was just the tip of the legal iceberg in this complicated case.

Some of the Westmoreland/Portland homebuilders were widows. These women, whose husbands had left them in very comfortable financial positions, formed an informal sorority in the two private places. In some cases they had brought substantial family fortunes to their marriages. Since several widows were in mourning when they moved to Westmoreland/Portland, they were not expected to attend the gala activities in the places. But they were permitted by Victorian standards to gather with each other for coffee, comfort, and conversation.

Among the first widows in the neighborhood was Maria J. Davis. In 1895, a year after the death of her husband, John, at the age of forty-nine, she moved into the home she and husband had planned. Maria Davis was a daughter of O. D. Filley,

mayor of St. Louis in 1859–1860. She kept active after her husband's death and was a member of the St. Louis Women's Club and the prestigious Wednesday Club.

Corinne C. Dyer, who built 38 Westmoreland in 1892, three years after the death of her husband, John Napier Dyer, could trace her lineage to one of St. Louis's first families. She was christened Corinne Georgina Chouteau and was a direct descendant of the cofounder of the city. In a move that was bold for the times, Mrs. Dyer moved her family of six children out of the Grand Hotel and into the new home, which the architectural firm of Peabody, Stearns & Furber designed at a cost of $22,510.28.

Just one month after investment broker Harold Kauffman's house rose at 51 Portland in 1907, his widowed mother's new house began to take shape across the parkway at Number 48. Nellie Bronson Kauffman's husband, John, had died three years before the decision was made to have the distinguished architectural firm of Mariner & LaBeaume design both houses.

Annie Lee Allen Chauvenet, who built the house at 20 Westmoreland, was the widow of Louis Chauvenet, who had died on August 2, 1904, at age fifty-two. His death left her with a nine-year-old son, Louis, Jr. Mrs. Chauvenet was accustomed to a comfortable life-style—her father, Thomas Allen, had planned Missouri's state-aided railroad system in 1850 and had built the Southern Hotel and most of the Iron Mountain Railroad. Her grandfather William Russell had made a fortune in real estate speculation before Missouri became a state.

Emma C. Copelin built 28 Westmoreland after the death of her husband, John G. Instead of seeking smaller quarters than the family home just west of Grand on Washington Avenue, Mrs. Copelin moved with her only child, Emma, into a home built for the two of them. When Emma married Harold Tittman, he moved into 28 Westmoreland as well, but the couple lived there for less than a year.

Other widows who built houses on Westmoreland/Portland were Mrs. Isaac Morton (Jeanette Filley, 43 Portland); Mrs. Joseph M. Schnaider (Elizabeth, 24 Portland); Mrs. Henry C. Scott (Bertha Drake, 31 Westmoreland); Mrs. George Holland (Nora Wilcoxson, 47 Westmoreland); and Mrs. Daniel K. Catlin, Sr. (Justina Kayser, 51 Westmoreland).

Life's rites of passage turn all too soon from joy to grief, and for most of life's residents these rites come and go with little fanfare. But for those born into wealth and prominence in the private places, each rite is bathed in floodlights.

7. WESTMORELAND / PORTLAND:
SURVIVAL AGAINST GREAT ODDS

Today these handsome structures still stand—a mellow tribute to the past and an oasis of privacy and beauty in the present age.
—*Globe Democrat Sunday Magazine*, April 22, 1973

That Westmoreland and Portland places still stand, majestic and virtually unscathed, seems only slightly short of a miracle. But the survival of these two premier private places can be directly attributed to the safeguards established by the founders and the tenacity of a few homeowners in the face of adversity. Were it not for these factors—plus some sheer luck—these two private places would have succumbed to the same forces that destroyed earlier private places, such as Lucas and Vandeventer.

Streetcars had had a devastating effect on the earlier private places. Electric streetcars, which made their St. Louis debut in 1890, brought with them noise, ugly overhead wires, and lots of people. Architectural historian Charles Savage, in *Architecture of the Private Streets of St. Louis*, notes that because the Lindell Railroad Company chose a spot just outside the gates of Lewis Place as a switching point for several of its lines, the stack-up was unsightly enough to keep buyers away from the private enclave. The planners of Westmoreland/Portland solved the streetcar problem by enacting strict zoning requirements. Efforts to control the streetcar nuisance continued for a half-century after the trolley's birth.

Ruben Wolff, who operated a popular grocery store that served Westmoreland/Portland clientele in the 1940s, remembers an attempt at traffic control on Union Avenue shortly after World War II.

When traffic started to pick up on Union and the buses started replacing some of the streetcars, the city put up signs making it illegal to park on Union, on either side of the street. That may have

helped their effort to preserve Westmoreland and Portland, but it sure hurt my walk-in trade quite a bit, because the chauffeurs couldn't park on the street anymore and wait while the lady of the house came in to do the shopping. But I guess that made it possible for us to do more telephone business.

The designers of Westmoreland/Portland knew from experience that the railroad, with its noise and smoke, could be an even bigger nuisance than the streetcars. They used their influence to keep the two biggest threats to neighborhood tranquillity—the Rock Island and Wabash railroads—in check. Rock Island Railroad property was purchased for the construction of apartments that acted as buffers; the Wabash was driven below ground, with tracks so well placed that detecting the rumblings of trains near fashionable Westmoreland/Portland's mansions was and is almost impossible.

Other threats could not be controlled by the planners' astuteness. One of the first challenges to the stability of Westmoreland/Portland was a natural one. Several pioneer homebuilders were in the winter of their years when their homes were built, and their periods of residence were cut short by death or enfeeblement.

For instance, Nellie Bronson Kauffman, the widow of John W. Kauffman, was fifty-nine years old when 48 Portland Place was completed in 1909. Her four children had moved away, and her son, Harold, had completed a home across the parkway. Nellie Kauffman remained in her house for only two years before finding it too large to maintain.

The builders of 53 Westmoreland, Leopold and Hannah Freund, were able to enjoy their new home together for only four years after they moved in, in 1910. Then they moved out of their large house and into the nearby Washington Hotel, primarily because of Leopold Freund's poor health.

Lewis and Ellen Mansur Tebbetts built 29 Portland even though Ellen Tebbetts was beginning to suffer the crippling

effects of rheumatoid arthritis. The new house proved too large for her to maintain, and the family moved out in 1902, nine years after their house-warming party.

The George Barnards enjoyed the comforts of their newly built home at 35 Portland for only two years before he died in 1915. Mary Barnard moved out one year later. Henry and Sarah Newman lived at 21 Westmoreland for less than two years before moving to El Paso, Texas, because of his poor health.

At least two widows remarried and continued to live in the homes they had built with their first husbands. When William Thornburgh died of heart disease in 1901, eight years after his house was built, his widow, Florence, elected to stay at 23 Portland. Two years later she remarried and lived in the house for another seventeen years with her second husband. Selwyn Edgar died of a heart attack four years after moving into a new house at 41 Portland. His widow, Iva, remarried later and lived in the house for fourteen years with her second husband.

A dozen houses have been destroyed in Westmoreland and Portland through the years, although all of them survived their creators. Most of these fine houses were destroyed in the 1930s and 1940s, when the city and the nation were feeling the pangs of the Great Depression, the onset of World War II, and a general apathy toward preserving landmark architecture. During the 1930s and in the years immediately following this dark economic period, the heirs to the estates of some of the pioneer homebuilders found it a burden to pay the property taxes, trustee fees, and maintenance costs of these great mansions. Subsequently, the houses were reduced to rubble.

The Faust heirs wanted nothing to do with the magnificent mansion at 1 Portland. In fact, Leicester Busch Faust and his sister, Mrs. Mahlon B. Wallace, came up with at least three plans for disposing of their late parents' home. After Leicester Faust and his family moved to far west St. Louis county in

1938, only a caretaker lived in the mansion. The Faust heirs first offered the home to the City Art Museum as an auxiliary showcase for fine art. But the Portland Place trustees pointed to the deed restrictions, and that idea was abandoned.

Faust and his sister then offered the mansion to the city as the official residence of the mayor. Mayor William Dee Becker inspected the mansion in 1943, but the city Board of Estimate and Apportionment decided that upkeep of the mansion as an official residence would be too great.

The Faust mansion was offered next to the St. Louis Science Academy. The academy was eager to establish a museum in the name of Edward and Anna Faust to house archaeological exhibits and the Indian collection of the late Dr. Henry Shipley, considered to be the finest collection of its kind in the Midwest. The residents and trustees of Portland Place were in a real quandary. They could not violate the deed restrictions by turning the mansion into a public museum, but they knew that if the home were razed, a gaping hole would remain in the block for a long time as supplies were not available to build a replacement during the war.

Taking a chance that the Faust heirs would have a change of heart, the Portland Place trustees refused to grant permission to the Science Academy. And the Faust heirs did not destroy their parents' mansion. However, it remained vacant until Dr. Harry Moore and his wife, Marjorie, purchased it on December 14, 1945.

While the Faust mansion escaped demolition, other Westmoreland/Portland houses were razed. One house was torn down in 1935, two in 1936, and three in 1941. The original 45 Portland survived its builder, Breckinridge Jones, by little more than six years. Hudson Bridge's 23 Westmoreland endured for sixteen years after he died in 1934. Number 26 Westmoreland survived its builder, George L. Allen, by fourteen years and his widow, Lillie McCreery Allen, by just two years. Charles Parsons Pettus died in the summer of 1923; his house, the original 33 Westmoreland, perished just eighteen years later. Joseph Dayton Bascom was not around to protect 45 Westmoreland after 1928. In 1936, four years following the death of his widow, Mary Frederick Bascom, the handsome Bascom mansion was erased from the horizon. The two most recent houses to be demolished were Samuel Kennard's mansion at 4 Portland, which was torn down in 1958, and the house built in 1896 at 2 Westmoreland for Henry Siegrist, which was dismantled in 1961.

Fire threatened some of the Westmoreland/Portland homes. In 1957, a maid working at 9 Westmoreland reported a fire

Architect W. Albert Swasey designed 4 Portland Place for the Samuel M. Kennard family in 1891. The house was torn down in 1958 after remaining vacant for nearly thirty years.

The Henry A. Siegrist house, built in 1896 from a design by W. Albert Swasey, was demolished in 1961. It had been unoccupied since 1947.

next door at Number 11. The house was extensively damaged and uninhabitable. The owners, Thomas and Jane Pettus, had the house torn down in 1958 and moved to Washington Terrace. The fire at 52 Portland on March 30, 1943, was minor. The Charles Bascoms reported damage of only $200. On November 16, 1966, fire damaged the mansion built by Jacob Van Blarcom in 1896. The damage to 1 Westmoreland, then owned by William S. Smith, was estimated at $4,000.

One of the most devastating fires in the neighborhood brought firefighters to 23 Portland on January 30, 1953, when flames raced through the house, virtually gutting it. The damage was estimated at $9,500. The house had been built by William and Florence Thornburgh and was owned at the time of the fire by Harry J. Tuthill, creator of the Bungle Family comic strip.

The Westmoreland/Portland enclave's most tragic fire

occurred shortly before midnight on Friday the thirteenth in December 1968. Two lives were claimed in an inferno at 5 Westmoreland, the home of Donaldson and Caroline Lambert. Donaldson Lambert was the eldest son of the late Maj. and Mrs. Albert Bond Lambert and an heir to the Listerine fortune. His father and an uncle, J. D. Wooster Lambert, had been among the financial backers of Charles Lindbergh's historic transatlantic flight in 1927.

According to neighbors, the fifty-six-year-old Mrs. Lambert was greatly afraid of burglars and had installed several extra locks on the doors to ensure security. She even locked herself in her second-floor bedroom each night. Donaldson Lambert was apparently downstairs when the fire started. Authorities surmised that he might have been watching television after his wife had gone to bed.

Although no cause for the fire was determined, it was suggested that Caroline Lambert may have been smoking in bed. When Donaldson smelled smoke, he ran upstairs and discovered that the bedroom and an adjoining room were ablaze. He apparently tried to kick down the bedroom door, but it was locked from the inside and would not budge. In his futile attempt to save his wife's life—which had already been taken by the fire—the sixty-eight-year-old Lambert may have suffered a heart attack.

The Lamberts' next-door neighbors to the east, Mr. and Mrs. William S. Smith, spotted smoke pouring through the windows and telephoned an alarm. Firefighters arrived to find Donaldson Lambert, clad in his robe, lying in the hallway outside the door of the master bedroom. Caroline Lambert's body, severely burned, was found on the bedroom floor. A small dog in the home escaped injury.

The fire was largely contained to the two upstairs rooms, although it burned through the second-floor ceiling into the third floor and on through the roof of the house. The Smiths attempted to buy the fire-damaged house but could not raise the money. Estimates for renovating the house ran as high as $89,000. The house, which had been built for Theodore and Lucretia Meysenburg in 1891, sat eerily vacant for more than a year. Neighbors remember that the icicles formed from water used to fight the blaze hung from the gutters as gloomy reminders of death until the spring thaw.

Just as the Lambert heirs had decided there was no recourse other than demolition, salvation appeared. Dorothea and Norris Allen had a special love for the house. Many years before, when the two had come home to St. Louis after World War II from the naval base at Long Island where Norris had served as commander, 5 Westmoreland had caught their eye. It was shuttered and vacant at that time, and its future looked bleak. Since the Allens had a long association with Westmoreland Place—her grandparents had built Number 9, where her parents, the Isaac Hedges, also lived—they thought about buying the house. Dorothea Allen remembers, "It was one of the smaller homes in the two privates places, but it had a charm all its own. The high-pitched roof and tall chimney stacks made the house appear as tall as any of the homes on the place." But the postwar price tag was $12,000. The Allens abandoned their attempt to purchase the house and moved in with her parents.

Nearly a quarter of a century later, when the its beauty had been marred by fire, Norris Allen stepped forward to save the house he could not afford to buy earlier. He contacted John R. Green II, the executor of the Lambert estate. "I informed him

that if the neighbor at Number 1 Westmoreland didn't buy the house, I would," Allen remembers.

I found out it would cost $3,750 to demolish the house, and I offered the lawyer for the Lambert estate that much for the lot and the house in its current condition. He accepted my offer.

There were a lot of skeptics who thought the job of renovating the house was too big a task, but I just knew I could redo the place for less than $89,000—especially if I did some of the work myself. So, with the help of a couple of handymen who worked for me, we set out to do the impossible. . . . I managed to get the job done for less than half of the $89,000 rehab estimate. And I later sold the house for $40,000. I just about broke even on the project, but the important thing was the satisfaction of knowing that I had kept a historic home from being torn down.

Smoke was a much more formidable challenge to the future of Westmoreland/Portland and the entire city than fire. Industrial, rail, and home chimney smoke had been a problem in St. Louis since town leaders held a meeting in 1822 to try to come up with a plan to clean up the air. A bill was introduced in the 1879 municipal assembly to require locomotives chugging through town to reduce the amount of black smoke they belched. But the powerful railroad lobby sidetracked the bill.

The Westmoreland/Portland trustees decided to attack the smoke problem on their own. A May 5, 1895, article in the *St. Louis Republic* reported:

In the good days to come St. Louis will doubtless be a smokeless city. . . . But the owners in Westmoreland and Portland Places have solved the problem without waiting for the aid of science and municipal pressure. No bituminous coal may be used in this new area. And there is no smoke blown into these streets since they both are north of Forest Park and the prevailing breeze is from the south.

While that evaluation was true for 1895, ten years later the relatively clean air above these two private places had been filled with thick smoke from the entire city. The vision of the founders of Westmoreland/Portland had been almost obscured by airborne soot.

In 1901 Mayor Rolla Wells appointed a chief smoke inspector for the city. The inspector carried an impressive title but had little authority. Darker days followed. In 1927 a nationally respected engineer called St. Louis "the dirtiest city in the nation." It was estimated that the average St. Louisan inhaled more than a tablespoon of grime each day. Aviators begged the city to keep the Lambert Field beacons burning during the daylight hours so pilots could find the landing strip—after they found the airport.

Those city residents who could afford to move began fleeing to the cleaner air of the suburbs. Westmoreland and Portland

In 1957 fire caused heavy damage to 11 Westmoreland, a Grable & Weber house built in 1891 for the Thomas Henry West family. The owners of the house decided it was cheaper to tear it down than to renovate it. The structure was demolished in 1958.

residents, too, began to abandon their beautiful mansions.

Dawn on Tuesday, November 28, 1939, found St. Louis immersed in a thick shroud of smoke. Panic overcame the city. Street lights were turned on at nine in the morning. This "black Tuesday" forced the city administration to act. The Smoke Elimination Committee quickly elected James L. Ford, Jr., a Westmoreland resident, to tackle the job of cleaning up the air. Mayor Bernard F. Dickman and Smoke Commissioner Raymond Tucker planned and initiated the city's monumental air-purification program, and the energetic Ford carried it out. A banker by profession, Ford admitted that he knew nothing about smoke abatement. But he also knew that, on bad days, St. Louisans could not see their hands in front of their faces.

Ford was offered $25,000 to conduct a survey. He refused the offer. He said it would be a waste of money to spend another penny analyzing the problem. The source of the problem was more than evident. "There's no sense in spending money to find out how filthy we are," Ford reasoned. "Just look out of a window. What's more, we don't need experts to tell us how to get rid of smoke. The way to do that is to burn smokeless fuel, or to burn other fuels in a manner that will not permit it to smoke."

With Ford leading the way, the city got tough and required that households burn coal with no more than 23 percent volatile matter, the so-called "smokeless coal." Thirteen inspectors were armed with cameras and stopwatches. Factories were allowed to produce only six minutes of heavy smoke a day, while their furnaces were being stoked. Railroad locomotives were permitted only one minute of smoke-belching inside the city limits. Offenders could be fined as much as a hundred dollars a day.

The results of the smoke abatement program were spectacular. Consumers reported getting as much as 30 percent more heat from the smokeless coal. Dry-cleaning, laundry, and house-painting bills decreased sharply throughout the city. Office supplies and furnishings did not have to be replaced as often in a smoke-free environment. During the winter of 1939–1940, St. Louis residents groped through 177 hours of smoke-induced blackness. After the smoke-abatement law was passed and enforced, residents during the following winter suffered through only 19 hours of dense smoke.

James L. Ford's other contributions to the stability of life in Westmoreland Place were monumental. In 1920 Ford bought 54 Westmoreland from the Walter McKittricks. In 1941, after the smoke cleared, Ford bought the house at 33 Westmoreland and presented it to his daughter Elsie Ford Curby and her husband, John. Westmoreland residents may have emitted more than a few hallelujahs, since the mansion, once owned by Charles Parsons Pettus, had stood shuttered and vacant for nearly five years. Next Ford purchased 52 Westmoreland for his daughter Jean and her husband, Edward C. Simmons II.

Elsie and John Curby may have shocked some of their neighbors when they announced their plans to demolish Number 33 and build another house on the site. Elsie Curby remembers:

The three-story Pettus mansion was gigantic. It included an art gallery which ran along Lake Avenue. It was an impossible house to manage for a young couple. We had been married for only five years at the time Father purchased the house. Raymond Maritz [of the firm of Maritz, Young & Dusard] had difficulty getting building supplies because of the war. But Mr. Maritz designed a much more manageable and much more salable four-bedroom house for us. In fact, people who were apprehensive about our tearing down a historic house let us know they appreciated the handsome and more practical home that rose to replace the old one. The Depression and

This picture was taken at 8:55 on the morning of December 22, 1939. Even though the Westmoreland / Portland covenant banned the burning of soft coal, the two private places suffered from the thick smoke that enshrouded all of St. Louis. A Westmoreland Place resident, James L. Ford, is credited with cleaning up the city's stifling smoke problem.

then World War II had a devastating effect on efforts to maintain big houses.

In fact, because of a critical shortage of supplies, the government put a ceiling of $500 per year per household on home improvements. It was during those war years that some of the grand mansions in Westmoreland and Portland and in many other private places began to show signs of wear. The meager sum of $500 was not nearly enough to maintain a twenty-to-thirty-room house that was subject to a leaky roof, sagging gutters, broken windowpanes, fallen plaster, peeling paint, creaking flooring, and other maintenance problems. The limit was especially constrictive because some carriage houses and

garages in Westmoreland / Portland are as large as many homes in the city.

Elsie Curby's sister Jean and her husband, Edward Simmons, took less drastic steps to make their home more livable. Mrs. Simmons remembers:

We moved into Number 52 right before Pearl Harbor. My father purchased the home from Mr. and Mrs. Robert D. Lewis. The interior was rather dark and foreboding, all dark woodwork. It had a stairway which ran all the way from the first floor to the third floor. It was lovely, but its openness didn't contribute anything to energy efficiency. The home was terribly difficult to heat. For heating economy we shut off the staircase at the second floor level. We really didn't need the third floor for living quarters, although our son often used the third floor as a playroom. A maid also used part of the third floor quarters for a while. We also removed a back stairway, converted one parlor into a large living room and turned the other parlor into a dining room.

The Simmonses also removed a four-column, two-story portico. After the alterations, Jean and Edward Simmons settled down for several decades of contentment with their house.

World War II had another devastating effect on the stability of the private places in St. Louis. During the war years, the once-loyal domestic army made up of butlers, maids, nannies, gardeners, laundresses, chauffeurs, and cooks left their service to homeowners and signed up for work at defense plants in the area. These domestics were able to double, triple, or even quadruple the salaries they had made as servants.

Beatrice Jackson came to cook for the senior George Conants in 1942, but she stayed with them for only a year. She recalls:

> I was making $15 a week with the Conants. They were really lovely people and I enjoyed cooking for them. But even after taxes were taken out I could make a little over $30 a week at the [small arms] plant. . . . A lot of the help in private family homes took those jobs at the arms plant because the money was too good to pass up. And many of them didn't go back to work in homes after the war.

Mrs. Norris Allen remembers that her parents, the Isaac Hedges, lost two members of the household staff during the war but were able to keep two. Many of the Westmoreland/Portland homeowners did not fare as well. The absence of servants soon became evident as hands that had never done menial labor attempted to hold house and property together. Homeowners in Westmoreland and Portland who had never mowed lawns, cooked, ironed a shirt, washed a window, stoked a fire, or tended a garden found themselves trying to keep up the interior and exterior appearances of their homes. The failure of some homeowners to maintain their houses' exteriors was one of the most obvious manifestations of the domestic exodus. The trustees relaxed the strict covenant rules that state that "no property owner shall cause or permit weeds, underbrush, grass cuttings, broken branches, roughage or refuse of any character to accumulate or remain anywhere in the Subdivision."

Ironically, the next concern for Westmoreland/Portland owners came from the buffers the founders had erected to protect their privacy. In 1959, when the city of St. Louis began to clean up the Mill Creek area, devastated by a tornado in

Ione Huse Hedges's father built 9 Westmoreland. She is shown above in 1948 with her husband, Isaac A. Hedges. The Hedges were among the Westmoreland/Portland residents who lost their domestic help to munitions plants during World War II. To the left is the dining room of 9 Westmoreland as it looked in the late 1940s.

1957, some displaced families began to move into the apartment houses ringing the exclusive neighborhood. As lower-income families moved into the already declining area, class and racially based apprehension increased, and so did crime. Houses in Westmoreland/Portland where doors had remained unlocked began to be outfitted with large, high-security locks. Many homeowners who had weathered other storms packed up and left. Property values plummeted, and many residents took whatever price they could negotiate before they fled to the western suburbs, just as their predecessors had fled from other ethnic invasions near Lucas and Vandeventer places generations earlier.

A third-generation resident of Portland Place remembers the challenging conditions of the 1950s:

> My brother was talking with one of the district policemen who said that at the district station, Westmoreland and Portland were referred to as "the Alamo" because of the crime wave that had gripped the neighborhood. I suppose the rioting in other cities around the country in the 1960s put some fear into some of the people who live around here.

By the mid-sixties the apartment houses around Westmoreland/Portland, virtually abandoned by their owners, had begun to look like bombed-out Berlin. Scores of homes were for sale in Westmoreland and Portland and in all the nearby private neighborhoods. Nay-sayers worked to convince the few stalwart souls who refused to move that the city was doomed, and appearances seemed to support that view.

Waterman Boulevard, from Kingshighway to Union, on the immediate north side of the Westmoreland/Portland enclave became an eyesore. The mixture of handsome single-family homes, duplexes, and apartment houses decayed like the portrait of Dorian Gray. Single-family homes were converted by landlords to rooming houses. With the city cooperating by failing to enforce building codes, the fear of muggings, rapes, robberies, and burglaries threatened the future of the genteel private places in the area.

Pershing Avenue, just north of Lindell Boulevard and west of Westmoreland/Portland, also took on a nightmarish appearance. This three-block thoroughfare with its majestic apartment houses from Union to DeBaliviere deteriorated into a devastated wasteland. As racial segregation broke down, middle-class white flight accelerated and the structures were filled with low-income residents. Belt and Clara avenues, which were tributaries of Pershing to the north, also fell into ruin. Owners of apartment houses cited their inability to collect rents from tenants and tenant vandalism as justifying their own abdication of maintenance.

Leon Strauss, president of Pantheon Corporation, redevelopers of buildings now housing more than thirteen hundred units near Westmoreland and Portland, thinks the decline of the large apartment houses began after the end of World War II:

> After the war there was an intense desire among apartment dwellers to get a patch of green. Aided by FHA and the highway department that gave us Highway 40, the people who lived in the West End apartment houses were able to buy little homes in the nearby suburbs. The tenants in these apartments in the 1950s were upwardly mobile clerks, department store workers, and office workers. We know they didn't have cars because some of the apartment houses had as many as ninety or more units and only a half-dozen parking spaces. That suggests that everybody was riding to and from work on the streetcars and buses. It's interesting that streetcars helped destroy some early first-class neighborhoods, but were actually a plus for the West End.
>
> So they moved out of the apartment houses in droves. They left landlords with no income stream. When a landlord found himself with thirty or forty percent occupancy, he either dropped the rent, cut the apartments into smaller, cheaper units, or in some cases the landlords just walked away from the properties and let them rot. In the 1960s and 1970s there were many apartment buildings just west of Westmoreland and Portland which had been condemned for occupancy.
>
> I'm sure some of the flight had racial implications. Landlords who had traditionally barred blacks from occupancy suddenly had to make the choice of whether to remain discriminatory and go without tenants or rent to blacks and take their rent money. Some buildings had a predominantly black occupancy and eventually became all black.

The crumbling of the city's West End reached its nadir at the same time as the downfall of what turned out to be the nation's biggest public housing fiasco. Located just northwest of downtown, the Pruitt-Igoe Housing Project had opened in 1954. Plagued with endless problems, most of them built in by the planners, a mass abandonment of the project was occurring just as the West End was being inundated with low-income residents.

Nonetheless, Westmoreland and Portland places beat all the odds. The restrictive traffic patterns, the brick and stone sturdiness of the houses, the sheer magnificence of the architecture, a band of residents who refused to flee, and a group of adventurous souls who moved in to take on new challenges once houses had been abandoned were all forces of salvation for Westmoreland and Portland. The proud houses have stood in the face of the deaths of their creators, the subsequent abandonment by heirs, the Great Depression, the smoke menace, crime, white flight, enveloping blight, and other elements that reduced earlier private places to ashes. And the future of Westmoreland/Portland today appears brighter than ever before. Houses are almost always sold before they go on the open market. Many of the current homeowners have standing offers on their homes, especially from devotees of outstanding architecture. One house in Westmoreland recently sold for a reported $650,000—a far cry from the $5,000 and $6,000 James Ford paid for the houses for his daughters in 1941. The heirs to one palatial mansion in Portland were asking more than $1 million for it in 1986.

To further ensure that the names *Westmoreland* and *Portland* will be etched in the history of classic American architecture, two private places were modeled from them, in Phoenix and Houston.

A *House and Garden* article written in March 1983 praised Westmoreland/Portland. In summing up a reason today's residents of the two premier private places have to be proud of their invincibility, the article stated:

> There are many sights to see in St. Louis—the Arch, Louis Sullivan's Wainwright Building, Eads Bridge—but the connoisseur of the house and garden should see above all else Portland and Westmoreland Places. St. Louis is unique among American cities for its private residential streets, and of the 50-odd examples that still survive, Portland and Westmoreland are the most magnificent, a high point in the history of American residential enclaves.

May it ever be so.

A COLOR PORTFOLIO OF WESTMORELAND AND PORTLAND

Designed by Eames & Young in 1890, 6 Westmoreland is one of a number of houses in Westmoreland and Portland in the Richardsonian Romanesque style.

The building permit for 7 Westmoreland
was issued on February 25, 1890, making it the oldest house still standing in
either Westmoreland or Portland.

Also begun in 1890, 9 Westmoreland, another Eames & Young design, took several years to complete because of the problems involved in moving the Missouri granite from the quarry over unpaved and often muddy roads. The portraits are of the house's original owners, Martha and William L. Huse. Their granddaughter Dorothea Hedges Allen and her husband, Norris, have lived here since 1959, making this the only house in either Westmoreland or Portland still lived in by a descendant of the original family.

The residence at 5 Westmoreland was designed by Eames & Young for Theodore and Lucretia Meysenburg, and construction on it began in August 1891. The carriage house was started nine months later, in May 1892. Horses were stabled there as recently as 1984.

The first building permit in Portland Place was issued July 24, 1891, for Number 39, the Queen Anne style house to the right. The central gable of the Tudor Revival house at 22 Westmoreland (below) was half-timbered when the house was built in 1891. The lower parts of the house were of mottled yellow brickwork. On the facing page is 29 Portland, which was designed by Theodore Link for the Tebbetts family, also in 1891. The half-timbered upper walls of this house were originally shingled.

Illustrated on pages 96–98 is the French Renaissance, or Châteauesque, mansion begun at 13 Portland for W. K. Bixby in late 1892. Although Bixby sold the house in 1904, his son William H. and his wife, Stella, purchased it in 1923. William H. Bixby lived here until his death in 1967, and Stella remained in the house until she died in 1987. The brick walls were originally of two shades, with contrasting terra-cotta around the doors and windows.

The carriage house and porte cochere of the Bixby house at 13 Portland.

Built in 1892, the Italian Renaissance residence at 23 Portland was designed by Eames & Young. The combination of richly carved ornamentation and short third-floor windows is derived from the Library of San Marco in Venice. The entrance from the porte cochere has a cozy inglenook with a fireplace to warm guests.

The short third-floor windows and stone swags of this residence at 25 Portland, built in 1892, can be seen on many of the Italian Renaissance buildings in Westmoreland and Portland. The Jackson Johnson family lived here for more than forty years. Three of Johnson's children, his brother, and a grandson also owned houses in Westmoreland/Portland.

Designed in 1892 by Peabody, Stearns & Furber, 17 Westmoreland, shown on pages 102–4, was the first of a number of palazzo-style residences in Westmoreland/Portland. The first residents were Maria Filley Davis, daughter of former Mayor O. D. Filley, and her sons.

The gallery, sitting room, porte cochere, and carriage house of 17 Westmoreland as they appear today. The carriage house, like many of the carriage houses in Westmoreland and Portland, has been renovated as a living quarters for the household servants. Plaques naming horses that have been stabled here remain on the walls inside.

Built in 1892, 38 Westmoreland is an example of Peabody, Stearns & Furber's use of the Queen Anne style and is similar in shape to the original 21 Westmoreland, the first house built in either Westmoreland or Portland.

In the French Renaissance, or Châteauesque, style, 19 Portland was designed in 1893 by Grable & Weber, who two years earlier had offered a Romanesque design for the original 11 Westmoreland.

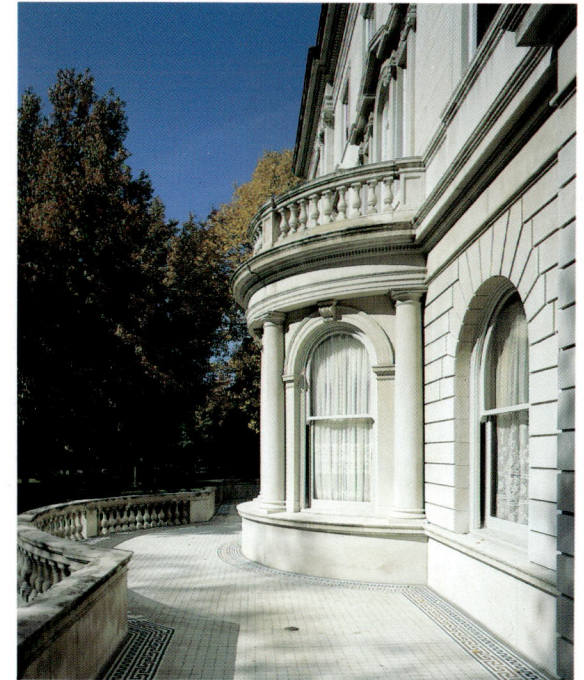

Another great palazzo, the house at 1 Westmoreland was designed by W. Albert Swasey in 1894. The conservatory to the right of the house in these photographs was added in 1900. Among the house's interior features are the mirrored center column in the large ballroom and the mosaics in the front entryway.

Begun in 1892 for the John D. Filley family, 40 Westmoreland is an example of Tudor Revival architecture.

Built in 1894, 29 Westmoreland originally had a columned center entrance, a stone porch on the east (right) side, a porte cochere on the west side, and a frieze of carved swags between the third-floor windows.

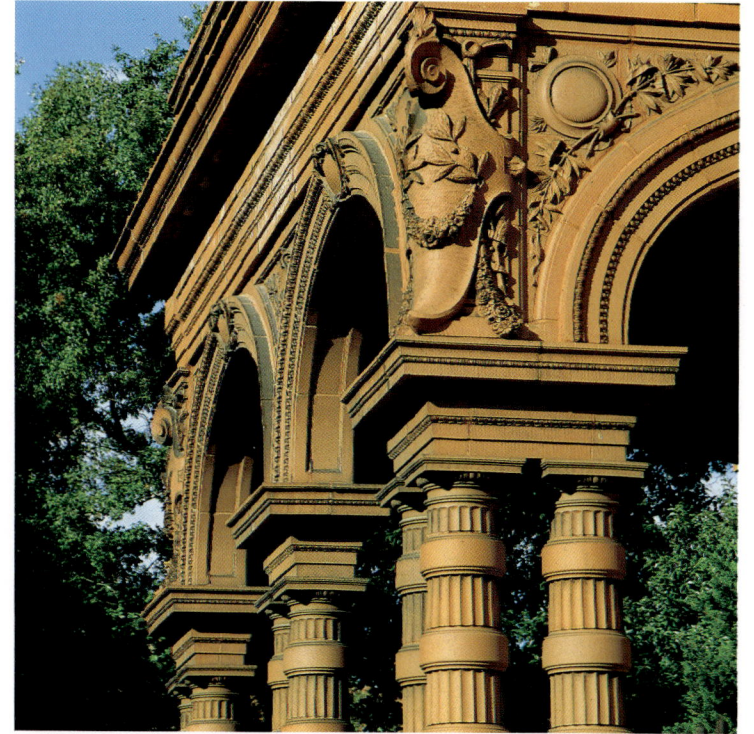

The only house in Westmoreland or Portland by architect John L. Wees, 10 Westmoreland was begun in 1895. The grand staircase originates in the reception hall and ends in a large gallery that occupies one-third of the second floor. The landing halfway up the stairs extends into a fourteen-foot alcove with a large art-glass window and a hemidome ceiling of art glass in a fine fish-scale pattern.

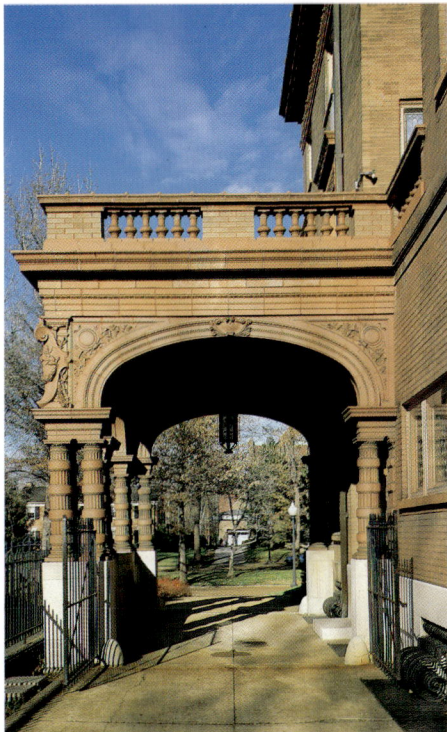

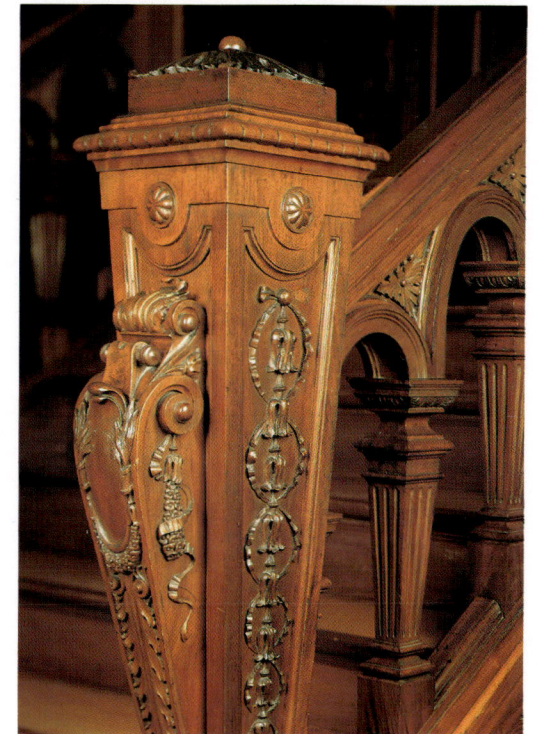

Built in 1896 for Judge and Mrs. Elmer B. Adams, 25 Westmoreland was later
the home of Mayor Rolla Wells and his wife, Carlota, for twenty-three years.

This house at 30 Portland was designed by Weber & Groves in 1897 for Elizabeth and Benjamin Clark.

Begun in 1897 for John and Belle Robb Holmes, 9 Portland has been home for members of the Birch and Laura McBride Mahaffey family for more than sixty years. Designed by Shepley, Rutan & Coolidge and John Lawrence Mauran, the house is built of Bedford limestone in a Beaux Arts style.

The residence and carriage house at 40 Portland were built in 1897 for Bettie and George W. Brown. The east part of the house (to the left in the photograph on the facing page) was added in 1908.

The Brown house was the last one to be built in Westmoreland or Portland in the Richardsonian Romanesque style.

The building permit for 15 Portland, built for the William D. Orthweins, was issued on July 26, 1898. The house was purchased by Marie and Joseph Desloge in 1941 from the heirs of Orthwein's daughter-in-law Jeanette. The Desloges continued to live at Vouziers, their estate overlooking the Missouri River, while maintaining 15 Portland for the family's social activities in the city.

Designed in 1898, 32 Portland is similar in shape and form to its neighbor at Number 30, designed the previous year. In 1931 the owner, Dr. Isaac D. Kelley, St. Louis's leading ear, nose, and throat specialist, was the victim of a widely publicized kidnapping that lasted eight days. The dining room at 32 Portland has a mural of exotic birds and flowers applied by Kathleen McBride Kelley in the 1920s and renovated by the present owners.

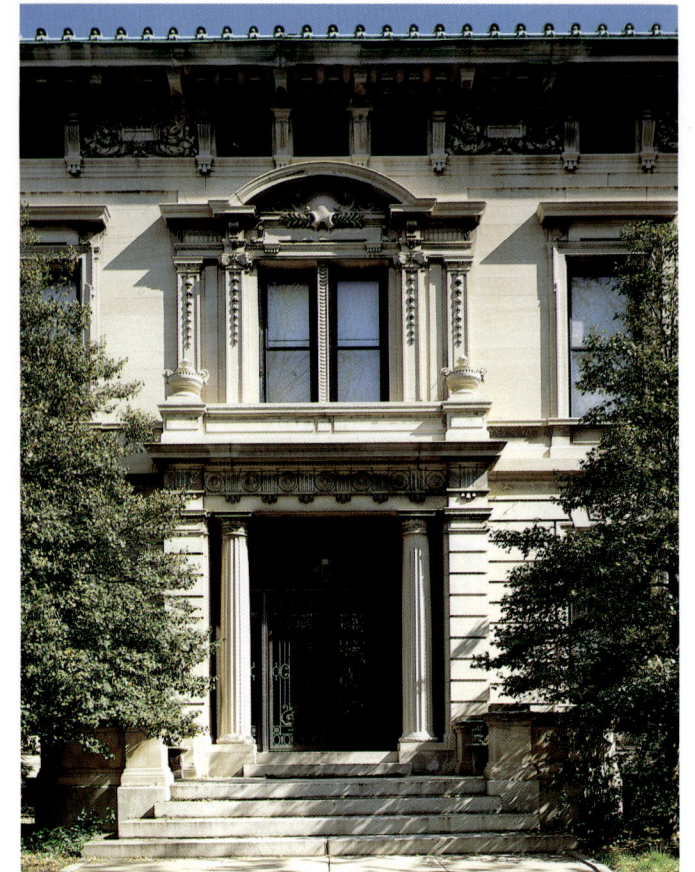

The Edwards Whitaker house, 13 Westmoreland, was designed by Ernst Janssen and built in 1899. Emma Whitaker Davis, the daughter of the first owners, and her husband, Samuel C. Davis, from next door at Number 17, lived here most of their married life.

A wooden balustrade originally connected the east and west chimneys of this house at 47 Portland. It was the first of a number of Georgian Revival style houses built in Westmoreland and Portland.

The building permit was issued in December 1905 for this residence at 12 Portland. It was designed by Mauran, Russell & Garden in the style of Frank Lloyd Wright's Prairie School. The third owner was William D. Crowell, who, as a later partner of Mauran & Russell, designed 33 Portland and 31 and 35 Westmoreland.

The Isaac Lionberger house at 37 Westmoreland, also begun in 1905, was originally three stories tall; the third floor with six large rooms and three baths was removed in 1949, and the carriage house was converted to a three-car garage.

The house at 38 Portland was designed in 1905 by Theodore Link. The original owners, Irene and Oscar Johnson, Sr., later enclosed the entrance loggia.

Number 52 Westmoreland was designed in 1905 for Herman and May Luyties, who a year later built a more expensive house at 36 Portland. The Westmoreland house was completed for Hariette and Carl Gray and was altered by Jean Ford and E. C. Simmons in 1941. It originally had a two-story portico, and the stonework alternated smooth and rough-faced courses.

Construction of the Georgian style house at 41 Westmoreland began in the same week in 1905 as did work on its neighbor at Number 37. These were the first of fourteen houses in Westmoreland/Portland designed by James P. Jamieson, the most prolific of the architects who worked in these two places. The Daniel Catlins (Jr.) lived here for nearly sixty years. The George Caleb Bingham portrait hanging over the mantel in the dining room is of Gen. Richard Gentry, whose great-great-granddaughter is a current owner.

The house at 20 Westmoreland, begun in 1906 and designed in plum brick by Lawrence Ewald, is reminiscent of H. H. Richardson's work in that rare material.

A Georgian style house designed by James P. Jamieson for Amy and Clarkson Potter, 42 Westmoreland was also begun in 1906.

Three houses were built in Portland Place in 1907. Number 44 was designed for Robert H. and Julia Keiser by Frederick Bonsack.

The fourth Westmoreland/Portland house to be built in 1906, 37 Portland originally housed Flora and David Gamble and many of their eleven children.

Number 36 Portland is similar to but larger than 52 Westmoreland. Both houses were commissioned by Herman and May Luyties, but they abandoned the Westmoreland house for the one in Portland. The latter house was built in 1906 and was designed by A. A. Fischer. It sits majestically at the corner of Lake Avenue and Portland Place. The carriage house overlooks a walled garden and pool.

Two houses in Portland were built for members of the Kauffman family in 1907. Number 48 was built for Nellie Bronson Kauffman after the death of her husband, John W. She sold the Kauffmans' elaborate mansion at Kingshighway and Lindell Blvd. to William K. Bixby, who had built 13 Portland.

Number 51 was built for Janet Morton and Harold Kauffman across the street from his mother's house. Janet Kauffman lived here for more than sixty years. These were the first of a dozen designs by Louis LaBeaume (with Guy C. Mariner and later Eugene S. Klein) for Westmoreland and Portland.

Ellen and George P. Doan were the first owners of 42 Portland. It was later home to the Solomon Roos family for forty years. This was another of the eight houses built in Westmoreland/Portland in 1908, and it was also designed by Mariner & LaBeaume.

Built in 1908, 46 Westmoreland is one of a number of "proto-Georgian" houses at the west end of Westmoreland designed by Mariner & LaBeaume. Its first residents were the William A. Stickney family.

The Tudor style house at 10 Portland has its main entry on the side. It was designed by Mauran, Russell & Garden in 1908 for William and Katherine Guy.

The house at 36 Westmoreland was built in 1908 on a lot
Samuel Fordyce sold to Louis Werner. It was designed by
Hellmuth & Spiering.

At 48 Westmoreland is another Mariner & LaBeaume house. It was designed for Rebekah and Allen West in 1908, at the same time as its neighbor at Number 46.

Built in 1908, 53 Westmoreland was commissioned by Hannah and
Leopold Freund. William A. Lucas's design is Italian Eclectic with yellow
Roman brick of the type used by Frank Lloyd Wright. The west wing (to
the left in this photograph) was added in 1914 by Mauran, Russell &
Crowell for the house's second owners, Charles and Elizabeth Bailey.

Harry Langenberg built 49 Westmoreland in 1908 as a wedding present for his wife, Alice. She lived there until 1980, longer than any other
resident in these places. The house is one of the three Mariner &
LaBeaume houses constructed in Westmoreland in 1908.

Constructed of poured concrete in 1908, 50 Westmoreland was designed by Mauran, Russell & Garden for Emily and Arthur B. Shepley. Though it has classical proportions, the house has very simple details.

The residence at 47 Westmoreland, started in 1909, was the last of Eames & Young's nine commissions in Westmoreland and Portland. It reflects their collegiate and monastic design sources. It was built for Nora Wilcoxson Holland, whose husband, George, died in 1902.

Designed by Mauran, Russell & Garden in 1909, 34 Westmoreland is a unique design in a style similar to the early Prairie School. The first two stories are of brick, while the third is stucco.

The house at 16 Portland was designed for Dwight F. Davis in 1909. It was sold to Andrew Johnson in 1927 after Davis left St. Louis for government service. Johnson added a solarium and second-floor dressing room to the east (left) side. Johnson was, like Dwight Davis, a tennis buff, and he brought many of the world's great tennis players of the 1930s and 1940s to the house's red clay tennis court. The carriage house contains servants' living quarters and a four-car garage.

The massive entry of the Tudor Revival house at 26 Portland, built in 1909, is reminiscent of a medieval gatehouse. William K. Bixby, the builder of 13 Portland, purchased this house in 1922 and lived here with his wife, Lillian, until his death in 1931.

The house at 24 Portland was designed in 1910 by Ernst C. Janssen for Elizabeth Schnaider, whose husband, Joseph, was founder of the Green Tree Brewery. It was converted in 1966 from "brewer's baronial," with gables, brick dormers, and leaded windows, to its present-day Georgian style.

147

The last and the grandest of the "palazzi," 1 Portland (shown on pages 148–50) was built in 1910 as a wedding present for Anna Busch and Edward Faust at a reported cost of $100,000. A second ballroom was added to the ground floor in 1915 for an additional $20,000. Inscribed in limestone on the porte cochere is "Tom P. Barnett, Architect."

Details of the magnificent mansion at 1 Portland.

The house at 30 Westmoreland was designed in 1910 by James P. Jamieson for Mary
Lionberger, who moved to Westmoreland Place from Vandeventer Place after her parents died.

In the style of an eighteenth-century French mansion, 33 Portland (illustrated on pages 152–55) was designed in 1911 by Mauran, Russell & Crowell. The first owners of this house were Claude and Dorothy Kilpatrick.

153

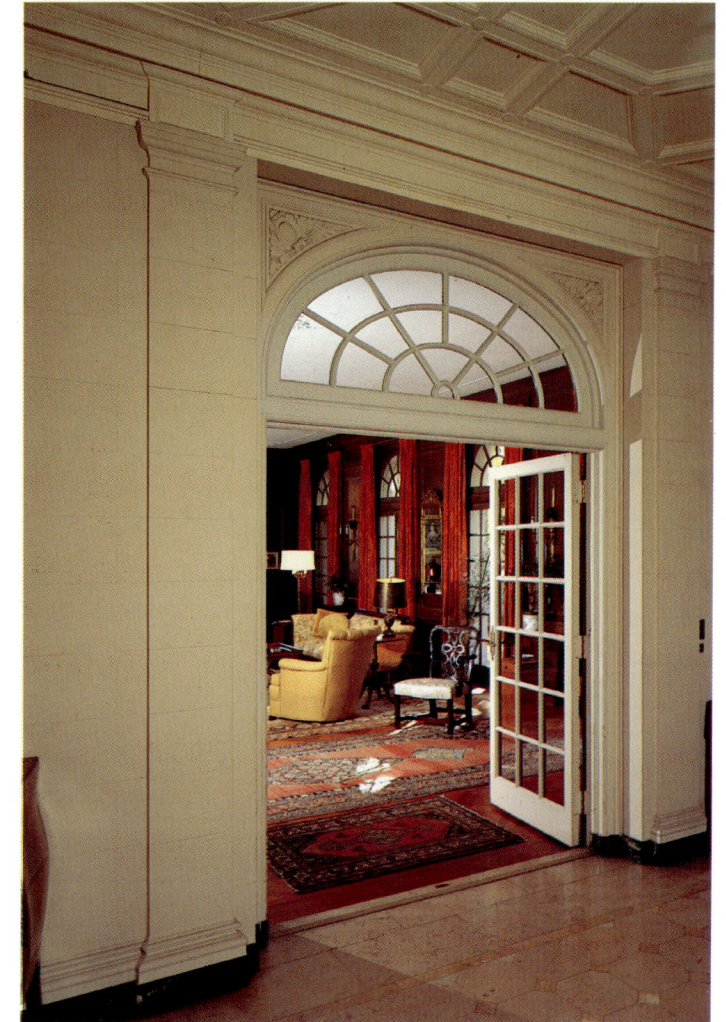

The eighty-foot-long house at 33 Portland has a sixty-five-foot-long hallway with marble floor, baseboards, and columns.

Built of rough-cut Missouri granite, 35 Portland was designed by Kivas Tully for Mary and George Barnard in 1911. This was the first of three Westmoreland/Portland homes owned by Dr. Isaac D. and Kathleen McBride Kelley. The current owners have decorated the entrance hallway with nineteenth-century French bronzes and a portrait by the English painter Sir William Beechey.

Begun in 1911, 43 Portland is another "brewer's baronial" residence by Ernst Janssen. It was built for Mrs. Isaac W. Morton (Jeanette Filley, daughter of former Mayor O. D. Filley) three doors east of the house of her daughter Mrs. Harold Kauffman.

This mansion at 8 Portland was built in 1912 for Lemuel and May Carter. Their daughter Margaret, later Lady Clifden, had linenfold natural oak panels from an old abbey brought from England in the 1930s and installed inside the house. The confessional door shown here has a bullet hole said to have been left by Cromwell in his 1642–1649 campaign to destroy abbeys and monasteries. The photograph on the table shows William McBride Love and his cousins Adelaide Mahaffey Schlafly and Katherine Mahaffey Walsh as children. Mr. Love grew up at 35 and 32 Portland and owned 8 Portland at the time of his death. Mrs. Schlafly and Mrs. Walsh grew up at 9 Portland and now live in Westmoreland Place.

The front door of the 1912 house at 46 Portland, designed by James P. Jamieson, originally had delicately patterned sidelights embellishing its much admired pedimented doorway.

Built in 1912, 50 Portland is a James P. Jamieson creation for Edith and H. Blakesley Collins. The living room of the current owners displays items from their eclectic collection of art objects. Hanging to the left in the photograph below is an oil painting by St. Louis artist E. Oscar Thalinger. The mask on the mantel is African; the plates on either side of it are Chinese export porcelain, Chien Lung circa 1748; the figures beside them are of Shakespeare and Milton by Thomas Parr, Staffordshire, circa 1840.

Designed for Sarah and John Foster Shepley by
Louis LaBeaume, 53 Portland was built in 1912.

The house at 35 Westmoreland was built in 1912 for John and Cora Liggett Fowler. It was designed by Mauran, Russell & Crowell and like 50 Westmoreland is a surprising early use of concrete.

The house at 54 Westmoreland was built in 1913 for Marjorie and Walter McKittrick. The brickwork in this design by James P. Jamieson is beautifully detailed with contrasting shades.

Begun in 1912 for Bertha Drake Scott (widow of Henry C. Scott), 31 Westmoreland was designed by Mauran, Russell & Crowell. Fourteen years earlier the same firm had designed another house for the Scott family in Vandeventer Place.

James P. Jamieson won a gold medal from the St. Louis Art League for his 1913 design for the Mallinckrodt house at 16 Westmoreland. The portrait reflected in the mirror over the living room mantel is of Andrew Sproule, the great-grand-father of the present owner.

Built in 1914 for Anne and Charles Nagel, 44 Westmoreland has been occupied for more than sixty years by members of the Edward K. Love family.

Designed by Hellmuth & Hellmuth, 52 Portland was built in 1915 for Ida and Charles Bascom.

The stained-glass window above the marble stairway in the entrance to 51 Westmoreland has inserts with the initials of Daniel Catlin, for whom the house was designed by James P. Jamieson in 1915.

Hellmuth & Hellmuth designed 6 Portland in 1915 for Mina and Alfred L. Shapleigh.
The design incorporates a prominent stair turret into the Colonial-Italian style.

The residence at 56 Portland was started for Mary and Herbert Edmunds in 1915 but finished for Lotawana and Eugene Nims, who lived here for fifty-three years.

The house at 17 Portland was built in 1916 from a James P. Jamieson design as a wedding present for Ella and Charles Wiggins, who lived here until the 1940s. Ella Liggett Wiggins's sisters Dolly and Cora had houses built at 33 Portland and 35 Westmoreland five years earlier. The three Liggett women were daughters of Liggett & Meyers tobacco tycoon John Liggett.

Built in 1919, 28 Portland is another James P. Jamieson design. Claude Saugrain Kennerly lived here for fifty years. The marble floor in the dining room nicely complements the Venetian glass chandelier.

The house at 32 Westmoreland was designed in 1923 for Almira and Edwin H. Steedman. Steedman's brother George lived next door at Number 34. Steedman family members occupied these two houses for more than fifty years, and another brother lived at 42 Westmoreland prior to his death in 1921.

Designed in 1927 by LaBeaume & Klein, 20 Portland was built for Emilie and J. D. Perry Francis. The staircase of this house, like that of its neighbors at Numbers 16 and 22, crosses over the main entry.

Built for Julia and N. S. Chouteau Walsh, 7 Portland is another of three
houses designed by LaBeaume & Klein for Portland Place in 1927.

The residence at 22 Portland was built for Mary and Marion Lambert in 1927 on a lot purchased from Wallace Simmons. The Lambert monogram is visible over the entry door.

Iva and Selwyn C. Edgar, Jr., built 41 Portland in 1929 in a
classic Georgian Colonial brick design by Hellmuth & Hellmuth.

Number 8 is the first of six houses in Westmoreland designed by Gale Henderson.
It was built for Marguerite and Ralph W. Coale in 1930. Its living room has a
fireplace that was originally in a Vandeventer Place mansion.

Built in 1931 for Frances Filley and Thomas S. McPheeters, 27 Westmoreland was the last house built on a hitherto undeveloped lot in either Westmoreland or Portland. It was also James P. Jamieson's fourteenth and last design in the enclave.

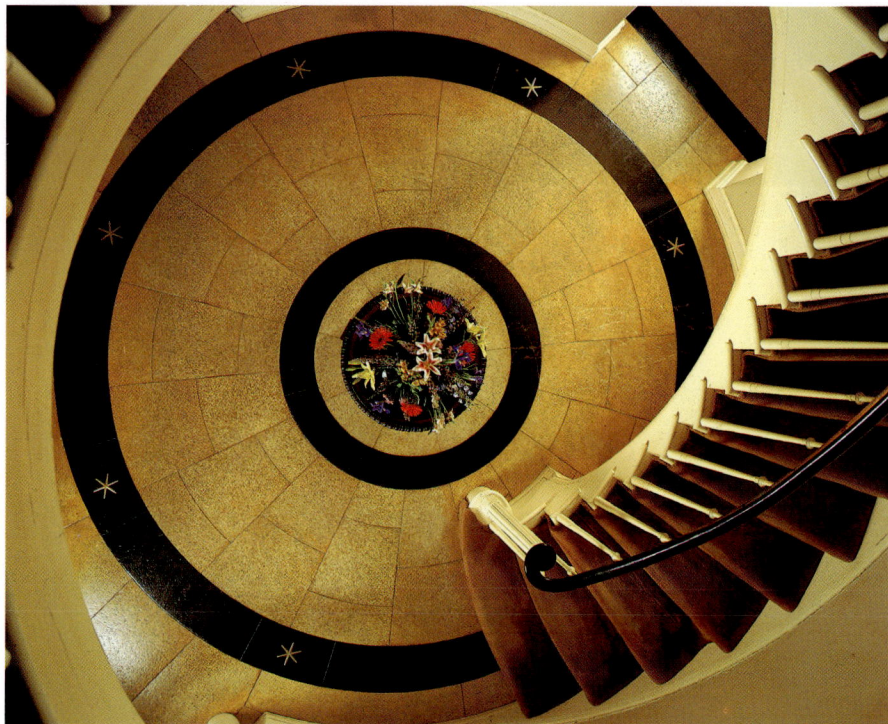

The current 12 Westmoreland, built in 1938, is the second house to stand on this lot. It was built for Erma and Arthur Proetz and was designed by Ralph Cole Hall.

The house currently at 28 Westmoreland was designed and built in 1939 by Gale Henderson for Eugenia and Sterling Edmunds to replace the original Emma Copelin house.

The current 45 Westmoreland was also built in 1939 and designed by Gale Henderson.

This Georgian Revival house, also designed by Henderson, was built in 1941 at 21 Westmoreland to replace the very first house built in either Westmoreland or Portland. The original house was demolished in 1941, but the carriage house still stands as the oldest existing structure in either place. The houses on this lot were owned by Edward C. Simmons and his descendants for ninety-four years.

The current 33 Westmoreland was built in 1941 by Elsie and John Curby because they desired a more manageable house than the one that originally stood on this lot. This house was designed by Maritz, Young & Dusard.

The second house to stand at 26 Westmoreland was built in 1941 for Elizabeth and Warne Niedringhaus from a design by Gale Henderson.

The house at 23 Westmoreland was built in 1950 for Harry and Constance Mathews to replace the Helen and Hudson Bridge house. It was the sixth and last house designed by Gale Henderson in Westmoreland. Former Mayor of St. Louis A. J. Cervantes and his wife, Carmen, resided here in the 1970s after having lived at 51 Westmoreland in the 1960s.

Work began in 1953 on the second house on the lot at 45 Portland, the only contemporary design in either Westmoreland or Portland. It was created for Isabel and Howard Baer by Frederick Dunn.

The Annie and Samuel Kennard house, built in 1891 at 4 Portland, was razed in 1958. This house, numbered 2 Portland, rose
on the same lot in 1960. It was designed by Alfred J. Johnson.

The original Florence and Thomas West house at 11 Westmoreland
was demolished in 1958 following a fire. This neo-Georgian
structure replaced it in 1960. It is an Alfred J. Johnson design.

THE ARCHITECTS AND ARCHITECTURE

by Esley Hamilton

The current appearance of Westmoreland and Portland places is the result not of a single vision or a sustained campaign of building but of construction stretching over more than a generation and of designs by more than two dozen architectural firms, many with sharply contrasting ideas of what was appropriate. Furthermore, during the time that these houses were being built, a major transformation occurred in people's thinking about what a city house should be. The once highly desired formality was replaced by a studied informality, and rather than drawing themselves up to their full height, houses settled down as though relaxing. Several of the houses in the old style did not survive this change in thinking, while others were altered to suit new tastes. Throughout, however, Westmoreland and Portland places were served by the best talent in design and craftsmanship that St. Louis had to offer, and it is ultimately this standard of excellence that gives the places their unity.

This chapter examines the architecture of the places in terms of the stylistic categories into which the houses can be classified. (All of the houses in Westmoreland and Portland discussed here are illustrated in the Chronology of Owners, which follows.) While several styles enjoyed popularity at the same time, there was a general progression that can be divided into three phases. When construction started, the popular styles were the waning Queen Anne and the fast-emerging Richardsonian Romanesque. These were soon displaced by more classical designs derived from the Renaissance, both Italian and French. The turn of the century brought renewed interest in Tudor and Georgian Revivals and also a search by some architects for a new nonhistorical style. In St. Louis, the leading architects adapted their vision to these changing trends.

From an architectural point of view, the key event of 1886, the year before the Forest Park Improvement Association was incorporated, was the death of the architect H. H. Richardson in Boston. Only forty-seven years old, Richardson had changed the direction of American architecture through his very per-

sonal use of the Romanesque style. Round arches derived from the early middle ages had been used for several decades—the Germans had called the style *rundbogenstil*—but Richardson's designs, with their massive rock-faced masonry, contrasting materials, squat colonnettes, and ribbon windows, were something new. Richardson came to the public's attention in 1872 with his design for Trinity Church in Copley Square, Boston, and in the succeeding decade and a half he produced many other influential designs. Richardson's repertory of styles included, in addition to his massive stone buildings, contrasting brick structures of clean-lined simplicity and shingle-clad houses combining picturesque massing with the rich but homogeneous surfaces that shingles produce. Probably through George Foster Shepley (1860–1903), who began working in Richardson's Brookline office in 1882, St. Louis acquired a number of Richardson designs during his last years, a brick house for Shepley's brother-in-law Isaac Lionberger, one with shingles for Lionberger's brother-in-law Henry Potter, and a monumental stone mansion on Vandeventer Place for Lionberger's father, John. (With the demolition of Vandeventer Place in 1948 and 1957, Westmoreland acquired its own bit of genuine Richardson architecture: the side porch from the John Lionberger house was reerected by Norris Allen in 1968 at 9 Westmoreland.)

The architectural critic Montgomery Schuyler, who was the cousin and namesake of the Very Reverend Montgomery Schuyler, dean of Christ Church Cathedral in St. Louis, wrote in 1891 in *Architectural Record* that while Richardson "was living and practicing architecture, architects who regarded themselves as in any degree his rivals were naturally loth to introduce in a design dispositions or features or details, of which the suggestion plainly came from him. Since his death has 'extinguished envy' and ended rivalry, the admiration his work excited has been free to express itself either in direct imitation or in the adoption and elaboration of the suggestions his work fur-

A section of the porch from the Lionberger house in Vandeventer Place is now preserved as part of a garage addition built in 1968 behind 9 Westmoreland. The Lionberger house was designed by internationally respected architect Henry Hobson Richardson.

nished." This was certainly true of Westmoreland and Portland places, where six of the earliest houses were in Richardson's most familiar stone style and several others were in the related Richardsonian brick mode. Theodore Link's gates for Portland Place, built in 1890, announced the intentions of the early builders, which were achieved to an extent that is not evident now that three of the most important Richardsonian houses have been demolished. By 1894, as one traveled north on Kingshighway, Westmoreland would have presented an unbroken row of Richardsonian houses, beginning with the brick Number 5 and continuing with Numbers 7, 9, and 11 in stone. Then, to the

The west entrance gate to Portland Place is on Union Boulevard. The architectural firm of Theodore Link designed both Portland Place entrances.

south of the Portland gate was the massive Kennard house at Number 4. The following year, T. W. Carter built still another Richardsonian house on the north side of the place. *St. Louis Through a Camera*, a book by James Cox published in 1892, includes a photo collage of these houses still unobscured by trees.

Aside from Link's gates, the earliest of these Romanesque designs was Alexander G. Cochran's house at 7 Westmoreland. It was designed by James Stewart & Co., a firm best known for general contracting, particularly for factories and office buildings. James Stewart (1821–1902) was a native of Aberdeenshire, Scotland, where his father was a successful granite supplier and contractor. The family business was inherited by an older brother (who later built Balmoral Castle for Queen Victoria), so James migrated in 1843 to Canada, where he became a building commissioner for the government, supervising construction of the parliament buildings at Ottawa. He came to St. Louis in 1865 and around 1873 formed James Stewart & Co. with his son Alexander M. In city directories James was listed as "architect" while Alexander was "draughtsman." Two other sons joined the firm as construction supervisors in the early 1890s, James Christian and John Lyall, who insisted on spelling his last name *Stuart*. By the turn of the century, the firm had become international in scope, with branch offices in London and sev-

eral American cities, and the family was drawn away from St. Louis.

James Stewart was approaching retirement in 1890 when the Cochran house was started, and someone else on his staff may have produced the design. Charles Savage has suggested Craig McClure, who was working as an architect in St. Louis in the late 1880s and who formed Stewart, McClure & Mullgardt in 1892 with Louis C. Mullgardt and Alexander M. Stewart (who retained his position in his father's company during the three years the new firm operated). City directories show, however, that McClure was not working as an architect during 1890 and 1891, being employed first as a clerk by the Waters Pierce Oil Company and then as secretary of the Missouri Mantel and Decorative Company. In any case, the design of the Cochran house is not the most sophisticated; it is basically in the widely popular Queen Anne style of the era, brought up to date by its rock-faced stone construction and by the low-slung arches, sometimes called Syrian arches, at its entrance.

A design based on greater knowledge of Richardson's intentions was the house next door, built for William L. Huse by Eames & Young. Huse's daughter Ione, who married Isaac A. Hedges, in an interview dated August 18, 1950, in the *Star-Times*, recalled the difficulties of building with the large stone blocks essential to the Richardsonian look: "Father decided to

use Missouri granite, because he discovered that its quality was equal to Connecticut granite, and he was determined to favor his own state as much as possible. The rough boulders were brought here, and we had to have a regular quarry set up to cut and shape the stones, and there had to be derricks to lift the blocks into place. We started to build in 1890, but it took them two years to complete it. I remember one piece of granite held up the construction for six months. It was a simply enormous boulder, and the horse-drawn wagons got stuck in the mud and they couldn't move it until the roads dried. The inside fireplaces and iron grillwork were ready long before the outside of the house, and they had to wait in the shop until the shell was constructed." The architects, William S. Eames (1859–1915) and Thomas Crane Young (1858–1934), were then only in their early thirties, but they had already been practicing together for five years. In 1890 both were made fellows of the American Institute of Architects; Eames had been the first president of the St. Louis chapter. Born in Clinton, Michigan, but raised in St. Louis, Eames was one of the finest designers St. Louis ever produced. He was also known as an affable companion, as the journalist William Marion Reedy reported in *The Mirror*, May 14, 1908: "Billy Eames is capable of whole-hearted, infectious abandonment to the spirit of fun, and is as much himself when surrendered to the bonhomie of the hunting and fishing camp as when he talks like a T-square to an assemblage of his fellow craftsmen or to a company of contractors and builders. Take him on another side—the aesthetic—and you find that he is not wholly the scientific architect, but one in whose conception of that art is fused the plastic sensibility of the painter and the poet." Eames had taken the grand tour of Europe following his graduation from Washington University, and his scrapbooks from that trip, now at the university, reveal his firsthand familiarity with many of the same buildings that had inspired Richardson. And Eames had the ability to adapt to other styles as the Richardsonian Romanesque waned in popularity. An early example of Eames's independence of thought is his brick house designed for Robert McKittrick Jones at 6 Westmoreland. The McKittrick Jones house was built across the parkway from the contemporaneous Huse house. It takes the lessons of Richardson's brick buildings a step further, with its symmetry, simplicity, and essential freedom from period styles. Number 5 Westmoreland is another, somewhat more conventional, example of Eames's brick style.

Just down from the McKittrick Jones house, railroad builder William Bagnell built another red brick house at 12 Westmoreland. Its twenty rooms were highlighted by a corner turret and, after a remodeling in 1898, a large oriel window over the front door. The architect for the remodeling, William A. Lucas, opened his office in 1892, two years after the house was originally built, but the original architect may have been Lucas's employer at the time, L. Cass Miller. In 1936 the Bagnell house, described as vacant and antiquated, was demolished.

The other Richardsonian Romanesque house (11 Westmoreland) was built for banker T. H. West by Grable & Weber. It was demolished in 1958 following a fire. Alfred Grable, born in 1825, was a generation older than both Eames and Young and had been practicing architecture in St. Louis since the Civil War. Auguste Weber (1857–1904) became Grable's partner in 1888, and the two designed houses on most of the city's private streets. Their design for West featured a large circular tower at the right front corner of the house, a third-floor veranda on the east side, and a matching stable with a Syrian-arched coach door.

Numbers 4 and 5 Portland also featured semicircular towers with short windows under conical roofs, and both houses had Syrian-arched entrances. Samuel Kennard's house at Number 4, the first started in Portland Place, was demolished in 1958. Built for a family of six children, it had eight communicating bedrooms on the second floor, with three baths, an unusual luxury even in houses of this size. The architect, William Albert Swasey (1864–1940), a graduate of the Massachusetts Institute of Technology, had come to St. Louis by 1885 and opened his own office two years later. He designed six houses in Westmoreland and Portland places, two in adjacent Lindell Boulevard, and fourteen in another nearby private street, Westminster Place. Although his practice grew to include office buildings and many other projects, Swasey left St. Louis for New York a few years after the 1904 World's Fair. The Swasey designs in Westmoreland and Portland set a high standard for elegance and craftsmanship.

In contrast to Swasey's relatively brief St. Louis career, the firm that designed 5 Portland had become a local institution. The partners in the firm of Barnett, Haynes & Barnett were George Dennis Barnett (1863–1922), John Haynes (1860–1942), and Tom P. Barnett (1870–1929). The two Barnetts were sons of George I. Barnett, who has been called the dean of architects in the West in the mid-nineteenth century, and Haynes was George D.'s brother-in-law. Though not the busiest architects in the city, they became known for the opulence and impressiveness of their designs, particularly those by Tom. Their house for T. W. Carter is an example of Tom's ability to immerse himself in a style and produce a thoroughly convincing design before moving on to something entirely different.

Of all St. Louis's architects, the one most closely associated with the Richardsonian Romanesque style is Theodore Link (1850–1923). His firm designed St. Louis's Union Station, which is widely acknowledged as one of the most impressive monuments of the style, although it also has numerous borrowings from French Renaissance châteaus. Link's gates for Portland Place predate that well-known work, as does his house for farm-implements tycoon L. B. Tebbetts at 29 Portland, which was started in 1891. The house originally had shingled walls above the Syrian arches and heavy stonework on its first floor, both characteristic Richardsonian features. The upper floors were refaced about 1920 with false half-timbering.

The house built for Brown Shoe Company founder George Warren Brown at 40 Portland is often cited as an example of Theodore Link's work, probably because of its superficial similarity to Union Station. But the Brown mansion was actually designed in 1897 by Frederick C. Bonsack, with the large east wing of 1908 by Albert B. Groves. Bonsack (1859–1917) began his career in 1880 as a contractor but turned to architecture in 1892. His marriage to Helen Niedringhaus, daughter of Frederick G. Niedringhaus, congressman and president of the St. Louis Stamping Company, associated him with that family's many business interests. Through them he designed much of the company town built at Granite City, Illinois, across the river from St. Louis.

The Brown house was the last one to be built in Westmoreland and Portland in the Richardsonian Romanesque style. Even after the success of his Kennard house, W. A. Swasey could claim in a booklet of his designs published in 1900, entitled *Examples of Architectural Work*, that "the Romanesque should be confined to large public buildings, requiring great stability and massiveness, and therefore not generally adaptable to the refinement and elegance forming the principal features in domestic architecture." By then the style had been completely eclipsed in popular favor. Richardson's own successor firm, Shepley, Rutan & Coolidge, and his chief rivals in Boston, Peabody & Stearns, had moved on to other styles. Both of these firms contributed houses to Westmoreland and Portland places, but none of them was noticeably influenced by Richardson.

Peabody & Stearns had appeared on the St. Louis scene well before Richardson. Robert Swain Peabody (1845–1917) was the son of the minister of King's Chapel, the first Unitarian church in the United States, and he came to St. Louis to design a new Church of the Messiah for the dynamic Unitarian leader William Greenleaf Eliot, the grandfather of poet T. S. Eliot. After Peabody & Stearns sent Pierce P. Furber to supervise their St. Louis projects, the firm was listed in St. Louis as Peabody, Stearns & Furber. They had the distinction of building the first house in either Westmoreland or Portland. Begun in 1889 at 21 Westmoreland for stockbroker and banker Henry Levi Newman, it was a rather plain, L-shaped brick structure ornamented with bands of stone—an example of the urban Queen Anne style that might have been built in any fashionable part of the city. But the Newman house lacked the elaborate ornamentation that gives the Queen Anne style its appeal today. The firm's house at 38 Westmoreland for Corinne Dyer, begun in 1892, was at first glance quite similar in design to the Newman house: an L-shaped brick structure with finials crowning the gables and tall chimneys. The Dyer house was smaller, however, lower (lacking the tall exposed basement), and more picturesque, with its quoined corners and windows and its scalloped bargeboard and semioctagonal porch.

One other house was built in the fast-waning Queen Anne style: 39 Portland, the oldest surviving house in that place (started three weeks before Link's Tebbetts house at 29 Portland). It was designed for real estate and investment-company millionaire W. W. Culver by Alfred Knell, a native of Canada who was then in partnership with Henry Isaacs. After the partnership dissolved in 1892, Knell claimed credit for some of the buildings usually attributed to Isaacs. Culver was his chief patron, commissioning an office building in downtown St. Louis and the buildings of the Culver Military Academy at Culver, Indiana.

A few months after the Dyer house was begun, Peabody, Stearns & Furber began work on a much larger mansion for John T. Davis at 17 Westmoreland. Neither client nor architect lived to see the house completed. Dry-goods magnate Davis died of Bright's disease in 1894 at age forty-nine; Furber died in 1893 at age forty. From the point of view of design, however, the palatial Davis residence was a new beginning rather than an ending; it reintroduced smooth, balanced Renaissance forms after years of knobby asymmetry. The Davis house was not only a revolutionary change in the architectural direction of Westmoreland/Portland houses, but, according to a survey of building permits, it was the most costly house ever built there. The cutting of the pink granite alone would have cost a fortune. But more important than the cost was the design, a faithful example of Italian Renaissance. This handsome style had been revived a decade earlier by the New York firm of McKim, Mead & White in their design for the Villard houses at Madison Avenue and 48th Street. (Both McKim and White had worked in the office of H. H. Richardson.) The Davis house is a fairly faithful adaptation of the Villard houses; the window designs are the same, although they are shifted to different floors, and the one-story central loggia is also similar.

John T. Davis had the distinction of being the first person in Missouri to employ America's foremost landscape designer, Frederick Law Olmsted. Early in 1894, at the request of Peabody & Stearns, the firm of Olmsted, Olmsted & Eliot prepared designs for 17 Westmoreland, including massed plantings around the curving entrance walk, a semicircular formal flower garden intended to be seen from the dining room windows, and ornamental trees on the east lawn. Although the plants themselves have long since disappeared, the plan still exists.

The Davis house became the first in a series of palaces built in the private places of St. Louis. Each rivaled, on more spacious lots, the palatial townhouses of Fifth Avenue in New York. More opulent than necessary even for the expansive life-styles of the wealthiest St. Louisans, these houses set standards of design and craftsmanship that have remained unsurpassed. Eames & Young began three of them in the same year that the Davis house was built. The building permits for the Thornburgh and McMillan houses at 23 and 25 Portland were issued on the same day, August 23, 1892. Completely dissimilar in materials and design, the two houses share the horizontality and classical detailing of the Renaissance. The Thornburgh house was the more startling of the two, with its yellow brick and white stone coloration. The carved and coffered interiors of the McMillan house feature more woodwork in the style of the sixteenth century than exists in most Italian palaces. None of these houses was a copy of a European original. The best designers of the time, particularly men with the abilities of William Eames, studied the works of the past not for purposes of plagiarism but to obtain a vocabulary of forms that they could incorporate into their own styles. The use of carved swags or draped garlands along the cornice lines of 23 and 25 Portland is one example of this design technique. The combination of richly carved ornamentation and a short third floor of attic windows is derived from the Library of San Marco in Venice, a work begun in the 1530s by Jacopo Sansovino. The Venetian library's proportions, however, are much narrower and the windows much less emphasized than those in the Thornburgh house. The McMillan house has the same design elements, but they are separated, with the stone garlands over the second-floor windows and the attic windows on a floor above that.

In 1895, Eames & Young offered a direct challenge to the grandeur of the Davis house in their design for a house to be located directly across the parkway at 20 Westmoreland. Commissioned by Louis Chauvenet, it was shown at the twenty-ninth annual convention of the American Institute of Architects, held in St. Louis that year. Smaller than the Davis house, the Chauvenet design had similar massing, with recessed entry bays and a lower third floor. In some respects it was even more opulent, with a projecting porch of paired columns and with coffered eaves under a broadly overhanging tile roof. Unfortunately, it seems to have been too much for the Chauvenets. A decade later a much more austere house was built on the site by Mrs. Chauvenet, whose husband had died in the summer of

Eames & Young designed this house for Annie and Louis Chauvenet in 1895. It was to be 20 Westmoreland but was never built.

1904. The house was designed in plum brick by Lawrence Ewald and looks back to Richardson's work in that material.

The short third-floor windows and stone swags seen in the Thornburgh and McMillan residences became unifying motifs of the houses on Westmoreland and Portland, motifs all the more remarkable because they are so seldom seen elsewhere. These motifs were used by Swasey in 1894 at 29 Westmoreland for dry-goods merchant Byron Nugent; by J. L. Wees the following year at 10 Westmoreland for bakery owner Lewis Dozier; by Widmann, Walsh & Boisselier in 1898 at 15 Portland for grain merchant William D. Orthwein; by Weber & Groves for Charles and Cornelia Fach at 32 Portland, also in 1898; by Ernst Janssen in 1899 at 13 Westmoreland for banker Edwards Whitaker; and by F. C. Bonsack that same year at 45 Westmoreland for Joseph D. and Mary F. Bascom. Swasey's Nugent house and Bonsack's Bascom house, like the Thornburgh house, had bay windows, really bowed projections in the wall surface, which had nothing to do with Renaissance precedent. These bay windows reminded some people of Richardson's towers and stair turrets, while others saw in them the bow-fronted houses of Boston's Beacon Street, houses that were then being copied by McKim, Mead & White. Swasey pointed out the compatibility of the Renaissance style with tile roofs, which were then coming into general use. Inside the Nugent house, Swasey designed the main hall in the same mode as the exterior, but the other rooms were copies of quite different periods. The Nugent mansion

and other houses of the time often resembled the decorative arts galleries of large museums by presenting catalogs of period styles. Nugent's frieze of carved swags was criticized at the time as being too large and heavy for the house. A later owner agreed and had most of this ornament chipped off.

The Bascom house suffered a much worse fate, being demolished in 1936. An article published in *The St. Louis Builder* while the house was under construction in 1899 said it was "destined to be one of the handsomest and most comfortable home structures in St. Louis." It was primarily buff brick, with a high foundation of Carthage stone and trim of white terracotta, including panels of garlands above the bow windows and a low third story shadowed by a bracketed roof of red Spanish tile. All the first-floor rooms were connected by large folding doors so that they could be combined into one large reception room. The hall and dining room had paneled wainscoting of mahogany, while the library was antique oak. A billiard room was in the basement, and the third floor had a ballroom measuring twenty-seven by fifty-two feet. The *Builder* described the exterior as French Renaissance in style, but inside the dining room was English, the library Italian, and the parlor Louis XVI.

The Dozier house was the finest residence created by John Ludwig Wees (1861–1942), but this native of Alsace-Lorraine designed many other buildings still known to St. Louisans. His designs for the Dozier house, dripping with terra-cotta ornamentation, were published in the *American Architect and Building News* on May 13, 1899. This was fortunate for posterity, because after Wees's death his original linen drawings "were washed until white and suitable for making pillowcases," a grandson later recalled. The commission for the Orthwein house was a similarly unusual excursion into residential design for the firm of Widmann, Walsh & Boisselier. Their specialty was brewery design, in which they had a long association with Anheuser-Busch. Frederick Widmann (1859–1925) was born in Germany, while Robert W. Walsh (1860–circa 1929) was a native St. Louisan, the son of another architect. The two partners lived in private places themselves, Widmann in the German enclave of Compton Heights and Walsh in Cabanne Place. Caspar D. Boisselier (circa 1854–1929) left the firm in 1906, but Widmann and Walsh worked together until the former's death.

The palatial Whitaker house at 13 Westmoreland was unusual for Ernst Janssen, who, like Widmann, Walsh & Boisselier, had a practice devoted largely to brewers and other affluent southside Germans. Most of his houses could be characterized as "brewer's baronial." Number 24 Portland was just such a house, designed in 1910 for Elizabeth Schnaider, widow of brewer Joseph M. Schnaider. A remodeling in 1966 removed the gables, leaded windows, and other features typical of Janssen's style.

FIRST FLOOR PLAN

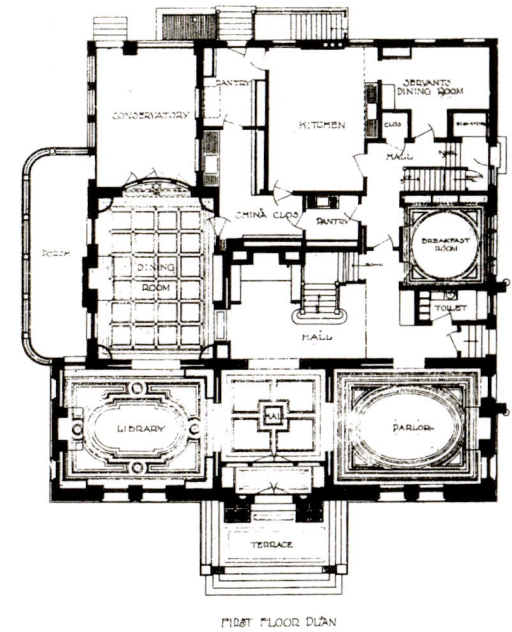

Architect J. L. Wees's renderings of the Rebecca and
Lewis D. Dozier house at 10 Westmoreland and of
the interior woodwork for the dining room and
parlor. The house was built in 1895.

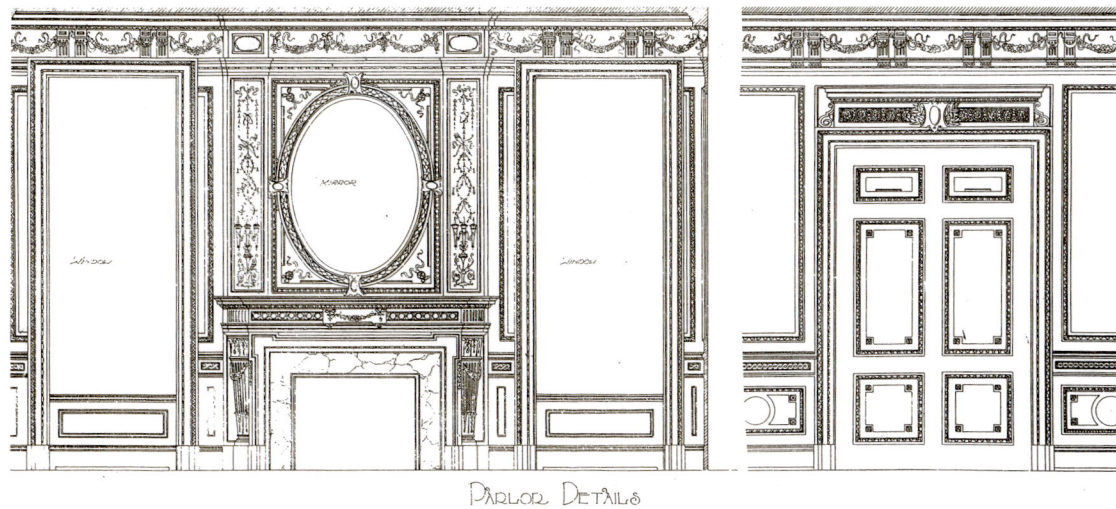

PARLOR DETAILS

Janssen's last house in the places was built the following year at 43 Portland for Jeanette Filley Morton. With its high hipped roof, broad gables, tall chimneys, and the matching pointed arches above its entry and side porch, it too has a somewhat baronial look. Janssen was a native American himself, born about 1855, but he had studied architecture in Karlsruhe, Germany, before beginning his St. Louis practice in 1879. Louis LaBeaume, a prominent architect of the next generation, claimed that the Whitaker house had actually been designed by Albert Guissart, whom he described as "a Beaux Arts man and a real artist." Guissart was then working for Janssen; a decade earlier his own short-lived firm, Torgerson, Guissart & Ginder, had won the competition for the new City Hall only to see the design contract awarded instead to Eckel & Mann, a St. Joseph firm.

Still other Renaissance palaces were built in the last years of the nineteenth century and the first of the twentieth. One of the grandest was the George Allen house at 26 Westmoreland, which was demolished by the heirs in 1938. Designed by Eames & Young at the same time that the Thornburgh and McMillan houses were on the drawing board, it had a more French appearance, with a high hipped roof, dormers behind a balustrade, and stone walls articulated by pilasters and a garlanded frieze. Many of the twenty-eight rooms in the Allen mansion were paneled in oak. The Van Blarcom residence, built for the wealthy banking family at 1 Westmoreland, had a similar balustrade and pilasters but was raised an additional story by a podium-like first floor. Swasey in his *Examples* described the style as "classic Architecture, leaning towards the Spanish Renaissance," but the St. Louis correspondent of *The American Architect and Building News* (August 17, 1895) pointed out that "the structure would look very much like the Farnese Palace in Rome if the pilasters were eliminated." Swasey explained that Jacob Van Blarcom had insisted the main entrance to the house be at the west end, off the porte cochere. Thus, the central place on the main facade usually reserved for the door in such designs had to be otherwise occupied. Swasey's solution was a semicircular bay window with a three-part window above. Just in case a visitor might mistake this feature for the entrance, a terrace with a balustrade blocked the approach.

The house designed at 25 Westmoreland for federal Judge Elmer Adams demonstrated how sensitive Swasey's designs could be to the adjacent houses and the context of the Westmoreland/Portland district in general. Although Judge Adams was one of the most distinguished and respected residents in the neighborhood, his house was to be built for a fourth of the cost of the Nugent mansion at Number 29. Until 1931, there was no other house between Numbers 25 and 29, and the inevitable

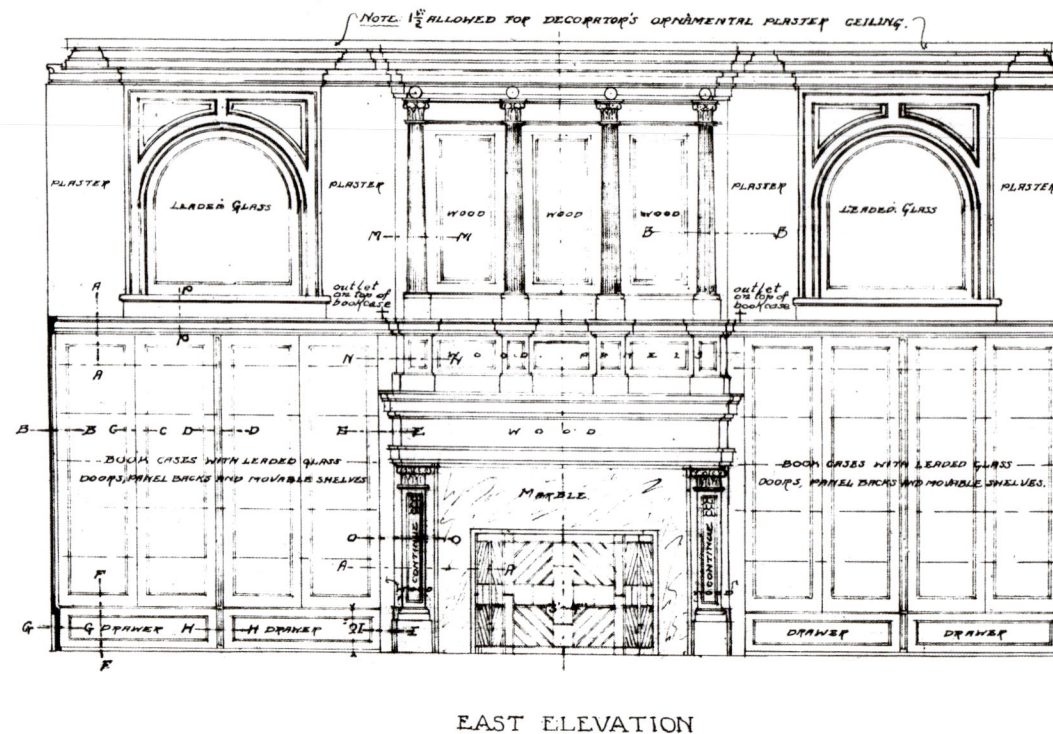

The Hellmuth & Spiering plan for the library woodwork for 36 Westmoreland. The house was built for Louis Werner in 1908.

EAST ELEVATION

comparisons were potentially unflattering to Judge Adams. Swasey, therefore, had to find ways to enable the Adams house to hold its own within its budget. He used brick instead of stone, two stories and dormers instead of three full stories, and one bow window instead of two. The house as built does, as Swasey intended, "uphold the dignity and attractiveness of the property."

Another pair of similar houses can be found next door to each other at 30 and 32 Portland, both designed by Weber & Groves. Number 30 is the simpler of the two, but it is still massive. It was designed in 1897. The more elaborate house next door was designed the following year. The third house in the row, Number 36, built in 1906 by the architect-builder A. A. Fischer, respects the general shape and form of the earlier two.

At the same time that Swasey's house for Judge Adams was going up, the firm of Shepley, Rutan & Coolidge was building a Renaissance palace next door at 23 Westmoreland for stove-manufacturing magnate Hudson E. Bridge. Like the Davis house, it took the Cancelleria as a model, adding a richly carved frieze above the third floor. The firm's St. Louis office was now headed by John Lawrence Mauran, a Rhode Island–born graduate of the Massachusetts Institute of Technology. Mauran had come to St. Louis in 1893 from Chicago, where he had supervised the construction of the Public Library and Art Institute,

both on Michigan Avenue and among the finest Renaissance-style buildings of the period. George W. Hellmuth paid the Bridge house a compliment in 1902 when he designed the nearly identical Copelin house across the parkway at Number 28. This symmetry can no longer be enjoyed, as both houses have been demolished.

In 1897 Shepley, Rutan & Coolidge, with John Lawrence Mauran joining them as a partner, designed the house for lumberman John A. Holmes at 9 Portland. This house follows the same design formula as the Bridge house, but incorporating two bows. This double bow was derived, it was said at the time, from the same firm's Blair residence in Chicago.

The Werner house at 36 Westmoreland, designed in 1908 by Hellmuth & Spiering, was one of the oddest designs among the Westmoreland/Portland palazzi. It uses the columns and entablatures of the other Renaissance-style houses but in an asymmetrical composition. George W. Hellmuth (1870–1955) is perhaps best known today as the father of George F. Hellmuth, the senior partner of the architectural firm of Hellmuth, Obata & Kassabaum. In his early years of working independently, the senior Hellmuth was best known for the grand residences he designed, including all but six of those in Westmoreland/Portland's neighboring Hortense Place. The Werner house was designed during Hellmuth's two-year partnership with Louis C.

Spiering (1874–1912). After Spiering's early death, Hellmuth took his younger brother Harry (1884–1963) as partner, and the two subsequently designed three more houses in Portland Place.

The last palazzo in the Westmoreland/Portland district was built for Anna and Edward Faust at 1 Portland. It rivals the John T. Davis mansion for sheer grandeur. The architects, Barnett, Haynes & Barnett, had by 1910 moved so far from the Romanesque Revival style that even the scale of their earlier design next door at 5 Portland now seemed alien. Even more dazzling than the size and clean lines of the exterior of 1 Portland, the interior caught the public's fancy, particularly after the opulent ballroom was added a few years later in the rear yard. Tom Barnett designed the ballroom and in later years took credit, probably deserved, for the design of the entire house. As another demonstration of his remarkable design facility, a few years later Tom Barnett created an entire farm complex in suburban St. Louis in the Pueblo Revival style for the Fausts' son Leicester.

Other alternatives to Richardsonian architecture appeared at about the same time as the palazzo style. One of them employed design elements from the sixteenth-century châteaus of the French Renaissance, notably the elaborately decorated dormers and chimneys and the profuse small-scale low-relief decoration around doors and windows. The style was introduced to this country by Richard Morris Hunt, who designed the house built for W. K. Vanderbilt on Fifth Avenue in 1883. The château style achieved great popularity in St. Louis in the early 1890s, beginning with the erection of the City Hall, whose design was based on that of the Hotel de Ville in Paris. The first house in St. Louis in the new style was W. K. Bixby's at 13 Portland. Now thought of as one of the most ornate houses of the era, the Bixby château was considered by its architect, W. A. Swasey, to be an example of restraint in ornament. According to Swasey in his *Examples*, "the terra cotta work in this house was the most elaborate made up to that time in St. Louis, and the manufacturers' successful efforts in carrying out my details and properly executing the work, gained a reputation for them which had a material effect in bringing out better and more correct designs."

Unlike its prototypes in France, the Bixby mansion was not originally white in color but was a striking combination of two shades of brick, with terra-cotta around the doors and windows. The stable in the back had a sawtooth pattern of contrasting brick outlining its gable. A year after the Bixby house was started, a more restrained Châteauesque house was built just to the west at 19 Portland for Oliver A. Hart, heir to a real estate and investment-company fortune. The architects were Grable & Weber, now joined by the younger Albert B. Groves (1866–1925). Groves had been trained at Cornell's School of Architecture and brought new ideas to the firm; he was proba-

bly responsible for this design, which, with its early Renaissance doorway and gable set between two turrets from a much earlier era, resembles a remodeled castle. The Châteauesque style was not to be seen again for more than twenty years, but its last manifestation was a noble one, the Mallinckrodt house at 16 Westmoreland, designed in 1913 by James P. Jamieson.

The other architectural style introduced in the early 1890s was the Tudor Revival. Like the Châteauesque, the Tudor Revival was derived from the transitional period in England between the Middle Ages and the Renaissance. Tudor Revival structures were sometimes built entirely of brick, but more typically they featured areas of half-timbering, a building method in which the wooden structural members are exposed to view and the spaces between are filled in with brick or stucco. This Tudor Revival style made its first tentative appearance in St. Louis in 1891 in the house designed for brick manufacturer E. C. Sterling at 22 Westmoreland by Rossiter & Wright of New York, with local assistance from Eames & Young. Ironically, the half-timbered central gable that was so startling to contemporaries was later covered with stucco, just as the mottled yellow brickwork of the lower parts of the house was also obliterated. Another debt to sixteenth-century England was seen in the large oriel over the front door, a cantilevered bay window. The following year Shepley, Rutan & Coolidge designed the house at 40 Westmoreland for John D. Filley, the son of St. Louis's pre–Civil War mayor Oliver D. Filley. Here the half-timbering can still be seen, although the yellow brick was again not typical of the style. The house that Peabody & Stearns had designed for Henry Newman in 1889 was transformed into a Tudor Revival composition in 1897 for Edward C. Simmons. Eames & Young spent about two-thirds of the original cost of the house to add a large east wing and to apply half-timbering to all the dormers and gables. Illustrations of the house, which was demolished in 1941, show it to have been somewhat top-heavy. Tudor Revival in a purer form was not seen on Westmoreland or Portland until the new century.

Beginning in the mid-1890s still another architectural style was talked about in St. Louis, although seldom seen. The "Colonial" style, actually Georgian Revival, was derived in part from eighteenth-century models in New England and in part from genuine English prototypes. This Georgian theme was revived in the 1880s by McKim, Mead & White. In St. Louis, the Van Blarcom house was called Colonial, but Swasey's 1896 design for Henry and Minnie Lawrence Siegrist, built two years after the Van Blarcom house and directly across the parkway from it at 2 Westmoreland, had a better claim to the designation. Swasey wrote in his *Examples* that he intended a "three-story Colonial house, introducing two bay windows, and a low

third story, with flat roof and balustrade, which the style called for." But Mrs. Siegrist wanted a tile roof, and four feet had to be added to the height of the third story to provide enough space for a ballroom that the architect had not originally contemplated. This amenity made the pale yellow brick house look more like the nearby palazzi, especially as seen from the eastern side, where the property bordered Kingshighway. The interior also had little in common with the republican simplicity of the Colonial era; it had an Elizabethan dining room, an Empire library, and a Moorish smoking room. The stair hall rose the height of the house to a circular balcony on the third floor. Swasey bragged that "this lavishness of decoration and appropriate furnishing make an interior hardly equalled in the West." This mansion was demolished in 1961.

The Georgian style, which ultimately was to eclipse all other traditional styles in popularity, made its appearance in Portland Place in 1902. In June of that year, Weber & Groves began the house for iron and steel magnate Frank N. Johnson at 47 Portland. The following January, construction began on Number 45 next door, another Weber & Groves design created for banker Breckinridge Jones. As the first houses to rise at the west end of Portland Place, they could be seen from Union Boulevard, and it is possible that Albert Groves had that view in mind when he designed them. Both were two-story red-brick buildings with contrasting stone and white-painted wood trim, gabled dormers with arched windows, massive end chimneys, rooftop balustrades, and columned side porches. Most notably, both had two-story porticoes—Johnson's a pedimented affair in Roman Doric; Jones's a semicircular porch in the Ionic order, a smaller version of the south portico of the White House. The spectacle of these fraternal twins was lost in 1935 when the Jones house was demolished, the first house in either place to disappear.

The Louisiana Purchase Exposition diverted manpower and attention from residential construction in 1904. Not a single house was built in the two places during that year. But 1905 saw construction resume with renewed vigor. Three of the houses built in Westmoreland/Portland that year were Georgian Revival; two were Tudor Revival. The first, at 52 Westmoreland, was started for chemical-company president Herman Luyties but completed for railroad executive Carl Gray. The builder was Alexander August Fischer, who by this year claimed to have built more than five hundred houses in St. Louis, and he was only thirty-eight years old. Few of the architects who worked for A. A. Fischer are known, but his houses all had a certain family resemblance. They were usually made of rusticated stone, often laid in alternating wide and narrow bands. Detailing was classical, with a columned porch or portico and a wide frieze broken by window tops. Number 52 had all these

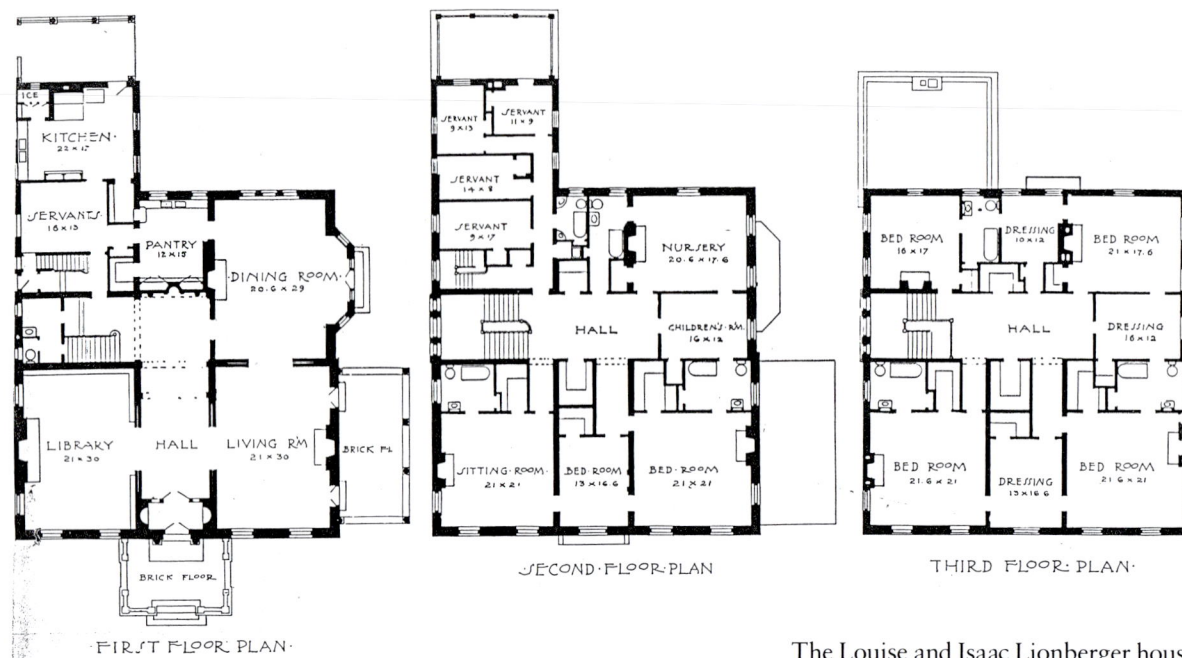

FIRST FLOOR PLAN · SECOND · FLOOR · PLAN · THIRD FLOOR · PLAN ·

The Louise and Isaac Lionberger house at 37 Westmoreland was designed by James P. Jamieson and built in 1906. The parapet and third floor were lopped off in 1949. The alteration eliminated four bedrooms, three bathrooms, and three dressing rooms. The floor plans are shown on the left.

characteristics, including a two-story Corinthian portico. Similar features can be seen in the contemporary Fischer houses at 36 Portland, the more expensive house begun the next year by Herman Luyties. In the 1940s, Number 52 lost its portico and had its rough-faced stonework smoothed down, alterations that have further clarified the basically Georgian character of the house.

The two other Georgian houses were built across the parkway from 52 Westmoreland at Numbers 37 and 41. Construction began the same week on the homes for lawyers Isaac H. Lionberger and Daniel K. Catlin, Jr. Both residences were designed by Cope & Stewardson, nominally a Philadelphia firm but in St. Louis actually headed by James P. Jamieson. John Stewardson and Walter Cope had popularized the use of "Collegiate Gothic" at American colleges, a style derived not from the Gothic era but from the Oxford and Cambridge colleges of the Tudor era and early seventeenth century. The firm came to St. Louis in 1899 after winning the competition for the design of the new Washington University campus, but by that year John Stewardson had died in a skating accident. Walter Cope died in 1902 of appendicitis. Jamieson opened the St. Louis office in 1900 and ran it in conjunction with the Philadelphia practice until 1912, when he began his own firm. A native of Scotland, Jamieson (1867–1941) had a dignified and reserved demeanor,

but his integrity and high standards of design and construction brought him a wide practice among the wealthiest and most influential people in St. Louis. He met many of his clients through his association with Washington University. Isaac Lionberger, for instance, was a director of the university. The Lionberger house was modeled after the Federal-era houses of Salem, Massachusetts, although it was more massive and solidly constructed. Its tall, lean New England proportions were lost in 1949 when the third floor was removed. The Catlin house next door was only two stories tall but made more imposing by the columned brick loggia in front. Although the Georgian style would seem to call for a center hall, both of these houses follow the general practice on these streets of having the hall oriented to the side entry, with the staircase at right angles to the front door. Jamieson designed the Georgian house at 42 Westmoreland in 1906 for Lionberger's nephew Clarkson Potter, the Tudor Revival house at 30 Westmoreland in 1910 for Lionberger's sister Mary, and the Renaissance residence at 51 Westmoreland in 1915 for Catlin's father.

Jamieson designed two more Georgian houses in 1909, another two in 1912, the year he opened his own St. Louis office, and a final one in 1913. The Dwight F. Davis house at 16 Portland displays the characteristics of the change that was occurring. The taller Victorian proportions of the earlier houses

were relaxing into lower, broader shapes, and horizontality was beginning to be emphasized by string courses, corner quoins, and friezes. The Dwight Davis house is Jamieson's finest essay in the Georgian Revival style. It succeeds in turning symmetrical facades to both the street and the garden, while providing a carriage entrance at one corner. Jamieson was known for designing double-fronted houses in the English fashion. Surviving sketches by the architect illustrate his plans for the interior of the Davis house. Some of the woodwork, particularly in the halls, is derived more from the seventeenth than the eighteenth century, but this was an anomaly frequently seen in houses of the period.

The house at 54 Westmoreland was started by Jamieson in 1913 for dry-goods merchant Walter McKittrick. Constructed on the corner of Union Boulevard, it is smaller than the Dwight Davis house but like it has beautifully detailed Flemish-bond brickwork. Jamieson's Robert Holmes house, built the same year at 46 Portland, has a pedimented doorway that was much admired in its time. Unfortunately, the home of the lumberman has lost its delicately patterned sidelights.

The house for H. B. Collins at 50 Portland is the anomaly of the group, a white stuccoed building started a few months after the Holmes house and using the same Georgian forms but in an asymmetrical way. The porte cochere and sleeping porch add an

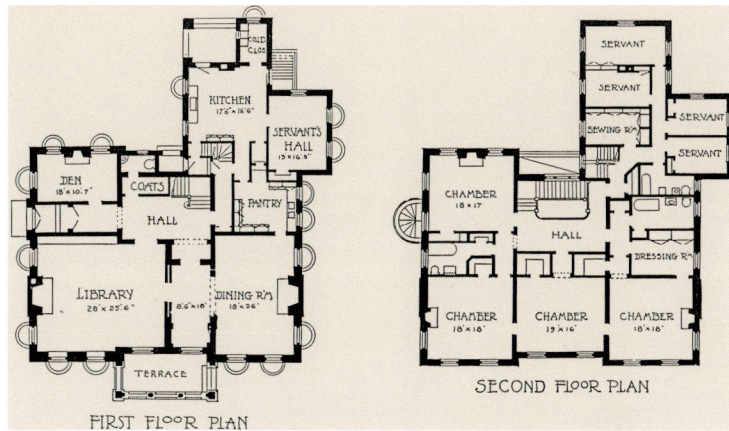

FIRST FLOOR PLAN

SECOND FLOOR PLAN

The floor plan for 41 Westmoreland. The house was designed for Gertrude and Daniel Catlin, Jr. The Catlins lived here for more than fifty years.

extra bay to the west end of the house; the front door is centered in the three-bay projecting wing, but the pediment above surmounts only two of the three bays. The garden front is also off-center. In this design Jamieson looked back to the earliest days of the Colonial Revival in the 1880s, when Georgian features were applied to sprawling Victorian floorplans.

By the first decade of the twentieth century, most of the major architectural firms in St. Louis were capable of designing competently in the Georgian Revival style. Milligan & Wray, for example, a firm known primarily for its school and hospital designs, did the house at 37 Portland for Washington University professor David C. Gamble in 1906. Like the Isaac Lionberger house but on a smaller scale, it is modeled on the Federal-era houses of Salem, Massachusetts. Rockwell M. Milligan (1868–1929) came to St. Louis in 1890 after studying architecture in Denver. He designed thirty-five hospitals around the country, and, succeeding the nationally known innovator William B. Ittner as commissioner of buildings for the St. Louis Board of Education, designed twenty-six schools.

A year after the Gamble house was started, Frederick Bonsack essayed the Georgian Revival style in a house across the parkway at 44 Portland for investment broker Robert Keiser. It is in striking contrast to his Romanesque Brown house two doors down, but it belongs more to the earlier Georgian Revival school than to the more authentic style being revived by Jamieson. Along with its tall proportions, Number 44 has single-paned window sashes, a practical feature but one not in keeping with the style.

George Hellmuth, by now in partnership with his brother

Harry, designed the Charles E. Bascom house at 52 Portland in 1915 and the Selwyn C. Edgar house across the parkway at 41 Portland in 1929. The projecting vestibule of the Bascom house is derived from a similar feature on the 1761 house of Gen. Philip Schuyler in Albany, New York.

Three other Georgian houses deserve mention: 42 Portland, designed in 1908 by Mariner & LaBeaume, and 8 Portland, 1912, and 44 Westmoreland, 1914, both by LaBeaume & Klein. All three are somewhat drier versions of the Jamieson style. Louis LaBeaume (1873–1961) was a native St. Louisan, the descendant of one of the city's early French settlers. Having studied architecture at Columbia University and in Europe, he returned to St. Louis to assist in the design of the Louisiana Purchase Exposition. LaBeaume's partnership with Guy C. Mariner lasted from 1904 to 1912 and was succeeded the following year by an association with Eugene S. Klein. Established in St. Louis society by birth and marriage as well as by his wit and personal charm, LaBeaume had an exceptionally productive career, although his design ability did not rank with that of Eames, Tom Barnett, or Jamieson at their best.

LaBeaume's most adventurous work came toward the beginning of his career, during his years with Mariner, when they developed a three-story house type that was often nearly square in elevation and usually had an off-center or side door. Charles Savage has called these houses "proto-Georgian," but they often used decorative elements from other eras without strictly following any one style. The first of these houses was built at 51 Portland for investment broker Harold M. Kauffman in 1907. Three more were built the following year: the adjacent William A. Stickney and A. T. West houses at 46 and 48 Westmoreland, and the Langenberg house across the parkway at Number 49. These houses, especially those placed close to the street, could be rather forbidding in appearance, and the new "style," if that's what it was, never proceeded further. In 1912 LaBeaume, working alone, attempted a different style of modern house for banker John F. Shepley at 53 Portland. It has two full stories with additional space in a front-facing gable and dormers on the steep roof, and aside from a segmental arch framing the entry and some patterns in the brickwork, it was virtually devoid of ornament. LaBeaume's later work with Eugene Klein generally retreated from these attempts to create a modern style.

LaBeaume & Klein designed three houses for Portland Place in 1927. The N. S. Chouteau Walsh house at Number 7 is Tudor Revival without any half-timbering, while the other two, adjacent houses for J. D. Perry Francis and Marion L. J. Lambert at Numbers 20 and 22, were in an eighteenth-century style. The plans of the two are similar, except that the Francis house has the kitchen and servants' rooms in a wing to one side, while in

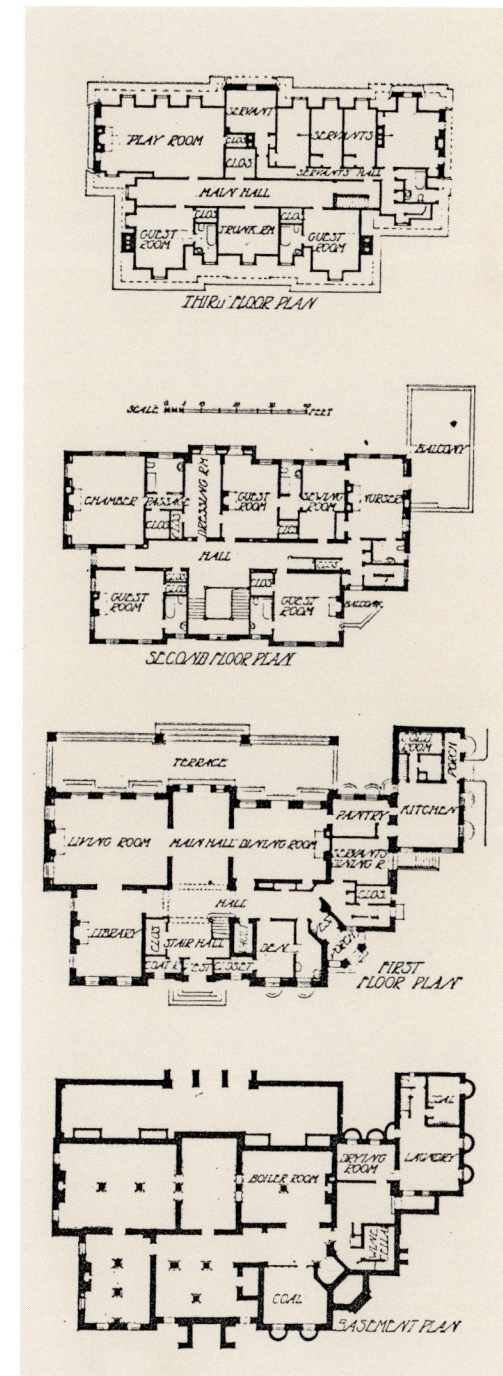

THIRD FLOOR PLAN

SECOND FLOOR PLAN

FIRST FLOOR PLAN

BASEMENT PLAN

The Cope & Stewardson floor plans for 16 Portland. The house was built for Helen and Dwight F. Davis in 1909.

the Lambert house these spaces are in the rear. In both, the staircase crosses over the main entry, a feature seen earlier in the neighboring Dwight Davis house. Externally, the Francis house is brick and has a pedimented doorway, a parapet, and double-hung windows, while the Lambert house is stuccoed and has casement windows. These features made the Lambert house distinctly French to observers of the time. Incidentally, the extensive press coverage the Lambert house received provides a check on the accuracy of the costs being reported on building permits. The Lambert permit, issued on November 29, reported the expected cost of the house as $70,000, but the *Globe-Democrat* the next Sunday gave the cost as $100,000. Probably all such figures on building permits are substantially below actual values.

Louis LaBeaume's career was full of accomplishments. He served on the board of the City Art Museum of St. Louis from 1916 to 1941, the last ten years as president. From 1926 to 1940 he was a member of the Plaza Commission, which shaped the area of downtown St. Louis around the City Hall. LaBeaume was keenly aware of his position as a traditionalist in a time of changing architectural values; at the time of of his death the *Post-Dispatch* recalled his comment that the Plaza buildings "were conceived just before the revolution in architecture and finished to be scoffed at by any who would." But he was an avid defender of his values, issuing a stream of books and articles.

The architectural ferment at the turn of the century in which Mariner & LaBeaume briefly dabbled is usually associated in this country with Frank Lloyd Wright and his Chicago associates. They established what has come to be called the Prairie School. But many other architects were looking, perhaps more tentatively, for alternatives to period styles, and modern scholarship is just beginning to recognize them. One such firm was Mauran, Russell & Garden, which was formed in 1900 when John Lawrence Mauran left Shepley, Rutan & Coolidge. He was joined by Ernest J. Russell (1870–1956) and Edward Gordon Garden (1871–1924). Garden was the brother of Hugh Garden, the accomplished Chicago modernist, and it is tempting to attribute the more adventurous designs of the firm's early years to him. Garden left the firm in 1908 and was replaced in 1911 by William DeForest Crowell (1879–1967). In its heyday, which extended to the death of Mauran in 1933, the firm was probably St. Louis's most successful, designing many important buildings downtown. In the neighborhood of Westmoreland and Portland, they were responsible for the Racquet Club, the local branch library, and four of the eight churches. Many of these commissions undoubtedly came to Mauran, who was married to Isabel Chapman, the only child of one of the prominent men in the city. The Maurans lived in the Chapman house

in Vandeventer Place and summered in Dublin, New Hampshire, near Mt. Monadnock. Theodore Roosevelt appointed Mauran to the Fine Arts Commission in 1908, a position he held for the rest of his life. In 1916 he was elected president of the American Institute of Architects.

The house that Mauran, Russell & Garden designed for George Carpenter, built in 1905 and 1906 at 12 Portland, offers a challenge to the Holmes house across the parkway, which Mauran had designed with Shepley, Rutan & Coolidge. It is fashioned of brown brick with a contrasting stuccoed third floor and an overhanging gable roof, both features found in Frank Lloyd Wright's early work, notably the Davenport residence of 1901 in River Forest, Illinois. The greater size and weightier materials of the Carpenter house make it seem more traditional, possibly Swiss. William DeForest Crowell, who later bought the Carpenter house, was often thought to have designed it, but he did not come to St. Louis until about 1910. The G. F. Steedman house built at 34 Westmoreland in 1909 is a variant of the Carpenter house design. Another direction for a modern style is seen at 50 Westmoreland in the Arthur B. Shepley house of 1908. It is constructed of poured concrete, a material that had been introduced into high-style architecture in St. Louis only a few years previously. Attorney Arthur Shepley was the brother of Mauran's former employer George Shepley. The Fowler house of 1912, at 35 Westmoreland, is another concrete house, with a concrete garage. Here the Italian influence is dominant, although no attempt was made to make the facade symmetrical. The second-floor loggia may have been suggested by Florentine houses. By 1914, Mauran, Russell & Crowell were executing their Mediterranean designs, such as the St. Louis Country Club, in stuccoed tile rather than concrete, and thereafter the style became a conservative rather than progressive one in the St. Louis area.

Two other houses were built in Westmoreland following the loosely Italian style of the Fowler house, sometimes called Italian Eclectic and not to be confused with the earlier palazzo mode. Both were designed by Jamieson. His L-shaped house at Number 51 for tobacco tycoon Daniel Catlin, Sr., begun in 1915, is one of the finest in the area. Its highlights are a Palladian-arched second-floor loggia and a spectacular curving staircase. In 1923 Jamieson executed a simpler example at Number 32 for machinery manufacturer Edwin H. Steedman.

Another house that should be mentioned in the context of the Fowler house is 53 Westmoreland, designed in 1908 by William A. Lucas for Leopold Freund. Its balustraded front terrace, stone-framed doorway, and bracketed overhang are all Italian features, but the long, low, yellow Roman brick (furnished by the Hydraulic Press Brick Company) was a type used by Frank

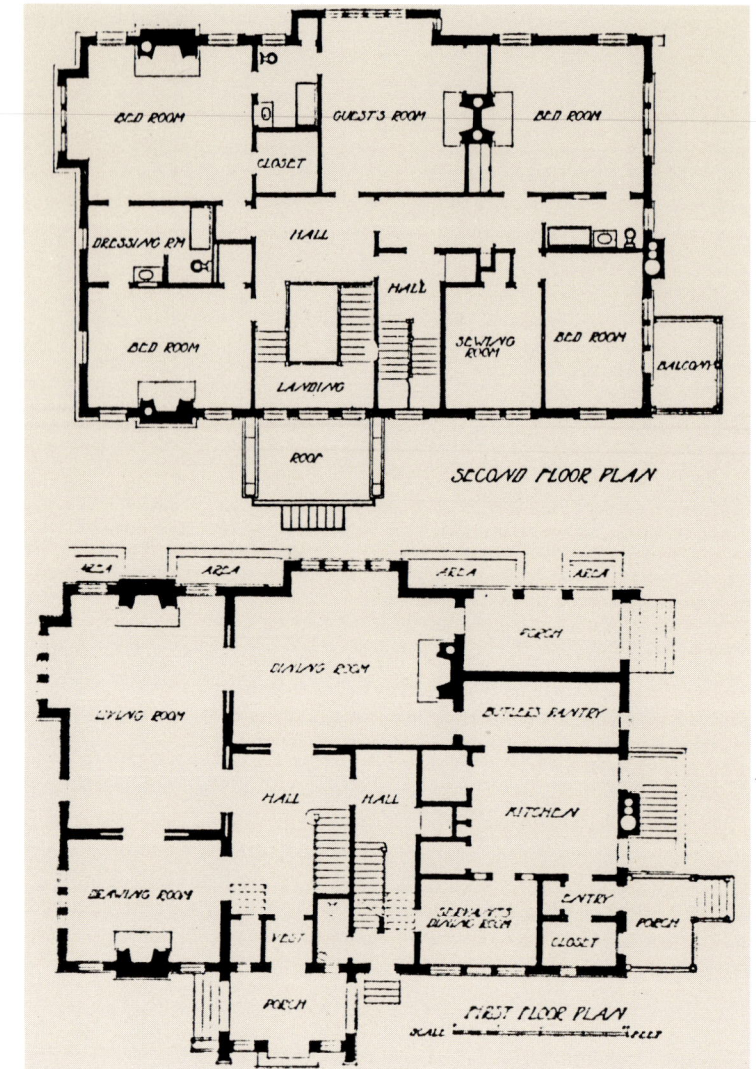

SECOND FLOOR PLAN

FIRST FLOOR PLAN

The floor plan drawn up by the Mauran, Russell & Garden architectural firm for the William Evans Guy family of 10 Portland.

Lloyd Wright in his early work. In 1914 Mauran, Russell & Crowell added a wing along Union Boulevard, making the facade asymmetrical. Lucas (1862–1940) was the son of a Hungarian father and a German mother and was trained in architecture locally. Much of his work was in medium-priced houses and flats, but he did work on a few other houses of this scale, including the Bagnell house mentioned earlier and a house in Compton Heights for Simon Freund, Leopold's brother and former partner in the Freund Bakery.

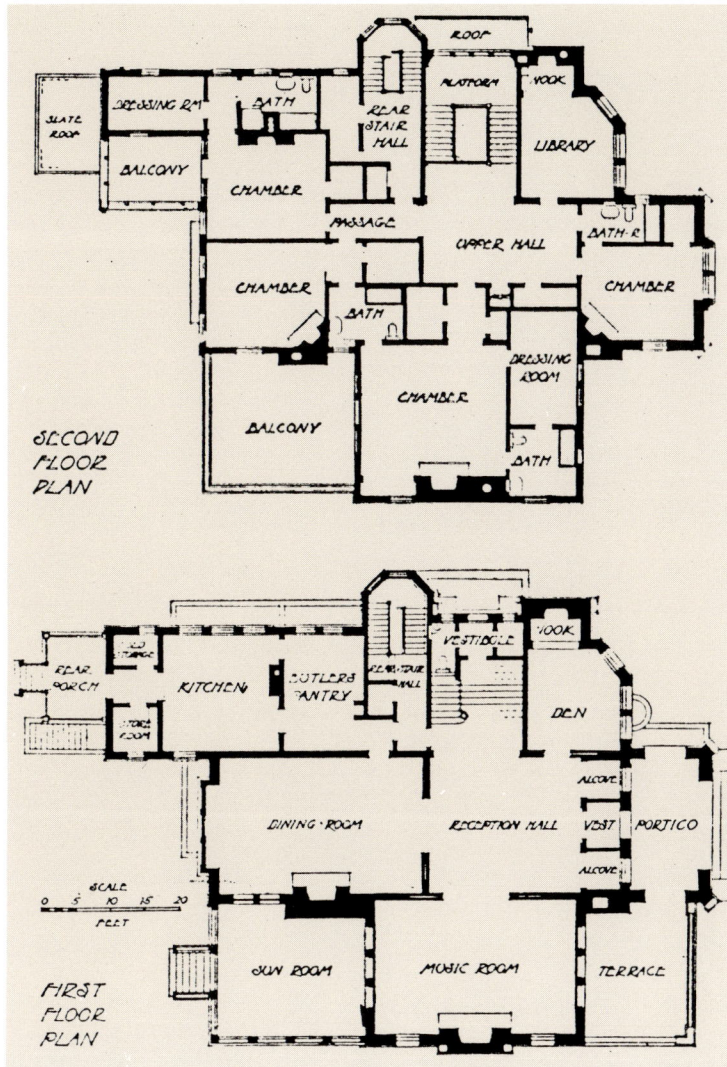

The Mauran & Garden floor plan for the Sadie and Charles Stix house at 26 Portland. The principal rooms around the main hall were laid out so the residents could enjoy a southeastern exposure.

The influence of Mauran, Russell & Crowell can also be seen in 6 Portland, which was designed in 1915 for hardware magnate Alfred L. Shapleigh by Hellmuth & Hellmuth. Its elevation is nearly identical to that of the house designed by Mauran, Russell & Crowell for Harry Lesser and built at 12 Washington Terrace in 1910. The Hellmuth brothers could also have noted that house's publication in *The Brickbuilder* in February 1914. Both houses vary the Colonial-Italian mix with a prominent stair turret.

Mauran, Russell & Crowell designed a house unlike any other in Westmoreland/Portland in 1911. Located at 33 Portland, it was commissioned by Realtor Claude Kilpatrick. Although it has virtually no design features in common with the Petit Trianon at Versailles to which it has frequently been likened, the house is derived from French eighteenth-century design in general, particularly from the Parisian townhouses and suburban villas of the first half of that century. The firm's new partner, William DeForest Crowell, had studied in Paris under a Rotch scholarship bestowed by the Massachusetts Institute of Technology. In plan, however, the Kilpatrick house could only belong to the period of the porte cochere; in addition to its wide central entryway, the design features a transverse corridor running completely across the house from the carriage entry to the staircase.

Other styles achieved popularity in Westmoreland and Portland, but that most frequently adopted for houses in this district during the first three decades of this century was the Tudor Revival. We have seen that the style made its first tentative appearance in the 1890s, heralded by half-timbering. The style had one attraction in common with the older Shingle and Romanesque styles: it easily accommodated irregular and asymmetrical floor plans that could be closely adapted to the needs of the occupants. On the other hand, most of the sixteenth- and seventeenth-century country houses that were the first models required considerable manipulation to fit onto narrow city lots.

The Tudor Revival reappeared in 1905 in the house designed by Theodore Link for millionaire shoe manufacturer Oscar Johnson at 38 Portland and in that designed by Weber & Groves for banker Charles Parsons Pettus at 33 Westmoreland. All brick rather than half-timbered, but very large, they must have made quite an impact along Lake Avenue, situated as they were on diagonally opposite corners and with wings extending back through their lots. This juxtaposition has not been visible since the Pettus house was demolished in 1941. Both houses had patterns worked into their dark-colored brick, and both employed the stone-framed casement windows characteristic of the style. The Johnson mansion was the more picturesque, with its gables and irregular massing. Its plan was also unusual, with a library and billiard room among the second-floor bedrooms. Link also designed the headquarters for the International Shoe Company, which Oscar Johnson headed, as well as several other houses for the company's owners. The rear wing of the Pettus house included an art gallery where Pettus displayed part of the collection that had been assembled by his uncle Charles Parsons, about 80 oils and 360 art objects including works by Reynolds, Raeburn, Hoppner, Church, and Inness. Through the will of Charles Parsons, Washington University acquired the collection

on Pettus's death in 1923.

The N. B. Kauffman house at 48 Portland was started in 1907, a half-timbered structure that looms over its slightly younger Georgian neighbors. The architects were Mariner & LaBeaume; Louis LaBeaume built a similar house for himself at 40 Waterman Place, which is just west and a block north of Portland. That house also served as a model for Saum Architects when they designed the Edmunds-Nims house at 56 Portland in 1915. Mauran, Russell & Garden joined the new fashion in 1908 with the Guy house at 10 Portland, a design that appears to be an anticipation of their house for dry-goods merchant Charles Stix the following year. The Guy house has no entry facing the street. The Stix house, at 26 Portland, has a massive entry portico surmounted by an oriel window, surely reflecting a study of medieval gatehouses. Collegiate and monastic sources, rather than country houses, seem also to have influenced Eames & Young in their Holland house at 47 Westmoreland, also started in 1909. While the scale of the Stix mansion rivals the palazzi around it, the Holland house adopts the more modest dimensions of Jamieson's contemporary Georgian. The recognition that a Tudor Revival style on a reasonable domestic scale was possible no doubt increased its popularity. The year 1910 brought Cope & Stewardson's Mary Lionberger house at 30 Westmoreland, 1911 the George Barnard house at 35 Portland by Kivas Tully, and 1912 Mauran, Russell & Crowell's Scott house at 31 Westmoreland (accenting its Tudor body with a Doric frontispiece, much in the way the Renaissance was actually introduced to England). Jamieson, whose mastery of half-timbering is seen in houses elsewhere in St. Louis, never had a comparable opportunity in Westmoreland or Portland, but the smaller, predominantly brick houses he did build here are attractive in their own way. The Wiggins house was built at 17 Portland in 1916 and the Kennerly house at 28 Portland in 1919. The McPheeters house was built at 27 Westmoreland in 1931, the last house on a hitherto undeveloped lot in either of the places. Like the Wiggins house, the McPheeters house has a second-floor loggia, a feature seen earlier in the Italian Eclectic Fowler house. Here the design source seems to be the staircase loggias found in French châteaus and townhouses of circa 1500.

Beginning with the Breckinridge Jones house in 1935, a dozen of the finest houses in Westmoreland and Portland places were demolished, the most recent in 1961. Ten new houses went up on these lots, all but one of them more or less Georgian in style. The most popular practitioners of that style during this period were Gale Henderson (1880–1969) and Raymond Maritz (1894–1973). These two talented architects had worked together from 1915 to 1920 but had then gone their separate ways. Henderson's first house in the places was the Tudor Revival one

Victor Proetz, whose brother Arthur built the second house on the lot at 12 Westmoreland, achieved international recognition as an interior designer. He designed the furniture and arranged the interiors for his brother's house, including a sitting room on the second floor (far left), the front bedroom (center), and the library (near left).

built in 1930 at 8 Westmoreland for R. W. Coale, with its striking oriel over the front door. He worked more frequently in the Georgian style, using its quoins, shutters, and white trim to accommodate modern floor plans that did not always adhere to Georgian symmetry. A good example of this is the house Henderson designed for Charles Belknap at 45 Westmoreland; it replaced the Bascom house there in 1939. The house achieves a suburban look by taking advantage of its wide lot and deep setback, with broad proportions and ample roof. One hardly notices that the Belknap house has only two bays to the left of the nominally centered door but three bays to the right. Henderson also designed four other replacement houses in Westmoreland, Number 28 in 1934, Numbers 21 and 26 in 1941, and Number 23 in 1950. He produced many similar houses in suburban Clayton and Ladue, often acting as his own contractor and even building some houses on speculation.

Henderson's former partner Raymond Maritz formed a partnership with Ridgely Young in 1921, and their firm dominated the market for large houses in the 1920s and 1930s. Although competent in the Georgian mode, the firm was most adept at styles requiring more picturesque massing, particularly the Tudor Revival and Spanish Colonial Revival. Maritz, Young & Dusard designed 33 Westmoreland for John and Elsie Curby, replacing the assertive three-story Tudor house by Albert Groves that had formerly occupied that site with a reticent two-story Georgian house. The Curby house was typical of the change in the appearance of the places that the replacement houses made in combination with the other newer houses of the late 1920s and early 1930s. Certain stretches of Westmoreland in particular now look almost suburban, while the older, larger palazzi

such as the Adams house at Number 25, once so carefully designed to fit in with their neighbors, now seem to be the intruders.

The house built in 1938 for Dr. Arthur W. Proetz at 12 Westmoreland is a great deal smaller than the Dozier house that looms next to it or the Bagnell house it replaced. Superficially, the Proetz house resembles the other twentieth-century Georgian houses on the block, but on closer inspection it can be seen to be a much more studied and personal design. Its architect was Ralph Cole Hall (1897–1977), who had been the partner of Dr. Proetz's brother Victor from 1924 to 1934. Hall and Proetz were both very knowledgeable about Georgian and early American design, but they were also able to manipulate period details to create a strikingly modern effect. This is evident in the Proetz house in the juxtaposition of the severely neoclassical Doric porch against the salmon brick house. The garden elevation, which is clearly visible from Lindell Boulevard across the site of still another demolished house, is also carefully composed around a two-story bay window. Victor Proetz (1897–1966) had left the partnership to pursue his interest in interior design, and he achieved international recognition for the London penthouse he created for Lord Louis Mountbatten (later Earl Mountbatten of Burma). As a designer, Proetz not only arranged interiors but also designed furniture; many of these pieces are now in the offices of the National Portrait Gallery in Washington, which was his last project. The rooms he designed for his brother were among his outstanding achievements, and the drawings for them are now in the collection of the St. Louis Art Museum. Before the current redevelopment of the old Siegrist property at 2 Westmoreland, the most recent houses to go up were at 2

Portland and 11 Westmoreland, both started in 1960 for Realtor Barbara Lucich following designs of Alfred Johnson. These are both conservative neo-Georgian designs typical of Johnson's work and would have looked more at home in the suburbs of the period. The last architecturally significant house in the Westmoreland/Portland complex, and the only contemporary design, is 45 Portland, designed for Mr. and Mrs. Howard Baer in 1953 by Frederick Dunn. In the 1930s Dunn had been in partnership with Charles Nagel, Jr., the son of the man who built 44 Westmoreland. Very much like Hall & Proetz, Nagel & Dunn were modern traditionalists (or traditional modernists, depending on where they placed their emphasis). After World War II, Charles Nagel became director of the City Art Museum of St. Louis and later of the National Portrait Gallery (where he hired Victor Proetz). Dunn continued to practice architecture, and although he was not widely known, he was highly respected as a modernist. At 45 Portland, Dunn had clients who appreciated his abilities. Mrs. Baer, the former Isabel Aloe, explained her design philosophy to the St. Louis Globe-Democrat in 1959: "After all, if you are able to get a good architect to design a home, it's really a piece of art. And I think houses are just like paintings. You shouldn't expect a painter of today to paint like they did in the seventeenth century. Houses also should reflect the era they're built in." Now more than a generation old, the modern design of the Baer house is already an architectural relic. But like many of the older houses around it and like those seventeenth-century paintings Mrs. Baer spoke of, it is a work of art, capable of giving pleasure to generations still to come.

CHRONOLOGY
OF OWNERS

The following is a listing of the architects and building-permit dates and a chronology of the owners and their spouses for all the houses on Westmoreland and Portland places. In the listings, spouses' names are joined by *and* with the couple's last name following the wife's maiden name, when the maiden name is known, or the wife's first name and middle initial. The names of nonspousal co-owners are separated by semicolons, with the relationship indicated when it could be determined. When one spouse continued in residence longer than the other, the death or departure date of the no-longer-resident spouse has been included in parentheses, when it is known. Dates indicate ownership of the lot from purchase to sale. Owners who sold a property before it was improved or within a few months of acquiring the property have not been included.

2 Westmoreland

Permit: 8 August 1896
Architect: W. Albert Swasey

1895–1901	Henry Ashley and Minnie Lawrence Siegrist
1901–1938	James (d. 1914) and Florence Platener Campbell
1938–1947	Elzey (d. 1946) and Lois Campbell Burkham (vacant 1947–1961)
1961	demolished

6 Westmoreland

Permit: 7 April 1890
Architect: Eames & Young

1888–1942	Robert McKittrick (d. 1940) and Grace Richards Jones
1942–1943	George W. and Virginia B. Hamilton
1943–1980	Edwin F. and Margaret Crane-Lillie Gildea
1980–	Gerald and Lorraine Dreifke

1 Westmoreland

Permit: 25 May 1894
Architect: W. Albert Swasey

1889–1921	Jacob C. (d. 1908) and Mary G. Van Blarcom
1921–1959	John C. Moon (d. 1933); Maude Moon Lee (daughter)
1959–1976	William S., Jr., and Virginia B. Smith
1976–1976	Earl D. and Carole Gales
1976–	William A. and Celia Rosemary Walker

5 Westmoreland

Permit: 22 August 1891
Architect: Eames & Young

1888–1936	Theodore (d. 1901) and Lucretia Block Meysenburg (vacant 1929–1935)
1936–1944	Walter (d. 1940) and Ruth McCracken Scott
1944–1951	Calvin F. and Delphine Polk Gatch
1951–1952	Malotte Houser Lehman (vacant)
1952–1969	Donaldson L. and Caroline Simpson-Polk Lambert
1969–1972	Norris H. Allen (vacant)
1972–1975	Earl D. and Carole B. Gales
1975–1984	William G. and Carolyn C. McCollom
1984–	Michael and Gretchen Freund Curran

7 Westmoreland

Permit: 25 February 1890
Architect: James Stewart & Co.

1888–1944	Alexander G. (d. 1928) and Mary V. Andrews Cochran
1944–1945	Crawford and Jane Burns Johnson
1945–1946	Emily Catlin Shepley
1946–1946	Martha Ferguson Butler
1946–1982	Daniel L. and Adelaide Mahaffey Schlafly
1982–1986	William and Patricia Handloss Stern
1986–	John Steven and Cynthia Sandburg

8 Westmoreland

Permit: 18 March 1930
Architect: Gale E. Henderson

1927–1956   Ralph W. (d. 1950) and Marguerite York Coale (d. 1955)
1956–1973   Wilbur and Irene Clifford Jones
1973–1974   F. Carl and Clay Hancock Schumacher
1974–1979   James T. and Ellen Corley Human
1979–1983   Paul and Ingrid Tucker
1983–   John and Judy Kujawski

10 Westmoreland

Permit: 11 July 1895
Architect: John L. Wees

1893–1914   Lewis D. (d. 1914) and Rebecca E. Lewis Dozier
1914–1920   Lewis D., Jr., and Elizabeth Overton Dozier
1920–1951   George and Fanita Hayward Niedringhaus
1951–1957   Granville and Opal Gamblin
1957–1975   John M. (d. 1974) and Angela Parato
1975–1979   Charles D. and Ernestina Parato Short
1979–   Sutter A. Gardanier II

11 Westmoreland (Second)

Permit: April 1960
Architect: Alfred Johnson

1959–1960   Barbara Lucich (nonresident)
1960–1967   Edwin, Sr., and Sally B. Guth
1967–1968   James B. Guth
1968–   Marjorie R. Brooks (d. 1981); George R. Brooks (son)

9 Westmoreland

Permit: 19 June 1890
Architect: Eames & Young

1888–1926   William L. (d. 1901) and Martha E. Brown Huse
1926–1959   Isaac A. and Ione Huse Hedges
1959–   Norris H. and Dorothea Hedges Allen

11 Westmoreland (Original)

Permit: no record (probably built 1891)
Architect: Grable & Weber

1888–1945   Thomas H. (d. 1926) and (1) Florence Terry West (d. 1898)
            (2) Virginia Hodges West (vacant 1933–1945)
1945–1947   Pierre L. and Lily Allen Papin
1947–1959   Thomas W. and Jane Messick Pettus
1958   demolished

12 Westmoreland (Original)

Permit: 21 May 1890
Architect: William A. Lucas

1889–1928   William (d. 1926) and Sally Adams Bagnell
1928–1936   George W. and Neosha Hobart Cale
1936   demolished

12 Westmoreland (Second)

Permit: 30 July 1938
Architect: Ralph Cole Hall

1938–1987   Arthur (d. 1969) and (1) Erma Perham Proetz (d. 1944) (2) Esther Schroepfer Proetz
1987–   Love Realty Co. (vacant)

13 Westmoreland

Permit: 9 June 1899
Architect: Ernst Janssen

1888–1926   Edwards (d. 1926) and Sophia Taylor Whitaker
1926–1946   Samuel Craft (d. 1940) and Emma Whitaker Davis
1946–1953   Baarent and Anna B. Ten Broek
1953–1972   Mary Douglas Carpenter Greve
1972–1975   Clifford and Mary Jane Greve
1975–   Fred and (1) Nancy G. Guyton (until 1978) (2) Nancy Rutter Guyton

16 Westmoreland

Permit: 26 June 1913
Architect: James P. Jamieson

1913–1974   Edward, Jr. (d. 1967), and Elizabeth Elliot Mallinckrodt
1974–   Andrew Sproule, Jr., and Sarah Otto Love

17 Westmoreland

Permit: 1 July 1892
Architect: Peabody, Stearns & Furber

1891–1932   John T. (d. 1894) and Maria Filley Davis
1932–1938   John T., Jr., and Edith January Davis
1938–1959   Samuel Craft Davis, Jr. (vacant 1955–1959)
1959–1976   Harry and Marjorie Moore
1976–1978   Heinz Peter
1978–1984   Reno R., Jr., and Cheryl A. Cova
1984–1986   Jeffrey and Debra McAlear Gluck
1986–   Leon and Mary Strauss

20 Westmoreland

Permit: 12 March 1906
Architect: Lawrence Ewald

1905–1916   Annie Lee Allen Chauvenet (widow of Louis)
1916–1923   Philip and Virginia Riddle Fouke
1923–1927   Lujafil Realty Co.
1927–1929   J. Clifford and Emily Catlin Wickham-McKittrick Rosengarten
1929–1934   James Alexander and Mary Anderson Summers-Liggett McVoy
1934–1936   J. Clifford and Emily Catlin Wickham-McKittrick Rosengarten
1936–1958   Charles McL. and Lenore Scullin Clark (d. 1955)
1958–1961   Robert W. and Jeanne Kelly Powers
1961–1962   Chester L. Wells
1962–1983   Richard S. and Emily C. Gordon
1983–   John D. and Linda F. Massa; William F. Massa

21 Westmoreland (Original)

Permit: 20 May 1889
Architect: Peabody, Stearns & Furber

1889–1893   Sallie (Sarah) and Henry Levi Newman
1893–1929   Edward C. and Carrie W. Simmons (d. 1920) (vacant 1926–1929)
1929–1936   The Virginia Investment Co.
1936–1941   Richard W. Simmons
1941   demolished

21 Westmoreland (Second)

Permit: 19 August 1941
Architect: Gale E. Henderson

1941–1949   Virginia Wright Simmons (widow of George Welch Simmons)
1949–1987   John H. and Lulie Simmons Crago
1987–   Dennis and Darcy O'Neill

23 Westmoreland (Original)

Permit: 1 August 1896
Architect: Shepley, Rutan & Coolidge

1896–1925   Hudson E. and Helen D. Bridge
1925–1950   L. Warrington and Marye Dodge Baldwin
1950   demolished

25 Westmoreland

Permit: 9 February 1896
Architect: W. Albert Swasey

1888–1923   Elmer B. (d. 1916) and Emma Richmond Adams
1923–1946   Rolla (d. 1944) and Carlota Clark-Church Wells
1946–1950   Wells Realty and Investment Company
1950–   Carroll S. and Laura B. Mastin

22 Westmoreland

Permit: 4 February 1891
Architect: Eames & Young

1889–1902   Edward Canfield and Cordelia Seavey Sterling
1902–1930   Alfred (d. 1927) and Bessie Johnson Clifford
1930–1957   E. Lansing and Mary Burkham Ray
1957–1968   John B. and Genevieve Mullins Mitchell
1968–1972   William B. and Genevieve Mullins-Mitchell Mattimore
1972–1981   Walter R. and Judith L. Clevidence
1981–1983   Matt B. and Florence F. Kallman
1983–   Rexford H. and Rachel S. Caruthers

23 Westmoreland (Second)

Permit: 3 October 1950
Architect: Gale E. Henderson

1950–1970   Harry Bailey, Jr., and Constance Andrews Mathews (Mississippi Lime Co.)
1970–1984   Alphonso J. and Carmen Davis Cervantes
1984–1987   Elwood L. Clary
1987–   Charles D. Schmitt

26 Westmoreland (Original)

Permit: 16 April 1892
Architect: Eames & Young

1891–1941   George L. (d. 1924) and Lillie McCreery (d. 1936) Allen
1938   demolished

26 Westmoreland (Second)

Permit: 3 March 1941
Architect: Gale E. Henderson

1941–1958   Warne and Elizabeth Terry-Shepley Niedringhaus
1958–1981   David D. and Louise Olin Braun Walker
1981–   Daniel L. and Adelaide Mahaffey Schlafly

28 Westmoreland (Original)

Permit: 1 August 1902
Architect: George C.W. Hellmuth

1902–1905   Emma C. Copelin (widow of John G.)
1905–1924   John Julius and Caroline Mastin O'Fallon
1924–1939   William Julius and Sarah Chambers Polk
1939   demolished

29 Westmoreland

Permit: 6 September 1894
Architect: W. Albert Swasey

1892–1917   Byron (d. 1908) and Julia Lake Nugent
1917–1931   Julian Lake Nugent
1931–1941   Edwin T. and Olga Clinton Nugent
1941–1966   Clifford W. and Catherine Manley-Pirrung Gaylord
1966–1976   Gilbert R. and Joan H. Pirrung
1976–1982   Robert B. and Cathleen Bardone
1982–   William W. and Soon Kim

27 Westmoreland

Permit: 14 July 1931
Architect: Jamieson & Spearl

1931–1979   Thomas S. (d. 1958) and Frances Filley McPheeters
1979–   Gerald J. Fivian

28 Westmoreland (Second)

Permit: no record (probably built in 1939)
Architect: Gale E. Henderson

1939–1955   Sterling E. (d. 1944) and Eugenia Howard Edmunds
1955–1963   Richard H. and Florence Waltke
1963–   Frank G. and Carmeline M. Viviano

30 Westmoreland

Permit: 18 March 1910
Architect: James P. Jamieson (Cope & Stewardson)

1908–1939   Mary Lionberger
1939–1944   Calvin F. and Delphine Polk Gatch
1944–1958   Ada Tyler Eaton
1958–   Edward J., Jr., and Katherine Mahaffey Walsh

31 Westmoreland

Permit: 15 July 1912
Architect: Mauran, Russell & Crowell

1911–1946	Bertha Drake Scott (widow of Henry Clarkson Scott)
1946–1975	William R., Jr., and Laura Rand Orthwein
1975–1978	V. Jose and Gracy Thomas
1978–	Harvey A. and Linda E. Harris

33 Westmoreland (Original)

Permit: 29 May 1905
Architect: Weber & Groves

1905–1935	Charles Parsons (d. 1923) and Georgia Wright Pettus (Cortland Realty Company)
1935–1941	St. Louis Realty and Securities Co. (vacant)
1941	demolished

34 Westmoreland

Permit: 9 March 1909
Architect: Mauran, Russell & Garden

1905–1935	George F. and Carrie Howard Steedman
1935–1962	Richard and Almira Steedman Baldwin
1962–1985	Eugene B. and Emilie Wilkey
1985–	Gary and Sheila Greenbaum Wasserman

32 Westmoreland

Permit: 31 May 1923
Architect: Jamieson & Spearl

1916–1961	Edwin H. (d. 1961) and Almira McNeely Steedman
1961–1982	Richard and Almira Steedman Baldwin
1982–	Athanasios Michael Athanasiades

33 Westmoreland (Second)

Permit: 14 August 1941
Architect: Maritz, Young & Dusard

1941–1971	John E. and Elsie Ford Curby
1971–	William Kearney Hall

35 Westmoreland

Permit: 17 May 1912
Architect: Mauran, Russell & Crowell

1911–1929	John (d. 1924) and Cora Liggett Fowler
1929–1963	Emma (widow of Henry) and Georgie (daughter) Elliot
1963–	Ben H. and Katherine Gladney Wells

36 Westmoreland

Permit: 12 August 1908
Architect: Hellmuth & Spiering

1903–1932	Louis W. Werner
1932–1935	Joseph L. and Elise Garneau Werner
1935–1941	James S. and Caroline Patterson Bush
1941–1975	Norris B., Jr., and Eloise Higgins Gregg
1975–	Kate May Gregg

38 Westmoreland

Permit: 13 April 1892
Architect: Peabody, Stearns & Furber

1890–1910	Corinne Chouteau Dyer (widow of John N.)
1910–1941	Samuel (d. 1928) and Katherine Shallcross Gordon
1941–1965	Samuel F. and Julia Lawnin Gordon
1965–1976	Bernard and Margaret L. Fehlman
1976–	James B. and Barbara J. Nierengarten Smith

41 Westmoreland

Permit: 3 November 1905
Architect: James P. Jamieson (Cope & Stewardson)

1905–1965	Daniel K., Jr. (d. 1964), and Gertrude Loring Hamlen Catlin
1965–	Homer E. and Elizabeth Gentry Sayad

37 Westmoreland

Permit: 6 November 1905
Architect: James P. Jamieson (Cope & Stewardson)

1905–1946	Isaac and Louise Shepley Lionberger
1946–1949	The Eighteenth Street Building
1949–	Robert Hays and Jean Malugen Shoenberg

40 Westmoreland

Permit: no record (probably built in 1892)
Architect: Shepley, Rutan & Coolidge

1890–1930	John Dwight and Frances Douglas (d. 1926) Filley
1930–1973	James H. and Ellen Filley Wear
1973–1976	Byron D. and Elma L. Sachar
1976–1978	Michael J. and Sally P. Soehingen
1978–1980	Michael and Cynthia Lewis
1980–	Ronald A. and Susan C. Brown

42 Westmoreland

Permit: 8 October 1906
Architect: James P. Jamieson (Cope & Stewardson)

1906–1919	Clarkson and Amy Holland Potter
1919–1923	James Harrison (d. 1921) and Virginia Chase-Wedell Steedman
1923–1958	Ira Edward and Marie Ewing Wight
1958–1970	Ira E., Jr., and Elizabeth Forest Wight
1970–1979	Carlton C. and Marion Hall Hunt
1979–	Robert and Mary Ann McDivitt

44 Westmoreland

Permit: 5 February 1914
Architect: LaBeaume & Klein

1908–1926   Charles and Anne Shepley Nagel
1926–1983   Edward K. and Laura Sproule Love
1983–   Charles and Martha Love Symington

45 Westmoreland (Second)

Permit: 4 May 1939
Architect: Gale E. Henderson

1937–1968   Charles and Helen Rockwood Belknap
1968–1975   Charles K. and Madelyn Hofling
1975–1987   Edward L. and Linda L. Eyerman
1987–   Howard V. and Katherine H. Stephens

47 Westmoreland

Permit: 2 September 1909
Architect: Eames & Young

1907–1924   Nora W. Holland (widow of George)
1924–1939   Kenneth Lemoine and Lucie R. Scudder Green
1939–1956   Henry and Dorothy Holloway Pflager
1956–1959   Henry B. Pflager
1959–1970   Francis C. and Barbara Barton Corley
1970–1974   Robert A. K., Jr., and Katherine Southworth Smith
1974–1986   Harry D. and Dorothy Schwartz
1986–   James T. and Linda Daake

45 Westmoreland (Original)

Permit: 24 April 1899
Architect: Frederick Bonsack

1889–1933   Joseph Dayton (d. 1928) and Mary Magdalene Frederick
             Bascom
1933–1935   Loco Realty Company (vacant)
1935–1936   Wm. S. Barnickel & Co. (vacant)
1936   demolished

46 Westmoreland

Permit: 31 March 1908
Architect: Mariner & LaBeaume

1905–1916   William A. (d. 1913) and Millecent Taylor Stickney
1916–1963   Wallace D. and Jessamine Barstow Simmons
1963–1975   Gerald F. and Frances G. Klapp
1975–1982   John R. and Mary T. Sutter
1982–   Richard and Linda Stein

48 Westmoreland

Permit: 31 March 1908
Architect: Mariner & LaBeaume

1908–1955   Allen T. (d. 1952) and Rebekah Semple West
1955–1975   Bradford, Jr., and Lucile Keeler Shinkle
1975–1980   Elmer J. and Freda Grommet
1980–1982   Carlos Frederico and Norma Joly
1982–1983   Thomas and Christine Brennan
1983–   Richard T. and Gail H. Hellan

49 Westmoreland

Permit: 8 December 1908
Architect: Mariner & LaBeaume

1908–1980 Harry H. (d. 1958) and Alice Morton Langenberg
1980– Victor R. Buzzotta

50 Westmoreland

Permit: 28 July 1908
Architect: Mauran, Russell & Garden

1908–1933 Arthur Behn (d. 1918) and Emily Catlin Shepley
1933–1954 Frederick and Florence Gottschalk Taussig
1954–1986 Thomas S. and Mary Taussig-Tompkins Hall
1986– Charles E. and Patricia Ranlette Valier

51 Westmoreland

Permit: 30 August 1915
Architect: James P. Jamieson

1915–1945 Justina Kayser Catlin (widow of Daniel K., Sr.)
1945–1948 Warren and Gertrude Catlin Chandler
1948–1953 Isaac D. and Kathleen McBride Kelley
1953–1960 Darwin R. and Mary Myrtle Howard
1960–1969 Alphonso J. and Carmen Davis Cervantes
1969–1974 Eugene A. and Barbara Timmerman Tuchschmidt
1974–1983 Joseph and Mildred Cohn
1983– James T. Human

52 Westmoreland

Permit: 20 July 1905
Architect: A. A. Fischer

1905–1909 Herman C. G. and May Carlin Luyties (nonresidents)
1909–1911 Carl Raymond and Hariette Flora Gray
1911–1941 Robert D. and Virginia Hinton Lewis
1941–1981 Edward C., II, and Jean Ford Simmons
1981–1984 Robert W. and Marie Rasner
1984– B. Morton and Cecilia Patton Bolman

53 Westmoreland

Permit: 2 June 1908
Architect: William A. Lucas

1907–1913 Leopold and Hannah Linz Freund
1913–1918 Charles H. and Elizabeth Bailey
1918–1919 Appolonia P. Ghio (nonresident)
1919–1919 John H. Grote (nonresident)
1919–1920 Nancy Clarke (nonresident)
1920–1977 Willard (d. 1949) and Genevieve Wilson Bartlett
1977–1984 Gary Werths
1984– Richard B. and JoAnne Kuhns

54 Westmoreland

Permit: 18 March 1913
Architect: James P. Jamieson

1912–1920 Walter and Marjory Holland McKittrick
1920–1946 James L., Jr., and Jean Wright Ford
1946–1975 Emily Catlin Shepley
1975–1986 Charles E. and Sharon Kozemczak Valier
1986– Stuart and Claudia Millner

1 Portland

Permit: 2 March 1910
Architect: Barnett, Haynes & Barnett

1909–1945   Edward A. (d. 1936) and Anna Busch Faust (d. 1935) (vacant 1938–1945)
1945–1957   Harry and Marjorie Moore
1957–   Otto R. (d. 1986) and Marian Sherrill Erker (until 1969)

2 Portland (Second House on Original Number 4 site)

Permit: 15 December 1960
Architect: Alfred Johnson

1960–1961   Barbara Lucich (nonresident)
1961–1971   Morris and Charlotte Mandel
1971–   James M. and Gloria Whittico

6 Portland

Permit: 19 July 1915
Architect: Hellmuth & Hellmuth

1915–1950   Alfred L. (d. 1945) and Mina Wessel Shapleigh
1950–1966   Royal and Jane Shapleigh Kercheval
1966–1972   Robert M. and Alice A. Walker
1972–   Jack L. and (1) Marjorie W. Croughan (until 1984) (2) Patricia Pepe Croughan

4 Portland (Original)

Permit: 15 May 1891
Architect: W. Albert Swasey

1890–1930   Samuel M. (d. 1916) and Annie Maude Kennard
1930–1958   Kennard Estate (vacant)
1958   demolished

5 Portland

Permit: 19 September 1894
Architect: Barnett, Haynes & Barnett

1892–1941   Thomas W. (d. 1924) and Mary Louise Lupton Carter (vacant 1939–1941)
1941   demolished
1943   joined with Number 7

7 Portland

Permit: June 1927
Architect: LaBeaume & Klein

1926–1932   N. S. Chouteau and Julia Crosby Walsh
1932–1942   Norris B., Jr., and Eloise Higgins Gregg
1942–1943   Edgar Monsanto and Ethel Schneider Queeny
1943–1953   George C. and Jean H. Wilson
1953–1972   Helen Rand (widow of Joseph O.)
1972–   Wilfred Leach

8 Portland

Permit: 16 August 1912
Architect: LaBeaume & Klein

1905–1965   Lemuel Ray (d. 1958) and May Dillon Carter
1965–   William McBride (d. 1985) and (1) Gloria O'Hearn Love
         (until 1970) (2) Lida Lee Christy Love

9 Portland

Permit: 10 August 1897
Architect: Shepley, Rutan, Coolidge & Mauran

1897–1925   John A. (d. 1915) and Belle Robb Holmes
1925–1959   Birch O. and Laura McBride Mahaffey (d. 1933) (Mesco
         Corp.)
1959–1982   Fristoe and Elizabeth Mahaffey Mullins
1982–   Kimball R. and Lisa Mullins McMullin

10 Portland

Permit: 15 April 1908
Architect: Mauran, Russell & Garden

1905–1929   William E. and Katherine Lemoine Guy
1929–1944   Arthur C. and Frances Billingsley Garrison
1944–1953   Edna Sutter Brinckenkamp; Antonia Sutter
1953–1976   Paul and Harriet Moore-Rodes Bakewell
1976–1986   John G. and Patricia Ann Horen
1986–   Thomas H. Brouster

12 Portland

Permit: 6 December 1905
Architect: Mauran, Russell & Garden

1893–1940   George Oliver (d. 1934) and Caroline Greeley Carpenter
1940–1941   Mabel Filley Simmons (vacant)
1941–1968   William D. and Monica D. Crowell
1968–1971   Bernard and Lois H. Royce
1971–1979   Arthur and Paula Littleton
1979–1982   Randall and Charlette B. Phillips
1982–1983   Robert and Priscilla Gontram
1983–   Martin R. and Deborah K. Berg

13 Portland

Permit: 30 November 1892
Architect: W. Albert Swasey

1891–1904   William Keeney and Lillian Tuttle Bixby
1904–1916   Walter J. and Agnes H. McBride
1916–1923   George M. and Katherine Fisher Brown
1923–1987   William H. (d. 1967) and Stella Fresch Bixby
1987–   Lynda G. Entratter

15 Portland

Permit: 26 July 1898
Architect: Widmann, Walsh & Boisselier

1898–1925   William D. (d. 1925) and Emily Thuemmler Orthwein
1925–1941   Frederick C. (d. 1927) and Jeanette Niedringhaus Orthwein
1941–1955   Joseph and Marie S. Desloge
1955–1957   John C. and Virginia Ball Gross
1957–1958   Ann C. Clark
1958–1962   Morris and Libby G. Bass
1962–1974   Harold B. and Nanette R. Huhn
1974–1987   Irvin H. and Helene Patricia Raisher
1987–   Dale and MaryAnn Billings

16 Portland

Permit: 15 February 1909
Architect: James P. Jamieson (Cope & Stewardson)

1894–1927	Dwight Filley and Helen Brooks Davis
1927–1966	Andrew W. and Helen Johnson Johnson
1966–1968	Butler and Martha Walker Sturtevant
1968–1969	Don B. and Susan Russe Faerber (nonresidents)
1969–	John T. and Virginia D. Byrne

19 Portland

Permit: 13 September 1893
Architect: Grable & Weber

1893–1898	Oliver A. Hart
1898–1923	Augustus B. (d. 1916) and Clara Ballentine Hart (d. 1918)
1923–1948	George K., Sr., and Eleanor Glasgow Conant
1948–1953	Duncan C. Dobson
1953–1959	Baarent and Anna B. Ten Broek
1959–1964	J. Marvin and Katherine P. Krause
1964–	Isabelle McGrath; Josephine McGrath (nonresidents)

22 Portland

Permit: 29 November 1927
Architect: LaBeaume & Klein

1927–1947	Marion L. J. and Mary Ryan Lambert
1947–1976	Sydney and Stella Hays Shoenberg
1976–1986	Joseph W. and Patricia B. Istwan
1986–	Robert D. and Susan M. Fry

17 Portland

Permit: 6 October 1916
Architect: James P. Jamieson

1916–1953	Charles and Ella Liggett Wiggins (d. 1942) (vacant 1948–1953)
1953–1956	Edward A., Jr., and Mildred P. O'Neal
1956–1959	Hal and Sara F. S. Ratcliffe
1959–1966	Gerard and Jane Tyne Brownlow
1966–1971	Richard S. and Helen H. Reamer
1971–1973	Richard F. O'Hara; Barbara A. Gove
1973–1975	Stanley G. Kann; Norman E. Delaney
1975–1987	Richard E. and Laura D. Hillman
1987–	Russell F. and Barbara J. Richmond

20 Portland

Permit: 27 July 1927
Architect: LaBeaume & Klein

1927–1945	J. D. Perry and Emilie DeMun Smith Francis
1945–1959	Dorothy McBride Orthwein
1959–	Joseph G. and Helen DeLargy Petersen

23 Portland

Permit: 23 August 1892
Architect: Eames & Young

1891–1903	William H. (d. 1901) and Florence Plimpton Thornburgh
1903–1920	William P. and Florence Plimpton-Thornburgh Stribling
1920–1923	Neill A. McMillan
1923–1941	Warren F. and Estella Brown McElroy
1941–1962	Harry J. Tuthill (d. 1956); Irene Morrison (sister)
1962–1967	Donald and Loretto Gunn
1967–1973	Arthur B. and JoAnn Osborn Twersky
1973–	Galen E. (until 1973) and Bonnie K. Mills

24 Portland

Permit: 26 March 1910
Architect: Ernst Janssen

1909–1922   Elizabeth Schnaider (widow of Joseph M.)
1922–1966   Robert A. Barnes (d. 1945) and Stella Schnaider Walsh
1966–   Charles W. and Susan Sallee Lorenz

25 Portland

Permit: 23 August 1892
Architect: Eames & Young

1891–1915   William Northrup (d. 1901) and Eliza McMillan
1915–1957   Jackson (d. 1929) and Minnie Wooten Johnson
1957–1974   Carolyn Skelly Burford
1974–   Christian B., Jr., and Diana Ellis Peper

26 Portland

Permit: 4 August 1909
Architect: Mauran & Russell

1908–1922   Charles A. (d. 1916) and Sadie Fraley Stix
1922–1942   William Keeney (d. 1931) and Lillian Tuttle Bixby (Essex
                  Investment Co.)
1942–1960   James S. and Caroline Patterson Bush
1960–1986   Oliver A. and May Pullen McKee
1986–   Thomas and Adele Daake

28 Portland

Permit: 22 October 1919
Architect: James P. Jamieson

1914–1964   Claude Saugrain and Edith Collins (d. 1945) Kennerly
1964–1965   Roy Pfautch
1965–1968   Edward and Shirley Block
1968–1976   Stephen and Jane Conant Post
1976–1979   Gastone G. and Linda Celesia
1979–1983   James T. Human
1983–1986   Robert W. and Priscilla Gontram
1986–   Brian and Kathleen Lacey

29 Portland

Permit: 12 August 1891
Architect: Theodore Link

1891–1902   Lewis B. and Ellen Mansur Tebbetts
1902–1911   Mary W. McKittrick
1911–1919   Uriel L. and Lillie M. Clark
1919–1948   Lee I. (d. 1933) and Helen Johnson Niedringhaus
1948–1954   Pierre P. Chouteau
1954–1971   Lemoine, Jr. (until 1970), and Grizelda Polk Skinner
1971–1981   Richard E. Young; Frank J. Brettle III
1981–1987   Darryl A. and Ellen Forshaw Ross
1987–   Emory L. and Winnie M. Kesteloot

30 Portland

Permit: 19 August 1897
Architect: Weber & Groves

1892–1921   Benjamin W. (d. 1905) and Elizabeth Evens Clark
1921–1949   James T. and Mary F. Caradine
1949–1969   Lee B. and Alice McBlair Hildebrand
1969–1971   Peter and Marjorie L. Geist
1971–   Eugene A. and Mary Ann Leonard

32 Portland

Permit: 26 August 1898
Architect: Weber & Groves

1893–1905	Charles and Cornelia Eitzen (d. 1901) Fach
1905–1928	Joseph G. and Caroline O'Fallon Miller
1928–1944	Isaac D. and Kathleen McBride Kelley
1944–1960	John L. and Mary Francis Wilson
1960–1978	Glenn A. and Dorothy Hager Delf
1978–	Jerome and Susan Dickens Schlichter

33 Portland

Permit: 30 October 1911
Architect: Mauran, Russell & Crowell

1910–1929	Claude (d. 1918) and Dorothy Liggett Kilpatrick
1929–1945	Frank O. and Helen Moore Watts
1945–1948	William S. and Blossom B. Medart
1948–1950	Lucille Walton Caselton
1950–1965	Fred C. and Patricia Varney
1965–	Walter W. (until 1968) and Lucianna Gladney Ross

35 Portland

Permit: 10 June 1911
Architect: Kivas Tully

1910–1916	George D. (d. 1915) and Mary L. Barnard
1916–1921	John T. (d. 1919) and May Patrick Milliken
1921–1926	Isaac D. and Kathleen McBride Kelley
1926–1978	Bradford (d. 1945) and Florence Johnson Shinkle
1978–	Luis and Rosa Schwarz

36 Portland

Permit: 26 September 1906
Architect: A. A. Fischer

1906–1922	Herman C. G. (d. 1921) and May Carlin Luyties (until 1912)
1922–1974	Charles W. (d. 1968) and Frances Wickham Moore
1974–1978	John G. and Patricia Reilly Levis
1978–1981	Paul C. and Carla Carton
1981–1984	Fred W. and Laura B. Weber
1984–	Joseph L. Bumbery

37 Portland

Permit: 25 April 1906
Architect: Milligan & Wray

1906–1927	David Coalter (d. 1908) and Flora Matthews Gamble
1927–1935	Felix E. and Beatrice Davis Gunter
1935–1944	New York Life Insurance Company (vacant)
1944–1985	Dana G. and Mary Jane Mastin Von Schrader
1985–	Dan A. Powell

38 Portland

Permit: 6 November 1905
Architect: Theodore Link

1904–1954	Oscar (d. 1916) and Irene Walter Johnson
1954–1961	Oscar, Jr., and Eloise Wells-Polk Johnson
1961–1971	Irene M. Morrison
1971–1980	William J. and Elizabeth Darst Costello
1980–	Daniel J. and Karen J. Comte Sullivan

39 Portland

Permit: 24 July 1891
Architect: Albert Knell

1891–1899	William W. and (1) Anna Scott Culver (2) Caroline Cleaveland Culver
1899–1905	Moses Rumsey
1905–1920	Marion M. Rumsey
1920–1949	Lou O. and Mary B. Hocker
1949–1972	Maurice and Fay Feldman Todes
1972–1973	John F., Jr., and Nancy Lee Box
1973–1983	Robert W. and Mary E. Wilkinson
1983–1983	Chalmer B., Jr., and Mary Jane Caudill
1983–	Lary and Concetta Kirchenbauer

40 Portland

Permit: 19 May 1897
Architect: Frederick Bonsack

1897–1936	George W. (d. 1921) and Bettie Bofinger Brown (d. 1934)
1936–1943	Washington University
1943–1956	E. Vernon and Eleanor Chase Mastin
1956–1961	Arthur R. and Marion Morriss Lindburg
1961–	Everett R. and (1) Peggy Leake Lerwick (d. 1967) (2) Shirley Ann Kelly Lerwick (d. 1985)

41 Portland

Permit: 9 April 1929
Architect: Hellmuth & Hellmuth

1929–1939	Selwyn C., Jr. (d. 1934), and Iva Dula Edgar
1939–1953	Kenneth Lemoine and Iva Dula-Edgar Green
1953–1962	Lenita Collins Morrill (widow of Charles H.)
1962–1972	C. Ford and Constance B. Morrill
1972–1978	John B. and Joanne Wrape Kistner
1978–	Thomas F. and Kathe W. Rafferty

42 Portland

Permit: 6 October 1908
Architect: Mariner & LaBeaume

1908–1916	George Patterson and Ellen Reilly Doan
1916–1917	Robert H. and Julia Maffitt Keiser
1917–1919	Charles W. and Jennie N. Whitelaw
1919–1959	Solomon and Selma Kalter Roos
1959–1982	Richard S. and Eleanor Sexsmith Waite
1982–1983	Thomas T. and Camilla J. Tucker (nonresidents)
1983–	David T. and Jill A. Cumming

43 Portland

Permit: 29 September 1911
Architect: Ernst Janssen

1908–1935	Jeanette Filley Morton (widow of Isaac W.)
1935–1979	Russell E., Jr., and Enid G. Simpkins Gardner
1979–1985	Howard S. and Ellen Louise Schwartz
1985–	Robert E. Hawkins

44 Portland

Permit: 27 June 1907
Architect: Frederick Bonsack

1907–1917	Robert H. Keiser; Laura R. Keiser (mother)
1917–1944	Robert H. (d. 1928) and Julia Maffitt Keiser
1944–1945	John and Genevieve Lamy Barlow
1945–1957	Lawrence and Bernice Lightner Post
1957–1959	George A. and Lula Windham Hannaway
1959–1974	Blanche M. Radford (Valuefact Inc.)
1974–1977	John P. and Barbara W. Inman
1977–	John J. and Virginia M. Kraska

45 Portland (Original)

Permit: 26 January 1903
Architect: Weber & Groves

1903–1945 Breckinridge (d. 1928) and (1) Frances Reid Jones (d. 1904)
           (2) Sarah Brant-Colwell Jones (vacant 1930–1935)
1935   demolished

45 Portland (Second)

Permit: 21 November 1953
Architect: Frederick Dunn

1953–1970 Howard F. and Isabel Aloe Baer
1970–   Saul and Rose Boyarsky

46 Portland

Permit: 4 April 1912
Architect: James P. Jamieson

1907–1927 Robert and Caro Nichols Holmes
1927–1940 Thomas H. and Cora South Brown-O'Fallon Wright
1940–1946 Emmet T. and Lillian Baker Carter
1946–1955 Bradford, Jr., and Lucille Keeler Shinkle
1955–1959 Edward L. and Emily Shepley Keyes
1959–1978 William O. and Lida Crawford Shock
1978–1981 Judith K. Hofer
1981–   Roger L. and Fran M. Koch

47 Portland

Permit: 20 June 1902
Architect: Weber & Groves

1901–1912 Frank N. and Mary F. Johnson
1912–1932 John T. and Edith January Davis
1932–1936 The Davis Estate (vacant)
1936–1947 Nelson B. and Olive Tripp Gatch
1947–1963 Leah L. Gardner (widow of Prince)
1963–   Murray E. and Lillian E. Finn

48 Portland

Permit: 13 April 1907
Architect: Mariner & LaBeaume

1906–1911 Nellie Bronson Kauffman (widow of John W.)
1911–1919 Thomas H. and Elsa Lemp Wright
1919–1927 Bradford and Florence Johnson Shinkle
1927–1928 Warne and Florence Lambert Niedringhaus
1928–1957 Florence Lambert-Niedringhaus-(Sharp) Ezell (d. 1938)-(Frederick C., Jr.) Orthwein (d. 1953)
1957–   John W. and Mildred B. Daake

50 Portland

Permit: 9 July 1912
Architect: James P. Jamieson

1912–1941 Henry Blakesley (d. 1918) and Edith Brooks Collins
1941–1944 Henry and Sarah Frances Collins Cook
1944–1976 Robert W. and Katherine Dallmeyer Otto
1976–1980 Robert T. and Bonnie Alexandra Eigelberger
1980–   Michael E. and Cecille Stell Pulitzer

51 Portland

Permit: 12 March 1907
Architect: Mariner & LaBeaume

1907–1971	Harold M. (d. 1936) and Janet Morton Kauffman
1971–	Rose M. Vassia; Lucy A. Vassia; Mary J. Vassia

52 Portland

Permit: 1 June 1915
Architect: Hellmuth & Hellmuth

1915–1977	Charles E. (d. 1956) and Ida Holliday Bascom
1977–	Roy Pfautch

53 Portland

Permit: 24 July 1912
Architect: Louis LaBeaume

1912–1924	John Foster and Sarah Hitchcock Shepley
1924–1931	William and Flora Dula Dean
1931–1948	Jerome G. and Catherine Edgar Meyer
1948–1952	Charles P. and Georgia Zeibig Whitehead
1952–1960	Henry and Dorothy Pershall-Jones Belz
1960–1970	Theodore M. and Martha Nicolaus Simmons
1970–1977	Carl C. Beck, Jr.
1977–1983	John E. and Ann L. Straw
1983–	Thomas L. and Virginia E. Gossage

56 Portland

Permit: 21 October 1915
Architect: Saum Architects

1915–1916	Herbert M. and Mary A. Edmunds (nonresidents)
1916–1969	Eugene D. (d. 1954) and Lotawana Flateau Nims
1969–1977	William A. and Betty J. Skaggs
1977–	William Wright and Janet M. Welch Clendenin

BIBLIOGRAPHY

In addition to the publications cited in previous pages, the following works provided valuable information in the preparation of this volume.

Coyle, Elinor Martineau. *Saint Louis Homes, 1866–1916: The Golden Age*. St. Louis: The Folkstone Press, 1971.

Cunningham, Mary B., and Jeanne C. Blythe. *The Founding Family of St. Louis*. St. Louis: Piraeus Publishers, Midwest Technical Publications, 1977.

Faherty, William Barnaby. *The St. Louis Portrait*. Tulsa: Continental Heritage, 1978

Forest Park and Its History. Visit St. Louis Committee, St. Louis Chamber of Commerce, 1943.

Forty-Second Annual Report of the Board of Direction [sic], St. Louis Mercantile Library Association, 1887. St. Louis: Nixon-Jones Printing Co., 1888.

Hunter, Julius K. *Kingsbury Place: The First 200 Years*. St. Louis: C. V. Mosby Company, 1982.

Lasdun, Susan. *Victorians at Home*. New York: The Viking Press, 1981.

Lionberger, I. H. "Glimpses of People and Manners in St. Louis 1870–1920." Missouri Historical Society.

Loughlin, Caroline, and Catherine Anderson. *Forest Park*. Columbia: University of Missouri Press, 1986.

Lowic, Lawrence. *The Architectural Heritage of St. Louis, 1803–1891*. St. Louis: The Washington University Gallery of Art, 1982.

McConachie, Alexander Scot. "The Cinch: A Business Elite in the Life of a City—St. Louis,

1895–1915." Ph.D. diss., Washington University, 1976.

Parry, Martin L. *A Way of Life, The Story of John Burroughs School, 1923–1973*. St. Louis: John Burroughs School, 1973.

Primm, James Neal. *Lion of the Valley: St. Louis, Missouri*. Boulder: Pruett Publishing Co., 1981.

Reinhard, Mary B. *The History of Community School, 1914–1979*. St. Louis: Community School, 1979.

Rodabough, John. *Frenchtown*. St. Louis: Sunrise Publishing Co., 1980.

Savage, Charles C. *Architecture of the Private Streets of St. Louis: The Architects and the Houses They Designed*. Columbia: University of Missouri Press, 1987.

Scharf, J. Thomas. *History of St. Louis City and County, Vols. I and II*. Philadelphia: Louis H. Everts & Co., 1883.

Starbuck, Carol Ferring. *Mary Institute: The Gentle Spirit and the Understanding Heart*. St. Louis: Milliken Publishing Co., 1984.

Thorndike, Joseph J., Jr. *The Very Rich: A History of Wealth*. New York: American Heritage Publishing Co., 1976.

Toft, Carolyn Hewes, and Jane Molloy Porter. *Compton Heights: A History and Architectural Guide*. St. Louis: Landmarks Association of St. Louis, 1984.

Westmoreland Park & Place Deed. Forest Park Improvement Association to William L. Huse, Thomas H. West, Edwards Whitaker, Trustees. Dated Nov. 6, 1888. Missouri Historical Society.

PHOTO CREDITS

All color exterior photographs are by Robert Pettus, with the exception of the photograph of the carriage house at 36 Portland and the photograph of the house at 42 Portland, which are by Leonard Lujan.

All color interior photographs are by Leonard Lujan, with the exception of the photograph of the entrance hall of 1 Westmoreland, which is by Robert Pettus.

The photographs in the Chronology of Owners are by Robert Pettus except for those listed below, which should be credited as indicated:

Annual Architectural Exhibition of the St. Louis Architectural Club (1900): 26 Westmoreland (original house)

Commercial and Architectural St. Louis: 11 Westmoreland

Inland Architect: 1 Portland

Edward D. King: 6 Portland

Missouri Historical Society: 21 Westmoreland (original house), 23 Westmoreland (original house), 44 Westmoreland, 5 Portland

William Julius Polk: 28 Westmoreland (original house)

St. Louis Post-Dispatch: 2 Westmoreland, 12 Westmoreland (original house), 45 Portland (original house)

St. Louis Public Library: 33 Westmoreland (original house), 45 Westmoreland (original house), 4 Portland

Swekosky Photo Collection, School Sisters of Notre Dame, St. Louis: 16 Westmoreland,

Stuart West: 6 Westmoreland, 16 Portland, 38 Portland

The balance of the black-and-white photographs, on the pages indicated, are courtesy of the following institutions and individuals:

Norris Allen, pp. 31 (bottom left), 87 (both), 185
The Bixby family, p. 55 (both)

Drawing by Gilbert Early based on 1932 sketch, p. 73
Mrs. Benjamin Edwards III, p. 74 (both)
Encyclopedia of the History of St. Louis, edited by William Hyde and Howard L. Conard, pp. 27, 31 (top left and right), 46, 51, 53 (left), 54 (right), 61, 77 (both)
Esley Hamilton, pp. 189, 190
The Lionberger family, p. 192 (right)
Missouri Historical Society, St. Louis, pp. 17, 18, 19, 21 (top and bottom right), 22, 23, 24 (left), 26, 29, 30, 31 (top center), 32, 34 (left), 35, 36, 42 (right), 43 (left), 47, 49, 50 (top two and bottom left), 52 (both), 53 (right), 56, 60, 64 (both), 65, 68, 69, 71, 72, 79 (right), 186
Robert Pettus, pp. 81, 82
The Pitzman Company, p. 33
William Julius Polk, p. 75
Rossman School, pp. 66, 67
St. Louis Art Museum Archives, Victor Proetz Collection—Gift of Mrs. Arthur Proetz, p. 196 (all three)
St. Louis Mercantile Library Association, pp. 24 (right), 25, 37 (top left), 50 (bottom right), 54 (left), 58,
St. Louis Post-Dispatch, pp. 42 (left), 45 (right), 78, 79 (left), 84 (right), 86
St. Louis Public Library, floor plans on pp. 192, 193, 194, 195
Selkirk Galleries, p. 57
Edward C. Simmons III, pp. 38, 62, 63
State Historical Society of Missouri, Columbia, p. 21 (bottom left), 34 (right), 37 (top and bottom right), 43 (right), 45 (left)
Swekosky Photo Collection, School Sisters of Notre Dame, St. Louis, pp. 20, 76, 84 (left), 188
Western Manuscript Collection, University of Missouri–St. Louis, p. 85

Map on p. 16 drawn by Pat Hayes Baer.

INDEX